MW00774888

SOLITUDE IMPROVED.

Solitude Improved

by

Divine Meditation

OR

A Treatise proving the Duty, and Demonstrating
the Necessity, Excellency, Usefulness,
Natures, Kinds, and Requisites
of Divine Meditation.

by Nathanael Ranew
Sometime Minister of Felsted in Essex, A.D. 1670

Soli Deo Gloria Publications
...for instruction in righteousness...

Soli Deo Gloria Publications
P.O. Box 451, Morgan, PA 15064
(412) 221-1901/FAX 221-1902

*

This edition of *Solitude Improved by Divine
Meditation* is taken from the 1839
Religious Tract Society Edition
published in London. This
Soli Deo Gloria reprint
is 1995.

*

ISBN 1-57538-012-0

RIGHT HONOURABLE AND MOST PIOUS LADY,

MARY COUNTESS OF WARWICK.

MADAM,

THIS ensuing discourse, first making its humble address in private, and having so favourable a reception, craves leave in the publication to make this second application.

The first occasion of this undertaking was from observation made of your exemplary and eminent practice of, and experienced sweetness felt in the breathings of your soul up this hill of holy meditation; it being so frequently, and with such complacency discoursed by you.

After a review made of the whole, I have both altered and added several things, which I most earnestly pray may (together with those helps of many better hands) issue in your Honour's and others' proving still higher artists, and richer proficients, in this rare way of heavenly self-entertainment.

I am ever,
Madam, your Honour's
most humble and most obliged servant,

NATH. RANEW.

TO THE CHRISTIAN READER.

PURPOSING some Improvement of Solitude in the late mournful year, when death was so largely commissioned to destroy by that dreadful pestilence, I made choice of this excellent subject of Divine Meditation. The best way of thinking and mind employing is this meditation. The right art and skill of it is a rare attainment. The due practice of it is a most noble self-entertainment.

A pious heart hath three happy ways of self-entertainment in solitary; three rare ways of being least alone, when most alone.

The first way of self-entertainment, is the ordinance of reading and searching the Holy Scriptures, the pure, perfect, and infallible word and will of Christ concerning us. There Christ hath prepared his rich feast of fat things full of marrow, and his royal banquet of heavenly truths. There he sets forth the great varieties of sure directions, precious promises, high examples, rare experiences, and the help of all his holy ordinances, to feed and satiate the hungry and thirsty spirit.

The second way of self-entertainment, is divine meditation, by either pondering of spiritual things, for improving knowledge, and exciting practice; or by a weighing all other things whatever, for reducing them to a spiritual end and use.

The third way of self-entertainment, is private praying, such as is both founded on and bounded by Christ's will in his word; such as is both prepared and assisted, made wise and warm by serious meditation.

Meditation stands between the two ordinances of reading and praying, as the grand improver of the former, and the high quickener of the latter, to furnish the mind with choice materials for prayer, and to fill the heart with holy fervency in it.

Natural philosophers observe, that to uphold and accommodate bodily life, there are divers sorts of faculties communicated, and these among the rest.

1. An attractive faculty, to assume and draw in the food.

2. A retentive faculty, to keep it, being taken in.

3. An assimilating faculty, to concoct the nourishment.

4. An augmenting faculty, for drawing to perfection.

1. Meditation is as the attractive faculty, to help to assume and take in spiritual food. This it doth by helping to act judgment, wisdom, and faith, to ponder, discern, and credit the things which reading and hearing supply and furnish.

2. It is like the retaining faculty, by assisting and corroborating the memory, helping to lock up the jewels of Divine truths sure in that treasury. Meditation makes a rational memory of things, which is the surest. There is in man a sensitive memory, in which he participates with sensitive natures, such as

beasts; they have a kind of memory. There is also an intellectual or rational memory, wherein man partakes of the like nature with angels; they have their faculty of memory. Meditation superadds to the sensitive memory, the help also of a rational memory, whereby spiritual things are secured as under double lock: what we rationally remember, is best remembered.

3. It is like the assimilating or digesting power, by helping to concoct spiritual food, and turn it into spiritual nourishment. This it helps to effect, by being instrumental to work things more powerfully on the will, in a free choice, firm purpose, and ready obedience of the excellent truths of Christ; and likewise by working on and into the affections of love, joy, and the rest, to cleave unto and be inflamed towards the things of Christ. A spiritual digestion is not by head work, but heart work, when the will deliberately and resolvedly chooses, and the affections earnestly embrace heavenly things. Meditation highly conduces to this spiritual digestion by its pondering, proposing, and edging efficaciously, such reasons and incentives as work the heart into compliance and obedience.

It is like, lastly, the augmenting and growing faculty, to help the good heart to grow better, and shoot up higher heavenward. The true Christian must grow all his lifetime. Natural things grow by new assumed nourishment, acted upon by the inward growing power. The real godly man hath an inward growing power, implanted by the new life given to him: but this, as by other means, so by frequent meditation, is much assisted and carried on. Meditation waters and cherishes the plants of heavenly graces. It helps them to root deeper, shoot higher, and grow stronger. Such Christians as meditate most will grow most, be growing to the end.

What in all Christianity is there that meditation is not a furtherance to?

That saying is excellent, worthy of duest weighing, "The meditating mind is the beginner of all goodness." On a sinner's part, it is the rise of his initial returning to God, of his first converting. In the saints and persons converted, it is their way to progressive converting and renewed repentance, Ezek. xviii. 28. "I considered my ways, and turned my feet unto thy testimonies," Psa. cxix. 59. The more consideration, the more conversion. The great inlet of man's first apostacy, (besides infidelity and pride,) was his incogitancy. Our first parents lost all for want of due thinking; not for the want of acting imagination, or any thinking, that could not be; but for want of that consideration which should have been. They did not consider all things to be considered.

The overflowings of impiety, aggravated by impenitency, and men's rushings into sin so eagerly and boldly, have been greatly from want of consideration. "No man repented him of his wickedness, saying, What have I done? every one turned to his course, as the horse rusheth into the battle," Jer. viii. 6. Their not returnings were from neglect of self-reflectings. In any nation, when God intends to work great returnings, he stirs up that people to self-bethinkings: "If they shall bethink themselves," 1 Kings viii. 47. He reminds them of considering, to bring them to returning. So a particular person, when he first comes in to God, he comes first to himself, and that is by con-

sideration and self-bethinking, as the prodigal, Luke
xv. 17.

In natures rational, the first mover is the mind by
consideration : in grace, the first mover is the mind
by holy meditation. The Christian that would set all
the wheels of the soul going and improve, that would
do great things, and have great attainments, great
things effected on the heart and in the life, much
light and wisdom, much warmth and fervour, high
resolution and courage, large proficiency in godliness,
must be much in meditation.

The greatest scholars of the world have not been
only great readers, but great students in musing and
pondering. The most eminent saints in all ages have
been this way excellent; as Job, David, Solomon, and
others in the Scriptures ; as Cyprian, Ambrose, Augustine, and other saints in succeeding ages.

Upon these, and sundry other considerations, this
ensuing treatise was taken in hand.

My purpose at first was only a private piece, for the
service of an honourable personage, very exemplary
in this pious practice. This occasioned also my taking
the greater liberty in the manner of expressions.
My intendment once accomplished, I entertained no
thoughts of a publication, till some intimate friends,
having the sight of the copy, importuned me to let it
come forth for the general use ; upon which, a review
of the whole being made, with divers alterations and
additions, to reduce it more to the help of all, I resolved to let it come abroad, though imperfect enough.
In the first framing, because I could not make use of
my study usual helps, sentences and quotations (the
ordinary trimmings) were wanting. And being not

willing to further trouble myself, make the treatise swell, and the price rise, I thought it best to let it pass as it is now presented to thy view.

The present age is full of books: there be books too many, and yet too few. Knowledge and wisdom will never in this world be perfect; yet we must ever tend to perfection, and press hard to the mark. And when so many still write after so many excellent treatises on the same subject, this ensuing may the better pass in the crowd. Though there be the greater lights of heaven, the sun, and moon, and stars of the first magnitude, yet the least appearing star is some lustre to the heaven, and light to the earth. Though some pieces of gold coin are current, being fair and down weight, yet those more worn and light may pass in greater payments.

Shall this ensuing treatise issue in persuading or provoking thee to the due practice of holy meditation, to make thee a true and real meditator, or a better and a higher meditator, to teach thee to take a turn often in the garden of God, and take the fresh air of paradise, to be mentally in serious musings, often mounting up to heaven, and return more enlarged and inflamed, more wise and warm at the heart,—let me only request this of thee, to improve some of that acquired warmth in thy way of fervent praying for him that is ever thy servant in the things of Jesus,

NATHANAEL RANEW.

CONTENTS.

PART I.

b

PART II.

PART III.

THE IMPROVEMENT.

SOLITUDE IMPROVED, &c.

PART I.

CHAP. I.—*Of Divine Meditation in general.*

On that noble subject, and necessary duty, Divine
Meditation, I have now chosen, by Christ's assistance,
to speak to you.

Of meditation in general, according to Scripture
latitude, in the various kinds and considerations of it
there expressed. My text, therefore, must not be
one single scripture, for the total foundation of what
I shall tender, but the universal vote, and passages
dispersed through the Bible : some of which are the
following.

" Meditate upon these things," 1 Tim. iv. 15.
Here on Timothy, and, by way of proportion, on
every person, is commanded meditation. " In his
law doth he meditate day and night," Psa. i. 2. If
the blessed man doth so meditate, then all who would
be blessed must do the like.

" I will meditate on all thy work," Psa. lxxvii. 12.
Both the word and works of God must be the godly
man's meditation.

B

" And meditate on thee in the night watches," Psa.
lxiii. 6.   And, " My meditation of him shall be
sweet," Psa. civ. 34.   God must be meditated on,
and that meditation should be sweet.

From these and the like passages scattered over
the Bible, the observation or conclusion is this:
Pious meditation is the duty of every Christian ; or,
It is the high institution of Christ, and greatly incumbent duty of Christians, to exercise themselves much
in holy meditation.

A rare and soul-enriching way : none know the
sweetness and blessings of it, but such as exercise
themselves in it.

Philosophers tell us, there would be no life or motion in the lower world, if the sun and celestial bodies
stood still.   Physicians say, if the heart did not continually beat in the body, there would be no life and
motion in the little world, man.   And experience
proves, if there were no springs or weights in watches
and artificial engines, they could perform nothing.
What the sun, moon, and stars are to life and motion
here below, what the heart is to the body's life and
moving, and what the springs and weights are to motions artificial, that in a high degree is meditation to
spiritual life and motion.

Of the various things tendered to us for truths, this
is the great trier, the percolation and refiner, the me-
lioration and improver.   Such things that come to us
·crude and raw, become mellow and concocted by
meditation.   It is the golden scale to give divine
things their due weight.   The soul's rare alembic, to
effect the highest operations, to extract the richest
spirits for heart use.

Meditation is of that happy influence, it makes
the mind wise, the affections warm, the soul fat

and flourishing, and the conversation greatly fruitful.

Who can fail to practise it, continue it, contend to
larger improvements in this heavenly art, that hath
once experienced and fed upon the surpassing sweetness and refreshments, the unspeakable solaces and
delights, both had and heightened in it!

To speak of it adequately I cannot ; it is such an
attainment that none know the all of it.   Nothing
but progress in the daily practice, can help to comprehend it.   There is still a going and a knowing
further.

I shall speak to four things only concerning meditation.

1. The precedents upon the file of Scripture, or
some rare examples of the practice, and but briefly.

2. The nature, ingredients, qualifications, and the
several sorts of meditation : and here I must be something large.

3. The grounds, and supporting reasons of it, to
manifest it.

4. The diverse improvements of it to divers sorts of
persons.

1. The precedents on the sacred file, recorded instances in Scripture.

There are, among others, four instances, which I
shall single out, four famous, holy, and eminent ones.

The first is that of the godly patriarch Isaac, Gen.
xxiv. 63, " Isaac went out to meditate in the field at
the eventide."   God is a most free Agent, as in all
other actings, so in conferring his Scripture honours.
He honours whom he pleaseth, and when and how he
pleaseth.   He is bound to give no account of his
matters.   And oft we see him in his goings and
doings, but cannot by searching find him out, Job xi.

7. Divine sovereignty and wisdom is pleased, in the Scripture records, to fix the first honour of this practice of meditation on holy Isaac.

Doubtless, his excellent father, holy Abraham, did use to beat this path to heaven, who walked so much with God. Doubtless, those other patriarchs and saints, living before Abraham, travelled much in this heavenly road. Enoch, for his walking with God, so highly honoured, was no stranger to this way. Questionless, it was one of his walks. He certainly used to go to heaven mentally, before he was translated personally. He used to ascend up by meditation, before his happy translation. But Isaac is he who first is mentioned, for acting this holy meditating. It may be he exceeded and excelled in this heavenly art and practice; and because it was a duty performed privately, and that was not known, God would reward and honour him openly, by making it known, and that some hundreds of years after, by Moses' holy pen.

It is probable there was something more than ordinary in it, which occasioned this first record of meditation. However, this was the holy pleasure of God so to fix it; to place it first on the file of godly meditators. Isaac is the first mentioned meditator in Scripture records.

The second instance, which is the fullest to all intents and respects, is that high and noble precedent of holy David, that man after God's own heart: among other reasons, I believe, for his beating so much this path to heaven; for the frequencies of his visits made this way.

He soon became a man of great troubles and disquiets; yet then in them he would resolutely cut out his way, and keep his course of holy meditation: witness those many psalms penned in and on occasions of his troubles, and styled his meditations.   He, after Saul's death, is crowned king of Judah, had his great multitudes of high employments, was a mighty warrior, and so must be exposed to highest hazards ; yet nothing, at any time whatever, should check or retard his course.   Though he had his head full of thoughts, his heart full of troubles, his hands full of work, nothing should hinder him in this high exercise of his so experienced sweet meditation.

In Psa. i. 2, he makes meditation the character of a blessed man, to meditate in God's law day and night.   And what he makes a rule for others, he makes good in his own example.

Psa. cxix. 97, " Oh how love I thy law ! it is my meditation all the day : " there is the practice of the first time, the day; and a full example, and practice, all the day.

And Psa. cxix. 148, " Mine eyes prevent the night watches, that I might meditate in thy word : " there is the practice of the other time mentioned in the character in Psa. i. 2.

Not a watch set in the night, but he had his meditation.   Oh most admirable frame of spirit !   A king and a daily meditator, and a night meditator also !

It was not family business, nor state affairs, not war's urgencies and difficulties, that so could crowd in and impose upon his thoughts, but he would have his spiritual retreats, his soul repasts, in meditation, mount up to heaven by it.   Trace we him with the eye of due observation over the book of Psalms, (the Psalms, which are the choice and rare records of his exemplary this way actings,) we find most excellent patterns, of all sorts, as for this holy exercise.   Singular meditations sometimes of the great works of God, as Psa. viii., and Psa. xix., and Psa. civ., &c., wherein the fire kindles and flies up, in the highest strains. His heart, like the most rare and exquisite engine and instrument, produces such raised and sublimated things, that transcend sometimes all the strains of rhetoric and poetry in the world, as some very learned men observe.

Sometimes his meditations (and there they ply more, as of nearer concernment) are on the word of God, as Psa. xix., and Psa. cxix., &c. ; and what passages and praises hath he, most high, and sweet, and savoury, that what can be fuller and higher, for the nature and properties of it !

Sometimes the most blessed God himself is the high subject of his meditating; and what transcendencies of thoughts, what raptures, what instances of highest soul transportings hath he this way recorded for us, purposely to put us upon pursuit of the like glimpses and tastes, by suitable first breathings and pantings after sweetest communion with him!

It is evident he was a grand master in this art of meditation, by the so exquisite pieces drawn to the life, and reserved for use and imitation in the book of Psalms.

The third pattern is that of the so wise Solomon, in Ecclesiastes, who gave his heart, as he saith, to seek, and search, and to know wisdom, Eccl. i. 13, 17 ; ii. 12. David's strain of meditation proceeds principally on matters in themselves spiritual, as God, his word, and ways, and sometimes on the works of God. Solomon's more upon things natural, and the ways and works of men, Eccl. i. 13, 14 ; but to demonstrate the insufficiency of all things in the world, and all the works of men, to make up true happiness, without the true fear of God, and keeping his commandments, Eccl. xii. 13. This is the sum and scope chiefly of that his book, that book of most deep and great considerations, and excellently useful meditations, for all to obtain wisdom by.

It is (of all) the choicest piece of Scripture, in this kind ; it sets us an accurate copy of regular and fruitful contemplation and meditation of all things under the sun, which we should strive to imitate and write after, chap. i. 14. It is left us thereby to learn from him, the so great experimenter and trier, the wisest and most exquisite weigher of all things, and the finder of their extreme insufficiency and vanity.

To teach every person, by this his so eminent and exemplary acting, his successful searching, to do in the like manner. To infuse his spirit, and lay it to steep strongly and deeply in this meditation of creature vanity, and the vanity of all men's labours under the sun.

Yea, to sink this down to the bottom of the soul, there to fix and root itself; thence, as by a most potent and predominant principle, to work and act up to more weanedness from the things of the world, and to more wariness of our being insnared by them.

The fourth rare instance is of the female sex, that of the blessed Virgin Mary. " But Mary kept all these things, and pondered them in her heart," Luke ii. 19. This is the remarkable and special example of meditation mentioned (that I know of) in the New Testament : we have none so punctual and plain, which I can remember, as this. Some signal honour is hereby intended to this so blessed virgin, to be so noted, more than others, in the gospel records ; and thereby held forth, as a pattern and provocation to all after-ages.

The Scripture's silence, as to other saints' practice in this duty, is not a negative or an exclusive of their doing it : because it is not said of every one, they pondered, or meditated, we must not thence infer they did it not.

David, in the first psalm and second verse, saith, the blessed man meditates in the law of God day and night.   He therefore makes it a necessary duty and certain character of every godly person, in some sincere measure and constancy performing of it.

As the people of God are all taught wisdom to salvation, so this peculiar wisdom, this way of meditation, of the great concerns of God's kingdom, and their most precious immortal souls, to give things of the highest importance their due weight in the balance of a holy meditation.

CHAP. II.—*Of the Nature and Description of this solemn Meditation.*

MEDITATION, according to the usual notion and acceptation, is taken for any serious or earnest thinking of any matter whatsoever, for what end soever, whether it be good or evil.   So meditating is used in the Scripture, not only in a good sense, but in an evil sense.   But ordinarily it is taken in a good sense, for a holy mind exercise, or acting the thoughts in any seriousness upon any matter in a spiritual manner. There is a double kind of meditation.

1. That which is more set and solemn, when a man is serious in thinking of any thing for some spiritual

end, and so as to allow some due space of time for a right performance of it.

2. There is that which is called meditation of ejaculation, which, though serious, yet is more short, and quick, and sudden, wherein the soul darts up to heaven, and makes a short visit thither.

I shall begin with the first, that which more commonly is called meditation. The other shall follow in its due place.

Therefore, having mentioned some Scripture instances or examples of meditation as to the practice of it, I shall come to handle the nature and description of the set and more solemn meditation.

Here first I will endeavour to present you with the true picture and description of meditation, in some Scripture lineaments and proportions; and afterward the explication and peculiar handling of them.

I shall give you the description in this manner. It is that ordinance of Christ, and obedience or duty of a Christian, whereby he acts his spirit into a right pondering of either heavenly and spiritual things, or any other things, in a holy manner, unto spiritual and holy ends and improvements only.

Here is the more *general* nature founding it; and the more *peculiar* nature and particular requisites finishing it.

The more *general* nature, in a double aspect: the first looks up to Christ; it is his ordinance, his institution. The second looks down to man; it is his obedience, his duty.

As to the *peculiar* nature and requisites, notice,

1. The object. I will consider the proper object of this meditation, in two parts: 1. Things spiritual and heavenly. 2. Things, though not in themselves spiritual, yet in a spiritual manner looked upon.

2. The acting on it. The acting on this object, by way of right pondering, where many particulars will be opened

3. The ends of this meditation ; for only spiritual ends, or the ends to be aimed at, must be spiritual and only holy.

As to the more *general* nature of meditation, it is, 1. Christ's own ordinance. 2. Man's duty and obedience. It is Christ's own ordinance, as those Scriptures forecited, and many others, which will be after named, prove.

Three things there are in an ordinance of Christ, which I shall speak of.

(1.) The rise and original, it is heavenly.

(2.) The nature, it is spiritual and holy.

(3.) The use and end, it is for a help.

(1.) For the rise and original, it is glorious and transcendent : it comes as far as heaven ; it is heaven-born and bred. It bears Christ's image and superscription, brings his broad seal and commission ; it is one bright beam of Christ's sovereignty, shining down upon us, one holding out of his golden sceptre, for us to touch the top of it. It comes with the King of heaven's *must*, it must be yielded to, done as the strict and high command of the great King of saints, given in indispensable necessity ; yea, with the very same cogency and necessity, that praying, hearing the word, or any other most usually yielded to duty doth.

Commonly (as by our daily practice we prove it) we lay not such stress upon divine meditation, as we do upon other Scripture institutions. As if there were a less weight of Christ's regal sceptre in it. As if it were not so current coin of his ; but rather like some light gold, which we need not receive except we please. Whereas this duty of meditation comes in Christ's

name, to every soul; and with a commission as full
and firm as any other gospel command or duty
whatsoever.

(2.) An ordinance of Christ is holy. Every institution is a participation, and carries a stamp and
beam of God's glorious holiness. Not only of his
regal authority, but of his inconceivable holiness and
purity. The holiness of God is that glorious attribute of his, whereby being free from all impurity, he
wills and orders all things for his name and glory.

The holiness of an ordinance, is chiefly that by
which it is laid and levelled full at the grand scope
and mark of God's highest praise and honour. It
must be looked on, and represented to us, as an appointment for the most high God, his highest interest. All religion is principally for living to the
living God, 2 Cor. v. 15. All ordinances are but
the higher and more eminent ways given us for exalting him; so many ascents and rising grounds,
whereby he may mount aloft, and become more transcendently great and glorious. If this be not the
predominant ingredient in our performances, we are
quite mistaken; and so take his blessed name in vain.
This therefore being the chief thing this ordinance
of meditation stands charged with, must accordingly
be minded and meant in it, God's institution of it.
First, for his own highest interest, his intending it
first for himself, who so infinitely surpasses all created beings and their total interests, whatsoever they
can amount unto.

(3.) An ordinance is helpful, for our heavenly
help; by grace and the Lord's condescension, it is an
appointment and institution for us. For our chief
interest, the highway of our soul's help; an intendment and a means to the main mark of happiness;

the singular way of our God's devising ; the sweet
way of our great Prophet's teaching ; Christ's first
setting me up a light, and therewith lending me his
hand of help : all gospel ordinances carry light and
help with them ; the Scriptures call them *ways*, Psa.
cxix. 3. They are God's ways, and they are also our
ways. They are first the King of heaven's highways,
his institutions and appointments for us ; and they are
our ways, our highways to travel up to the city of God,
heaven ; our ways to walk in to our chief happiness.

I must look upon Christ's ordinances, not as mere
impositions and significations of Christ's sovereignty ;
not as burdens and tasks, the products and effects of
severity ; but such as are the demonstrations of his
graciousness and pity. He sets me and shows me
the way, who justly might leave me to lose my way,
and to lose myself ; to lose both my labour and life,
heaven and happiness, and that for ever.

From these three forementioned considerations,
what extreme need hath every one, to give them the
keenest edge, to make meditation more penetrative and
powerful ! to both facilitate it to us, and fortify it in
our hearts !

Ah ! when we are to meditate, how do we still find
our spirits all overrun and tainted with carnal and
hellish repugnancies and recoilings against it ! Rom.
vii. 21. How biassed and acted with strong diversions
from it ! How sunk down suddenly, in deadness and
flatness in it ! How overcome with fainting fits and
feebleness in it, from the poisonous fumes and dangerous damps ascending out of the hell of corruption,
lying at the bottom of our spirits ! And how still
abused by the frequencies of our heart's deceitfulness
and miscarriages about it ! The more high, holy,
and profitable any ordinance of Christ is, the more

fearful and sad are the demonstrations of the enmity and hell in our hearts acting against it. "Lord, I am hell," said a devout meditator.

Ah, what floods, what seas of considerations have we need of, to quench these hellish sparks that rise up in our bosoms! What need of all the heavenly fire we can make and kindle, to extinguish this hellish fire, that so quickly burns and flames up! As we see the sun to extinguish the fire on the hearth; celestial fire our culinary fire.

Chap. III.—*Meditation our Duty, our Obedience.*

MEDITATION is not only Christ's institution and ordinance, but every one's incumbent duty and necessary obedience : not like the free-will offering, a matter merely arbitrary, and as a dealing by way of courtesy. Not for a casting in, as a redundancy, over and above all other duties ; but it is and must be performed as a duty of indispensable necessity, 1 Tim. iv. 15 ; Psa. i. 2.

1. A duty in reference to Christ. Necessity in reference to Christ himself; an obedience to his law, a subjection to his crown imperial, a homage and service due to him, as the sovereign Lord of our souls, and of that meditating and pondering faculty he endowed them with.

Meditation is Jesus Christ's reservation in the great gift and grant of our soul's thinking power. He hath endowed us with that so noble faculty of

minding and musing, and also with a large mind-
charter, and liberty of thoughts, for our own occasions
and sober recreatings, in our contemplations or studies.
But yet, it is always provided, that a holy tribute, out
of the whole of our thoughts, is still duly to be paid
in, and that as an acknowledgment both of holding
our thinking faculty upon him, and our best way of
employment of it; and this to be done in the due
seasons, both ordinary and extraordinary. The neglect
of this duty, is a denying of his right and royalty over
my thoughts, and over that which is so eminent an
endowment of the mind, and given in to the spirit by
God; for it is chiefly thinking of him that is so high
and all-sufficient, and the surpassing excellent things
of God, as being the soul's best acting. Certainly
thus the saints in the Scripture acted highly upon this
account, of their paying in the reserved dues of Christ,
their liege Lord, 1 Cor. vi. 20. His dues and their
duties moving strongly to act highly in this work
and way.

2. It is a duty to myself, and my own soul concernments.

In all doing duty, there is a doing myself right,
paying in to my own soul its due. Neglecting in any
kind my duty, is a wronging my own soul. "He that
sinneth against me wrongeth his own soul," Prov.
viii. 36. Performing it is a doing my soul right.
Yea, holy duties are the highest doings of right to our
souls. There is no way of doing better to myself, than
going in the King of heaven's highway. His ways
are my soul's best ways, wherein I act best for myself,
and when I perform them in the best manner.

CHAP. IV.—*Of the Requisites in Meditation.*

THERE are these three things I shall mention as the requisites for holy meditation as a duty.

1. What I call a foundation, or preparative to it.

2. Those things that are for the forming and framing it as to the parts and proportions.

3. The things that finish it up.

1. As to the foundation, or preparative to it, this must be laid above in heaven, by the dispositive or preparative work of fervent prayer. The foundation of this soul affair must be, as a learned man saith of the foundation of the world : The foundation of the world, he saith, is the third heaven, which is of a " constant, incorruptible nature, of no pre-existent principles, and so not liable, as other things are, to corruption and resolution ; and which, as to the convex or outward superficies, or the highest part, is only bounded or terminated by its own limits, or terms of essence and quantity; but in its concave or hollow superficies, or the lowest part, contains all inferior things, and is fixed immovable." If the foundation of the great world is laid by the third heaven, the foundation of this great work of holy meditation must be laid in heaven, laid by the soul's strong mounting up thither, and fixing itself there by fervent prayer, as the great preparative to this meditation. Fervent prayer : the word in the Hebrew used for meditation, signifies also prayer; prayer and meditation being so near akin, and the one helping mutually the other.

(1.) To begin with a bringing the soul into the

c 2

glorious and tremendous presence of the great God, and under his so pure and all-seeing eye.

(2.) To act the soul, and lay it as it were to steep in self-abasings and humblings, for its former miscarriages and failings in, and present unfitness and indisposedness for, what is now undertaking.

(3.) To exercise fresh self-denyings, as to any sufficiency of ability to perform any thing herein acceptably and profitably.

(4.) To act vigorous and strong recumbencies on Jesus Christ, for both his teachings and touchings of our spirits, and upholdings likewise in the work.

(5.) To procure and beget a warm temper in us, such as may make the heart to glow all over in the duty.

2. As to the forming of the duty in the parts and particulars of it.

(1.) It must be founded on, and rise from, the spring and great principle of motion and action, which is the will, in a both free choice and firm purpose. A resolvedness and rooted purpose: thus David, " I will meditate in thy statutes," and, " I will meditate in thy precepts," Psa. cxix. 15, 48. The evil heart saith, I will not meditate: Satan saith, (so far as he can hinder,) You shall not : and the profane world saith, You need not. But the holy heart saith, I will meditate. This is my free and firm purpose, and nothing, by Christ's assistance, shall divert me.

The philosopher saith, that in every virtuous action there must be a choice of will; it must come free from the spring of the will, and run in resolution ; otherwise it is not a virtuous action.

The Scriptures, for all religious actings, call for willingness : " Thy people shall be willing in the day of thy power," Psa. cx. 3 ; or, as it is in the Hebrew, A people of willingnesses, thy people : and in divers places call for readiness in what we perform to God. No work in the world can challenge such an intense degree of readiness and freeness as Christ's work, and such ways as have a clear and lively stamp of his royal will and command. No higher character is given in Scripture of real godliness, than freest choice of will and readiness. To choose the good part, Luke x. 42. To choose the things that please God, Isa. lvi. 4 ; and as in abundance of places is to be seen.

A carnal heart acts from carnal wisdom and self-interest, or from passion and self-biassing affection, but not from pure freeness and deliberate choice of will. That is not the spring and rise of his duties, as it is in a good and holy heart. A good heart acts from purpose, a well and deep set purpose : with purpose of heart to cleave to the Lord, Acts xi. 23. And Psa. cxix. 106, " I have sworn, and I will perform it, that I will keep thy righteous judgments." So the will, for holy duties, must put forth in purposes, firm purposes, varieties of fresh purposes ; act all the still needful and conducing purposes, any duty in any respect calls for. There are many rare and rich attendants and properties, ingredients and excellencies, divine and heavenly beauties, appertaining to holy duties, which the will must intend and make its free, firm choice of, which the purposes of the will must lie level to and make after, as the proper and proportionate marks and higher tendencies.

CHAP. V.—*What the Will must intend in Meditation.*

I SHALL name five particulars : there must be,

1. An aim and firm purpose to make the duty a
right work, to make sure it be made true.

2. A free and full purpose of a wise work, to have
it a work of spiritual wisdom.

3. A firm purpose for a vigorous and spirited performing.

4. A strong purpose of watching and earnest striving against all diversions and interruptions.

5. In a firm purpose of utmost endeavour of success, and having the right and kindly end and fruit of
the duty.

1. A right work.

1. The will's purpose and intendment must be to
make the duty of meditation a right work ; to make
sure it be made true and sincere, John iv. 24. Not
a carcass, a painted piece, without soul and substance, a formality without power. Not a mere work
performed, as it were to flatter God, who looks for a
duty, as they in Psa. lxxviii. 36, 37 are said to flatter God with their lips, but their heart was not right
with him. We are ready to flatter him with our
modes of meditation, and fashions of thinkings, with
our formalities, without realities and truth, and the
work's being sincere. It must not be a flattering of
God, but a true pleasing him, from being true itself.
It must not be a work daubed over with the untem-
pered mortar of our own heart's self-deceitfulness, setting up a thing to show like it, and be something near
it only, and putting thereby a cheat upon ourselves.

Nor must it be a thing only to stop the mouth of our consciences, keep them from calling on and challenging of us; but we must design it strongly and firmly, to purpose, through God, to proffer to and please him with a sincere work. "Walk before me, and be thou perfect," Gen. xvii. 1. This must be understood, certainly, of every walk and path we go in: not a walk in some one way, or divers, and not all; but in every walking sincerity must be a property, a qualification designed and firmly resolved; and we must not be satisfied unless it be right meditating, such as Scripture requires, and saints in Scripture practised; yea, that they told God himself that they performed, Psa. cxix. 23. And doubtless David durst not tell the heart-searching God he meditated, if he had done it formally and hypocritically, and not been sincere and upright in it.

2. The intendment of the will must be for making this duty a wise work, to make it a work of spiritual wisdom. The apostle, in Eph. v. 17, says, "Be ye not unwise, but understanding what the will of the Lord is." And in 2 Tim. iii. 15, there is mention of wisdom to salvation : and in Prov. ix. 12, wisdom is called on for ourselves.

(1.) Wise in respect of God. Certainly, as Solomon did things of great excellency to show himself very wise; so when the most high God's honour is concerned, and when he will be present at our performances, and comes as it were purposely to them, shall we present him with any foolish piece; not design a wise work, and not be seen acting wisely?

(2.) Wise in reference to ourselves. Should we not also strongly purpose to make this duty a wise work, a work of sure wisdom for ourselves, and lay it fully level to the grand mark of eternal salvation for

ourselves? Solomon, in Prov. xvii. 21, saith, " The
father of a fool hath no joy :" so the parent of a foolish acting will have no joy : it is the godly, prudent
acting, whose fruit is peace, and which issues in
heavenly joy. Oh how sweet and comfortable is that
duty, in which we have acted up to the rule of sound
wisdom !

3. A spirited and lively work. There must be a
firm and strong purpose and intendment for a vigorous
and spirited, a lively and warm work. " Fervent in
spirit, serving the Lord," Rom. xii. 11. In every
duty we must have a purpose of striking fire, of making
the heart burning hot : it must not be lukewarm, in
an indifferency, that is but lazy ; nor blood-warm, that
is but low. But the soul's purpose and design must
be for highest heat and fervency, greatest vigour and
activity. As artists in some high operations, seek for
the hottest fire.

As warmest preaching and warmest hearing, as the
disciples' hearts burned within them, when Christ opened the Scriptures, Luke xxiv. 32. And so warmest
reading and warmest meditating. In David's heart,
while he mused, the fire burned, Psa. xxxix. 3. So
when we meditate, we should intend a warm work, to
be very warm at the heart.

4. A striving against all lets. In a strong purpose
of earnest striving against all lets and interruptions.
The whole work of a Christian here, must not only be
vigorous and sedulous, but striving and contentious.
" Strive to enter in at the strait gate," Luke xiii. 24.
Every single and particular duty must bear a part of
striving to enter in at the strait gate ; for this is to be
applied to every particular duty, though Christ speaks
only in general, bidding us strive.

Two things make up the notion of striving.

(1.) Intention and earnestness.

(2.) Contention against opposition. When a man strives, he acts earnestly; and when he strives after or for a thing, he strives also with that which is against him. Striving is against something that lets or opposes. In all soul work, and peculiarly in this of meditation, the throng of difficulties is great, the oppositions are many, therefore the purposes and resolutions of heart must be strong and high. None ever carry on their work well, who are not first well resolved, and still renew and link one firm purpose to another, to hold on their course to the last.

5. A purpose for the kindly issuing of meditation. The will must purpose firmly to endeavour still the kindly issue and success of the duty. Look, saith the apostle, ye lose not the things wrought, 2 John 8. Who would set up at the labour in vain? Christ's sweet promise is, " The seed of the blessed of the Lord shall not labour in vain," Isa. lxv. 23. The way, among others, of having it performed, is by grounding our endeavours in strong and rooted resolutions for that running and pressing on, and looking after our duties doing; until the work winds up, and issues in the spiritual ends, in the sweet success it is appointed unto; such as increase of holiness and grace, and improvement of communion with God. Success sets the crown on the head of the work: resolve to get the crown still set on the head of every duty, that it may shine in the glory of success.

These are the five special branches this root of resolution should put forth; these, as so many precious corner-stones, should lie at the bottom of this building, the better to bear it up. These should be as so many great arteries branching forth from the heart, to convey vital spirits into the body of this heavenly duty of meditation, and keep it alive, and warm, and improvingly active.

CHAP. VI.—*Of the proper Objects of Divine Meditation.*

FROM things of a remoter relation to the subject in hand, I pass to such as are the nearer, the more intrinsical and peculiar. And here comes first to be handled, the matter, or the object of this meditation. When the wise king Solomon was to build the temple, first he is providing the rich and precious materials, then he proceeds to the framing and fitting of them, and then to erecting and finishing that glorious structure. That which next is to be done, is first to look out the materials of our work, and then the framing and finishing up is to follow. The materials, or objective parts, are far more rich and precious than those of Solomon's temple. They are, as our description of meditation holds them forth, either,

1. Such as are more properly and purely spiritual and heavenly in their own nature.

2. Or things considered in a spiritual way, and to a spiritual end and use.

It is not the consideration of things as to their entity or being, that is metaphysical: metaphysics treat of entities, of the mere beings of things. Of the first Being, namely, God; and of secondary beings derived from God, the first Being. It is not the consideration of things as rational; the rational respects things have one to another, this is logical: logic, that considers respects of things, as causes, effects, subjects, adjuncts, and the like.

It is not the consideration of things in their particular natures and natural properties : this, natural philosophy contemplates.

It is not the consideration of things civil, moral, or political : these, moralists and statesmen are exercised about.

Neither is it the consideration of particular crafts and trades : this is mechanical, and but a work prudential and human, not divine. But this meditation hath objects of a far higher sphere and rank ; things of a divine and theological consideration.

Nay, nor yet is it the mere study of things theological and divine. A man may be a student in divinity, beat and busy his brains about the high points and mysteries in it, may read and muse on matters divine, and yet not be a meditator, such as we speak of, not act divine meditation. A man may act upon things as notions, and as matters of knowledge ; or, to make a universal knowing person, he may act contemplation for curiosity ; for such a use, as the heathen man Aristotle made of reading Moses' first chapter of Genesis ; whereof he passed his undue and heathenish censure, that Moses affirms all, but proves nothing : he read first, and then pondered, and then censured. But he acted not meditation, not that we speak of : it was not a consideration of spiritual things as spiritual, and for spiritual ends ; but only as a wise man acts his thoughts upon things as new, for new notions and improving knowledge. Many thus consider things Scriptural and divine, study them, as we call it, study books of divinity, study things in the Scripture ; but they act not the duty of meditation. They act upon things as matters intellectual and rational, not as heavenly and spiritual. Act for notion and speculation, and not for holiness. Act curiosity, not Christianity.

The right meditator far transcends any mere student; he acts a more noble part, hath a more noble and sublime manner of operation. Aristotle's studying Moses' writings, and David's meditating in the law of God, how far do they differ! So a heathen's, or a Mohammedan's, or a Jew's, or any such person's studying matters in the Bible, differs greatly from meditating in it.

Nay, many protestants are great students in divinity, that never meditated: they dwell upon the study of it, but touch not with the least of their fingers the hard work of holy meditation.

But to return to our matter in hand, and to speak to this subject of meditation: formerly it was said, that spiritual things, or things in a spiritual and heavenly manner considered, are the proper and adequate object of this meditation.

And here, oh how large and fair a prospect hath the spiritual eye to expatiate and recreate itself in! The infinitely glorious and all-sufficient God, the Father, Son, and Holy Spirit, as the Scripture reveals: the vast world, the frame of heaven above, and earth below, with all the innumerable things contained in them.

Their sundry natures, properties, and uses, with the so beauteous and various excellencies of them. The mighty sustentations and preservations of all things created, as to their beings, their faculties, and their acts.

The most wise, righteous, and holy governing of them, with a most steady and never-erring hand, unto their particular ends; and with a most certain winding them all up ultimately, in the supreme scope of the great Creator and Governor.

Then that peculiar government of the rational creatures, angels and men : the unspeakably sad fall of some angels, and all mankind ; the recovery of some men, and their eternal salvation, by Christ the Redeemer, God in our nature : here, here is matter of meditation, the great mystery of godliness, as in 1 Tim. iii. 16. And particularly, the four last things, as they are called, namely, death, judgment, heaven, and hell.

Besides, there is for meditation, the whole book of Holy Scriptures, now complete in the New Testament times ; with the ordinances of Christ, and the covenant of grace. And lastly, the meditation of that so great concern, our own particular estates, how matters stand with us, and are like to be with us to all eternity ; which eternity challenges and imposes on every person the greatest intensity and frequency of thought. But though this be so great, yet again what is there in all the vast circumference of the whole world ; I say, what is there, although ever so small, but by a wise and holy heart may be an object improvable to an excellent use and end ? As the art of chemistry can extract rare and efficacious remedies out of putrefactions and poisons.

That soul must be a pitiful, vain, and barren piece, that wants matter and mind to move and act fruitfully, in so large a sphere and compass as meditation hath : it affords the whole latitude of all things properly spiritual ; and it comprises likewise all other things, which, in some respect or other, wisdom can improve by this rare art.

No artist in any way of operation, with all his rare

instruments and efficacious engines, can operate more
eminently than an artist in this holy kind may do.

Of this the Scriptures give plentiful proof in the
many precedents left us in it for imitation. So we see
it in holy David, in many of his psalms, (besides
those concerning the word of God, his greatest subject of meditation, in those made of God's great works,)
yea, the works of his common providence and guidance; as the growing of the grass, and herbs, and trees;
the singing of the birds among their branches; in the
waters, the playing of the leviathan, the innumerable
creeping things in the seas, and the going of the ships
in them, as in Psa. civ. The wise Solomon hath his
meditation of the horseleech, with her daughters,
Prov. xxx. 15. The ant in her industry, sending the
sluggard (that turns on his bed, as the door on the
hinges, that often moves, but never removes, Prov.
xxvi. 14) to her to learn industry, Prov. vi. 6.

Yea, sometimes the most inconsiderable things the
Scripture takes notice of, for us to mind the hairs on
the head, which all are numbered; the sands of the
sea, which though so weak and small, is thereby
bridled; the dust of the earth, by God's power, as
in a measure comprehended, Isa. xl. 12. And not
only God's great works and high actings, but the lowest
actions of men, and the meanest actings of the inferior
creatures, are in Scripture held forth as occasions for
this meditation, as advantage-grounds for the ascending of thoughts, and raising up the mind heavenward.

All this pains taken by the Spirit of God, in the
Scriptures, is to show what a wise and fruitful spirit
may extract, by this holy art of meditation; yea, to
teach us how constantly thought-busy we should keep

our hearts, (like that wonder in nature, the so wise and laborious bee,) still ingathering some celestial sweetness from every flower of Scripture or providence, or any other object we stay upon.

CHAP. VII.—*Of the Requisites for Meditation.*

FROM the object and matter of meditation, we must next come to the requisites and qualifications, and the things contained in it, and constituting it.

Here, by the way, there were two sorts of meditation mentioned.

1. That which is set and more solemn.

2. That which is short, sudden, and ejaculatory.

1. The first, that which more properly is called meditation, is that so frequently we have spoken of in the Scripture, and mentioned in our divinity books, and in discourses. Meditation in the ordinary acceptation of the word, taken for a work of time, seriousness, and solemnness, that must have a due proportion of time, labour, and diligence, to effect that upon the heart it is to be used for.

2. There is that which is called ejaculation, sudden, quick acting, or ascending of the soul to heaven. This is a holy spark that flies up out of the heavenly fire, burning suddenly in the heart; this is but meditation rather more improperly so called. Of this I shall speak something hereafter.

But that we are now to proceed upon, is the meditation more properly so called, more set, solemn meditation, a business of time and seriousness.

I shall mention eight particulars or requisites for this meditation.

1. There is requisite a holy awe and reverence, a putting on a reverential frame of heart suitable to the holiness of the duty.

2. There is requisite a retreat of the thoughts, calling off the mind from all its preceding excursions or engagings other ways.

3. There is requisite the setting of a strong guard and so sure a watch upon our slippery spirits as we are able, to secure it against all diversions.

4. Meditation, as to the form and nature, proper notion and essence, consists in application of the mind and thoughts, and setting them upon the subject or matter intended to be considered.

5. Meditation, as to the nature and essence, consists, as in application of the mind to, so in the intension and due seriousness of thinking on a fit object.

6. In a diving and searching of thoughts, scanning for a best discovery.

7. In an abiding due stay of the thoughts upon the work in hand, without precipitation and undue hastening.

8. It is requisite there be an infusing and intermixing the life and beauties of such affections as are suitable and proper for the duty.

1. Meditation must have the dispositive and preparation of holy awe and reverence; a still engaging the spirit to, and imposing upon it, and framing of it, unto all that holy awe, and highest reverence, which this so excellent duty calls for, both in the entrance, and over all the performance. I say highest reverence, as that which is to be done in the infinitely pure presence of a God; a God whose eye is observing in a special manner our heart-temper, not only in

a duty performed in his view, but a temper presented and tendered to himself, as a homage and honour. As a way of ingratiating ourselves with him, as a way, and one of our sweetest ways, of higher intimacy and communion with him. The spirit of a creature perfect, much less of a sinner, cannot have too strong an infusion, too deep a tincture, of holy reverence.

CHAP. VIII.—*Two other Requisites.*

2. THE next requisite is in sounding a retreat of the thoughts, and calling off the mind from all pre-engagements, not only evils and vanities, but all business and duties. Nothing must detain the thoughts, or divert the thoughts, when we design and intend meditation. God complains of men when bodies are brought, and hearts are left out : well may he complain, if we go about meditation, a mind, a thought exercise, if we let the mind and thoughts be sent abroad, and not called home.

The philosophers say truly, that intention can be only of one thing at one particular, individual time. Divinity tells us, there must be no allowance of disintention, neither a giving way to a seizure of impertinencies to keep possession of the mind ; that will keep off that which is incumbent, and our present duty.

David, in Psa. cxix. 113, says, he hated vain thoughts, when they were intruders, when they crowded in : much more as they were excluders, and crowded out good thoughts. Therefore, most of all, when they obstructed and interposed at the time of his

meditation. Therefore, being so rare an artist in heavenly meditation, he still would shake out and empty the
vessel of his heart of other previous improper thoughts.
Do as Nehemiah ; when Tobiah had laid up his stuff
in the temple, he throws it all out to make way for
the proper furniture.

Musing in this sort, therefore, must have its preparative, its stand, and its retreat off and from all impertinent thoughts : a making the coast clear, a setting
the mind free, disburdening and disclogging it : casting
off all weights when we are to run this race, and mount
up the hill of divine contemplation. Now is the
time to call to by-thoughts to void the room, and
leave it free for other thoughts to enter.

3. When meditation is to be performed, there must
be a strong guard set, a sure watch kept upon all
avenues and passages, on all the inlets and outlets of
the heart.

As Jehoiada the priest set a guard round about the
young king, when he was to be crowned, 2 Chron.
xxiii. 7, so when this duty is endangered, and ready
to be hindered from having the crown of a right performance set upon it. The Scripture rules impose
circumspection, great caution in all our concernments,
but more peculiarly in things pertaining to God, and
his worship. Take heed to thy foot, &c.; so, Take heed
what you hear. And, Take heed how you hear. So
there must be heed, and a great take heed how we
meditate. The strongest guard is little enough, yea,
too deficient and weak, for the holiest heart, and the
best exercised in this part of godliness. Oh how
inconceivably evil is every heart in its leakings and
runnings-out, in its rovings and wanderings, in its
slipperiness and inconstancies ; and likewise in its
sinkings and fallings, instead of keepings-up in its

heat and heavenly vivacity, and keepings-on in any evenness and equality!

No sieve is more unapt to hold water, no hand more unable to hold sand, or oil poured into it, no bone, which often hath been out of joint, is more apt to dislocate and slip out of place, than is the best heart to slip off, rove, and range from this duty, in diversions and admissions of impertinencies.   When we are most serious and intent, suddenly our carnal spirits give us the slip, and are gone : like the bird, if the cage be but open ; or the prisoner, if the doors be not fast and watched.   Or, if the heart get not out in diversions, it falls flat in deadness and sudden coolings : like the iron in forging, no longer hot than the workman keeps blowing : like melted metal, which cools as it runs and is pouring forth.   This made David in the Psalms so often and earnestly to call for quickenings, from the sense of his frequent heart-coolings and sinkings.

The acting of meditation must not be going up a hill of ice, where footing is both slippery and cold, but like the going up the burning Mount Etna, where the footing, if not firm, yet is that which the travellers (as they say) feel warm.   Or like Moses' going up the mount to God, which was steady and earnest till he came to the top.   Still a due guard must be kept about our hearts in this so important soul affair.   An intense care must be used, and a holy fear against all diversions, all heart-sinkings, and against all disappointments also, that we lose not the real benefit and comfort of this work.

CHAP. IX.—*Meditation in applying the Mind to a proper Object.*

4. MEDITATION stands in an application and bringing the thinking power of the soul upon the object, or thing to be meditated of. Taking that great engine of the spirit, and setting it to act upon some fit subject.

The thinking faculty is a rare endowment; an engine whereby the reasonable creature can draw up and take in any object, and act or exercise itself about it for that use or end we aim at in our thinking.

In all meditation there must be an applying and conjunction of the mind and the thing. As sensitive seeing must have some union, virtual union, with the thing seen ; so intellectual seeing, seeing by the eye of the understanding, must be by a bringing the thoughts upon that is to be thought upon. The Scripture hath this expression, of setting the heart upon a thing, Hag. i. 5. So it is in the Hebrew, that which we translate " Consider your ways," is, Put or set your hearts upon, &c. In consideration or musing there is not only a taking of the heart and thoughts from foregoing minded objects, but a putting or setting it on some new thing, setting that on there where it was not set before.

The sinful heart of itself will run any way ; upon earthly things, upon evil things, or upon impertinent and unseasonable things ; not come to or keep upon that it should intend and mind : therefore it must be taken as by strong hand, and set upon spiritual things, set on musing and meditation of heavenly things. A carnal heart is like the loadstone, it cleaves to nothing but steel or iron, and both of them easily unite : but

the heart must be of another property, and act in a
higher way.   And a good heart, though it thinks too
much earthward, runs often wrong; yet it will set
itself in its thinkings right, on right objects, make
itself and them to meet and unite.   David tells us
how he did, he inclined his heart to God's commandments, Psa. cxix. 112, both to keep them, and to
meditate on them.   He took and bent his heart, as a
thing bending too much to other things; set his mind
on musing on it.   He found his heart and the law of
God too far asunder, and so would continue, unless he
brought them together and made them one.   If he
had not brought his heart to the word, he had never
meditated: the object cannot apply itself to the mind,
but the mind must bring itself to the object.   No holy
duties will come to us, we must come to them.   Many,
in a secret folly and sluggishness, would have things
do alone of themselves, without their stirring or acting: but they mistake; it is something like to Mohammed the deceiver, who once told the people that
were met by his means, to see him have a mountain,
upon his call, to remove and come unto him; but
when the mountain would not come, he boldly then
tells them, If the mountain will not come to Mohammed, Mohammed must or will go to the mountain.
What he did attempt in pretence, and act in impu-
dence, but was fain to go at last to the mountain, that
would not come to him; I say, like to this we are
ready to do in slothfulness, we look that duties should
come to us, that they do themselves, and we do
nothing.   But that which will not come to us, we
must go to it; we must bring and set our hearts to
this and all other duties.   There must not be a letting the mind lie still; that so matter of meditation
may come to us, and make us meditate; but we must

bring and set our hearts to objects of meditation, and make this happy meeting, of excellent objects, and this excellent musing power. This is the more to be contended for, because this work of holy meditating hath so many busy adversaries, but chiefly in the constant progress and carrying of it on.

Ah, it is extremely against the grain of a natural heart, to be broken off from its customary wildness, wanderings, and rangings of thoughts ; to cage up itself, and become tame, and tuned to serious musings and thinkings heavenward. In the best heart, that sin that so easily besets us will be ready quickly to interpose, and cut off the passages otherwise open.

Oh how the heart strives to beset and block up all passages, when we are beginning to enter on this work ! All the whole garrison of disinclinations and repugnancies, the hellish heart, venoms, and contrarieties take instantly the alarm, and endeavour to hinder the heart's conjunction with spiritual objects by this meditation. The soul under its complications of lusts and corruptions, is as if you had a bowl of many biasses clapt upon it, all ready to draw diversely, but all from the duty in hand : and as natural corruptions will be acting contrarieties and diversions ; so old customary evils, haunts, and wonts, will be calling upon us, coming to give us their visits, calling us off to some other way.

Satan also, and the power of darkness, will not be absent at this time, that may turn so much to his prejudice; but he will be sure (if he any way can) to divert thee totally, and cause the whole current of thy thoughts to run out in useless impertinencies.

Great circumspection must therefore be still used in our settings upon this duty : a work well begun is half done.

CHAP. X.—*Meditation must be a serious
Thinking.*

5. MEDITATION includes, as an application, so an intension and seriousness of thoughts.

Serious objects, and serious work, must have thought-seriousness; an earnestness, and acting the vigour of the thinking power. We can think slightly, but this we call not meditation; but serious and earnest minding must be ever an ingredient of due performed meditating.

In Scripture it is sometimes expressed by the term of considering. "I will consider thy testimonies," Psa. cxix. 95; that is, mind them with a serious and earnest thinking. So Psa. lxxvii. 5, "I have considered the days of old;" he acted in not a slight eyeing, but serious musing.

Thus Solomon in his Ecclesiastes often expresses it by the term considering; "I considered all the oppressions that are done under the sun;" and, "I considered all travail," Eccl. iv. 1, 4. Consideration (besides the bringing of the mind unto a thing) includes also seriousness, an intension of the mind upon the object. Sometimes in Scripture it is expressed by the word pondering, "Ponder the path of thy feet," Prov. iv. 26; that is, earnestly mind them. So Mary is said to ponder the sayings of Christ in her heart, Luke ii. 19; she made it a work of great seriousness.

There is a slight and easy thinking, an acting of thoughts cursorily, and when a thing is out so soon as in, and the thought off so soon as on; and there is a serious thinking.

The mind of man hath not only an ability to act, but can put forth an exceeding great seriousness. That as in things natural they have not only power to act, but can also act intensely and vigorously. Thus in things inanimate, as in fire, how hot and in-tense may it be! In brute creatures, how earnestly can they act, when they put forth their strength! As the horse in running, the eagle in flying. In things artificial, to what intense degrees can divers instru-ments and engines operate, and discharge themselves! Oh what can this engine of the mind of man effect! what heights of seriousness can it arrive at! what contributions of earnestness can it pay in, when it is highly concerned, when it is edged by some real or supposed grand interest; as some weighty affair, urgent business, some imminent danger to be escaped, some rare pleasure, high preferment, vast sum of treasure, or such like engagements! Yea, what can the mind, as to a high seriousness, act sometimes upon objects totally unworthy of the thoughts! vain thoughts can be very eager and intense.

If we can be so serious in matters inferior, certainly divine and spiritual matters must needs claim a far greater share of seriousness. There should be no earnestness of thoughts on any ground or interest whatsoever, like to this meditating earnestness.

There are several spheres of seriousness of thoughts which we may observe men move in; steps and ascents of seriousness.

(1.) Countrymen, in their lower ways, have their plodding seriousness: how earnest do divers of them appear in minding of their occasions, which they account great!

(2.) Citizens, in their higher ways, have their higher and more improved seriousness. Oh what are the various earnestnesses, how strange and amazing to consider are the daily beatings of brains, and intendings of thoughts, on daily occasions by multitudes of persons in a vast city !

(3.) Students and scholars, in their ingenious ways, what intense and earnest musings do many of them habituate themselves to ; and what improved heightenings of the ways of studying do they contend unto ! The highest seriousness makes the best scholar.

(4.) Statesmen and soldiers, what seriousness do their grand and important affairs for the public (that lies at the stake to be preserved and advanced) engage and draw forth ! How great is the great politician's seriousness about his designs !

(5.) Debauchery and vice hath its sinful seriousness. Sensuality, uncleanness, contemplative fornication, hath in all places and ages given highest evidence of unparalleled seriousness : what ever hath raised and wound up the seriousness more ; as in amorous poetry, and wanton romances, and such-like filthy writings appears ! All sorts of vices and lusts, the lower they lie in the sink of the sinful heart, the higher they act in saddest seriousness and studyings for satisfaction.

(6.) The black train of hell and devils have their unspeakable heights of seriousness and musings for souls-destroyings.

But whatever spheres and heights of seriousness there can be, spiritual things of right must challenge of every Christian a far other and better seriousness. The perfect rule of religion obliges Christians to outdo all others in their greatest seriousness.

(7.) Doubtless the saints in all ages have excelled in this kind. In their retirements and happy

engagements between Christ and their souls.   Such as
Enoch, who walked with God, such as the other
holy patriarchs, such as Job, and other eminent ones.
And peculiarly David, that so rare artist in this way.
What may we also say of the holy prophets, blessed
apostles, glorious confessors and martyrs, and the
eminent saints and excellent lights of the church?
these no doubt have been highly serious in their
heavenly meditations.

Certainly the rare artists of the world, neither
Apelles in painting, nor Phydias in carving, nor De-
dalus in contriving the Labyrinth at Crete, nor
Archimedes in devising his mathematical instruments,
nor Plato, Aristotle, and the great philosophers, did
arrive at greater seriousness in study, than the worthies
of Christ in the passages mentioned before ; neither
than that seriousness of such as lived after the
apostles, as holy Ignatius, Cyprian, Justin Martyr,
Ambrose, Augustine, and others of the ancients, rare
men in contemplation.   And such as not only the
blessed reformers abroad, Luther, Melancthon, Bucer,
Martyr, Calvin, Zanchy, and others of them were,
but such of our own martyrs, holy Cranmer, Latimer,
Bradford, and the rest of that glorious army ; and as
many after them, in the several parts of these nations ;
one of whom would say, he thanked God, that for
twenty years together he had studied nothing but the
Bible and his own heart.   I believe none of those
philosophers and artists ever acted any seriousness to
that height and sweetness, that the holy ones of
Christ have done.

CHAP. XI.—*Meditation must be a Searching and
Scanning.*

6. THIS meditation, besides application of the mind
to the object, and intension or seriousness on it, includes a searching and scanning, or diving deep, an
extension of thoughts, a looking about, or endeavour
of comprehensiveness, in respect of the object, so far
as we can. To make as perfect and full a view
of it, and to see into the dimensions and extents of
that we think on. Thus when a man studies a thing,
he endeavours an extensive and a comprehensive seeing and having the fullest view. He sets it not before him to see a little, but the most he can.

The Scripture phrase I cited of Proverbs iv. 26,
and that of Luke ii. 29, of pondering, includes this
particular likewise we now are to treat of. In pondering, there is both first the mind's applying itself to a
thing, and the intending its acting, and then this third,
of an acting, of searching and diving into it, or
knowing what we can of it.

Pondering is an expression taken from goldsmiths
and tradesmen, that desire to know the full weight of
a thing, and thereby the value or worth for their profit and use. Thus the merchant weighs his mer-
chandise, the goldsmith weighs his silver and gold, the
jeweller weighs his rich pearls, rubies, and diamonds,
to know them more exactly. There is exceeding
great weight and worth in heavenly and spiritual
things : meditation must hold the scales, to weigh, so
well as we can, these so rich and precious things, these
diamonds, and pearls of heavenly treasure; yea, weigh
them as things that unspeakably surmount all other

things. As Prov. ii. 4, Wisdom must have a searching for as for hid treasures : as the searching for and
searching in the gold and silver mines ; in which there
is not only great earnestness of search, till the rich
vein is discovered, but being once found, there is a
following it with exactest industry, and utmost
curiosity, to find not a part or quantity of the treasure,
but all the riches scattered over the whole mine, part
after part. A Christian in his exercise of meditation,
must act the part of the exquisite miner, to dig deep,
dig over all the mine, and gather up the riches of it,
the lesser and greater quantities, as they come to view,
in the mines of spiritual treasure. Travellers tell us,
that in the Persian Gulf, at a certain season of the
year, great store of a kind of shell-fish is to be found
near the shore, in which shell-fish they find the precious pearls bred in their shells ; but the way of finding them is by diving : there are men that have an art
of diving down to the bottom of the sea, and bringing
up their baskets filled with these shell-fish ; the shells
being opened, they find and take out the orient and
rich pearls, of several proportions, some of them very
great and rich ; whereby they greatly enrich themselves
and those that deal in them. Meditation is the
spiritual merchant's art of trading for heavenly riches,
pearls of great price ; but there must be a diving deep.
If we have not this art of diving, we shall lose the
rich pearls : the deepest diving down in the practice of
meditation, comes up with the greatest returns of soul
enrichments.

    Solomon, in Eccl. vii. 25, hath a very emphatical
expression, to hold forth this we are upon : our translation hath it, "I applied mine heart," but the Hebrew
hath it, I compassed, and my heart that is compassed
to search, and seek out wisdom : or, I and my heart

compassed; so in the margin we have it.   There is coming upon a thing, and a compassing a thing; the heart in meditating is to compass in a thing as well as it can.   They say in philosophy, that wisdom lies in perspection, introspection, and prospection ; that is, in viewing throughly, all over, viewing inwardly, and viewing what may be eventually, what may be the issues of things : it pries into a thing, and looks round about a thing; makes the mind endeavour an extensive and comprehensive knowing, as was said.   Meditation in spiritual things should be like Nehemiah when he came to Jerusalem, and would go view it ; he went and viewed first one part, and then another, till he had gone round.   So meditation looks largely, views what it can take in and consider.

As God took Moses to the top of Mount Nebo, showed him all the land of promise, part after part round, Deut. xxxiv. 1 ; thus when we go up this mount of meditation, we must search, view, look round, take in as large a prospect as we can.

Chap. XII.—*Meditation is a Dwelling of Thoughts.*

7. Meditation includes a dwelling of the thoughts upon the object, drawing out the golden thread of holy thinking to its due length ; giving the mind its full scope and allowance of abode on the meditated matter.   Meditation is, in Scripture, and often particularly in the book of Ecclesiastes, expressed by the phrase of considering.

In consideration, there is, 1. Application of the mind to an object. 2. Intension upon it. 3. Pondering of, or searching into it. And this, 4. thing, the dwelling of the thoughts for some due space of time, for viewing and reviewing; for second thoughts, bettering of thoughts, and better completing this great soul affair of meditation. This meditation needs must have that allowance that all great musings and considerings have. Such as rare artists, exquisite engineers, deep philosophers, and great statesmen, all noble and ingenious ways must have for their times of studyings: they must have their due space of time for thinking, and lengthen out their mindings in that time; to make, as we say, no more haste than good speed. A staying awhile will make an end the sooner, make the work the surer.

Meditation is not a hasty hurry of thoughts: that is precipitation, not meditation. It is not gathering half-ripe fruit, that which hath not its time for the influence of heaven to come down upon it, and its own internal principle and power of its nature, to produce a kindly maturation, a kindly ripening. We will not have (for want of time) our bread dough-baked, or meat raw-roasted; knowing that what is not rightly prepared for the body, may breed distempers, if it bring not death. It is not the way to thrive, look well, and be strong, lively, and cheerful: why should we gather our soul's precious fruits half-ripe? feed our souls with dough-baked bread for want of a little time? Some things must have infusion for taking forth the spirits and tinctures of colours. Others a due time for percolation and straining, for a separating of the finer parts from the feculent and dreggy: and some things a longer space, in a slow and constant fire in the operation, or the cost and labour is lost.

Intensions for effecting things greatly beneficial and admirable, are most freely allowed a larger proportion of time, both for frequencies and repetitions of musing seriously.   But oh how too ordinarily do the best of saints fall short of the actings of rare artists, in their higher operations, in their stands and abodes of thoughts for more curious observations, and intellectual satisfactions! usually we are too hasty and eager to have duties over.   The soul is in pain till it be delivered of them.   In meditation it is hard (sometimes at least) to take off the thoughts for it from pre-engagements of other thinkings, and apply them to the duty; but harder to become duly serious in acting in it; harder yet to dive and ponder; and hardest of all to hold up an abiding of thoughts, and dwell long enough, and after views to make reviews, to re-act the same thinkings, to taste things over and over when the freshness and newness is past, when by long thinking the things before us seem old : we are ready to grow dead and flat in a performance, except we stir up ourselves often in it.   It is hard to hold on and hold up, unless we hold up a wakeful eye, a warm affection, a strong and quick-repeated resolution ; yea, and without often lifting up the soul to Christ, for fresh recruits of strength to hold on.   David, that so excellent artist in this way, saith he will meditate, often saith he will.   See Psa. cxix.   Doubtless he not only said I will, when he was to make his entrance into this hard work ; but likewise for continuance in it, to keep up his heart from flagging, till he well ended his work.   It is not the digging into the golden mine, but the digging long, that finds and fetches up the treasure.   It is not the diving into the sea, but staying longer, that gets the greater quantities of pearls.   To draw out the golden thread of meditation to its due length, till the spiritual ends be attained, this is a rare and happy attainment.

CHAP. XIII.—*Of Affectionateness in Meditation, or the Life and Lustre of it in the Intermixings of suitable Affections.*

8. I NOW observe that, for finishing the work, there must be intermixtures of the life and beauties of such affections, as are proper and suitable for the duty. It must be an affectionate acting, warm and zealous, lively and vigorous. So David's meditation, while musing the fire burned, Psa. xxxix. 3. Not only it should be so eventually, but by way of concomitancy; when we meditate with the mind, we should be warm at the heart: the fuel and fire of holy affections must come to the offering up this sacrifice. There must be an affectionate acting, which brings the life and beauty into the body and face of the duty.

They say beauty must have these four things. 1. Perfection, or entireness of parts, no part wanting. 2. Proportions due, no part too great, too little, or unsuitable : and proportion of colour, white and red in a just proportion. 3. There must be right order of parts, that nothing be misplaced. 4. There must be spirit and vivacity appearing in the face, as a chief ingredient or superaddition to all the rest, as that which adds singular grace and lustre to all. So besides the parts and chief lineaments, there must be that which completes the beauty of meditation ; those things which are as, not only the beauteous colours, but the freshness, liveliness, and spirits dispersed and appearing over all the face of this rare piece, this excellent performance. That as the heart, with its diffusions of heat and spirits in a due proportion, makes a comely, graceful, and lovely colour, which in heart-distempers, faintings, and sinkings, disappear and vanish; so the holy heart, with its diffusions of heavenly warmth and spirits, heavenly affectionateness, makes meditation comely, beauteous, and lovely.

If meditation be only head-work, and not heart-work, it is like a picture without life; like a student that studies in a mere acting of wisdom only. The right and genuine meditation is an affectionate thing: as the head acts, the heart glows. The life-veins of warm affections run and disperse themselves through the whole duty, and give lustre to it. This we may see in the meditations of that great artist in this kind; in holy David you may see a beauty and excellency of holy affection mixed and interwoven, like the gold in the tissue with the silk, and sparkling in his thus acting; affections appearing set as so many rich stones, rare beauties, and glories among his various musings.

There are three sorts of affections that shine gloriously in David's and other holy men's meditations left upon record in Scripture, which needs must be patterns to provoke us to imitation.

1. The affection of desire.
2. Of love.
3. Of delight.

Chap. XIV.—*Of the First Affection, Desire.*

THAT affection of desire wound up, and let out to
pantings and longings heavenward, and being above,
in this heavenly exercise of meditation.   David, with
his meditating of God and his word, tells us what
longings and heart-pantings he had.   " My soul
breaketh for the longing that it hath unto thy judgments at all times," Psa. cxix. 20.   How was this?
to have the book of the law?   No, it was to be exercised in it, to an improving of meditation on it, Psa.
i. 2.   Ah, he could not meditate enough, act freely
enough, far enough.   The commandment was so
" exceeding broad," as he saith, Psa. cxix. 96, so
very broad, and his heart so narrow : sin so encompassed and straitened him, that his soul breaks that
he could have no larger thoughts.   Such an edge and
eagerness of affection, such a large, strong, and vehe-
ment desire, should be an attendant, an assistant of
meditation, one strong feather added to the wing of
contemplation to make it mount up fast to heaven.

Ah, say Christian, Lord, that my soul could meditate still better, fly further, mount higher, be more
upon the wing, make sweeter and more happy discoveries, and prove a greater proficient in this heavenly
way ! Meditate with desires and breakings of soul, to
dart up the highest you can to heaven, and stay
there.

CHAP. XV.—*Of the next Affection, Love.*

THE next affection, which sends a great artery of
vivifying heat, a glowing heat, into this meditation, is
that of heavenly love; love to the duty and the excellent things to be meditated upon. Love is the great
heart fire, made to warm every holy service: " Oh
how love I thy law! it is my meditation all the day,"
Psa. cxix. 97.   Love led him into this pleasant soul
walk of sweet meditation, and love kept him company, kept his heart warm in it.   The fulfilling of
the commandment is love, Rom. xiii. 10, and love is
the fulfilling of this commandment of meditating; it
is performed in love.   This heart-vital heat of love
must move to and in meditation; must glow through
the whole work all the time of it.   Meditation is
either of the infinite beauties of the most blessed
God, the infinite perfections and surpassing glories of
his essence and attributes, and of the three Persons
in that essence; or else of the precious word or works
of God, his general providence and government, or
his peculiar governing of the reasonable creatures,
especially that so stupendous work of redemption by
Christ, and all those things which are reducible to
his praise; which must needs, being so beauteous,
have their supassing loveliness.   And therefore there
is great reason to act love abundantly towards them;
to have meditation still richly perfumed with actings
of burning love all over it.
    Oh let love ever come in and act its part in medi-
tation, wherein the soul's eye is not only glancing, but
wishfully viewing the surpassing beauteous things of
heaven, or such things as may lead up to heaven.

Ah, if I cannot ascend in a flame of love, yet let me in meditation fly up in some sparks of love. If my heart cannot burn in the flame of love, let it keep warm upon the embers of love. Let love give it a spirit, vigour, and liveliness. As Solomon's temple was inwardly all overlaid with gold, let this rare work of contemplation be overlaid and inlaid with love : as Solomon's chariot in the Canticles, the midst of it paved with love, Cant. iii. 10 ; so let this chariot of contemplation, the midst of it be paved with love.

Chap. XVI.—*Of the last Affection, Delight.*

The last affection, to make a threefold cord, to draw up the heart in meditation, and that winds the work up higher, and that is a great superadded beauty and glory, is the affection of delight, joy, and pleasure.

Meditation must not be a dull, sad, and dispirited thing ; not a driving like the chariots of the Egyptians, when their wheels were taken off, but like the chariots of Aminadab. Make me like the chariots of Aminadab, that ran swiftly, Cant. vi. 12 : so let us pray, Lord, in meditation make me like the chariots of Aminadab, that my swift running may evidence my delight in meditating. Holy David makes delight such an ingredient or assistant here, that sometimes he calls this exercise of meditation by the name of delight, Psa. cxix. 16 ; speaking in the foregoing verse of this meditation, " I will meditate in they precepts ;" in the 16th verse, " I will delight myself in thy statutes ;" which is the same with meditation, only with superadding the excellent qualification due meditation should have : this name is given from this noble concomitant.

As Wisdom's ways are all paths of pleasantness, so this path hath its pleasantness and sweetness. Contemplation hath its rare and most pleasant walks : no habitation hath such rooms, such galleries within, of pleasure ; nor gardens without with such walks and curiosities ; no situation, or stand, such prospects and varieties of delightful eye-objects as meditation enjoys. All objects that nature or art can present to the eye, are mere shadows and nothings compared with the rich and rare furniture the eye of meditation is provided with. The traveller, whose feet and helps have carried him the farthest, whose eye and observation hath viewed and taken in ever so much variety and curiosity, that hath recreated and satiated itself ever so largely, with any of the most taking things the whole world's fulness comprises, hath not, cannot come near to, and compare with, the transcendencies of purest, highest, soul-refreshing delights this high operation and more sublime acting conveys and gives in ; where the object is spiritual, the eye spiritual, the heart holy and spiritual, and the way of acting upon this spiritual object is spiritual, as every way or ordinance of Christ is. Or where the object is excellent, the faculty exercised on it is excellent, the medium or way of applying the faculty to the object is excellent, there the delight and pleasure is most rare and excellent.

There are sundry sorts of pleasures ; there are sensitive pleasures of the external senses, as of hearing, seeing, tasting, and the like : these are very various and very great, but too often bewitching and besotting.

There are fancy, imagination pleasures, which are

rare and higher than those of the outward senses.
Imagination and fancy, which is a quick, sudden,
short, and shallow apprehension of things, (it is not
judgment that ponders,) but a sudden slight taking
in and acting : this is (especially in some sorts of persons) a very high spring and strong feeder of delight
or pleasure ; of pleasures that come like things fresh,
quick and spirited to the body and senses. Fancies,
oh how they perfume like richest scents, please like
briskest and most racy wine ! fancies (though often
very fond and vain) yet are great inlets of delight.

3. There are intellectual pleasures, rational joys
and delights. These are more high, sublime, and refined, and therefore more sweet, such as the pleasures
of understanding new, rare notions, excellent speculations, and apprehensions of solid and precious
truths, and the mind's musings on them, tasting, feeding on them : this in itself is a more transcending delight than the two former ; though fancies weigh more
with some, yea, though sensual pleasures take most
with abundance.

4. But there are beyond the former, namely, those
that are spiritual pleasures. Delights found and felt
in a holy and spiritual heart, in one that hath a principle far above sense and fancy, and natural reason :
that a renewed mind, a spiritual understanding, a wisdom from above, only reaches and relishes ; and these
are best and sweetest, when they are not only taken
into the soul by an act of apprehension and conceiving of them, but when they pass into the more
inward room, or office of the mind, into the judgment ;
when they are there detained in consideration, and by
meditation give down their delicious sweetness, like
grapes in the wine-press. Meditation is such a soul
engine, such an instrument of such a manner of

operation, that nothing in the world, the highest objects of sense, fancy, or mere natural reason, can act with that complacency and delight.

Solomon, in his Ecclesiastes, that rare record of his large and infallible experience of all things for pleasure and delight, tells us he found nothing so sweet, and which he could act upon with that delight, as when he acted up in meditation, Eccl. xii. 13. David oft expresses what joy he acted in this soul engagement; yea, tells us as he did, so he will delight himself in it, and the heavenly objects of this heavenly work. Heavenly things and a heavenly heart meeting in meditation, will act and make the purest pleasure.

Meditation therefore must have this attendant of delight; which like a flame, like the chariot of Elijah, carries up the soul in musing into heaven.

CHAP. XVII.—*Some other Particulars added in some special Scripture Expressions.*

BESIDES these three affections of strong desire, ardent love, and holy delight, that, like heat, and spirits conveyed from the arteries (arising in the heart) into all the body, to add to and complete what we have in some measure expressed, there are these three or four things I shall a little speak to.

1. Meditation should be a work very savoury to the soul.

2. It should be sweet and pleasing to it.

3. It should be with satiety in it.

4. With an admiration, as the crown on the top of it.

1. It should be performed, not as a thing that is disrelishing, but savoury to the spirit in the doing, Rom. viii. Those that are after the Spirit, savour the things of the Spirit.

There are some things that are unsavoury in themselves; others, though savoury, yet not savoury to some palates. The things of heaven are none of them in any degree unsavoury in themselves. Meditation is not so in itself, but to a carnal spirit it is one of the greatly unsavoury things, greatly displeasing and disrelishing ; but to the spiritual man it is not so, but a work singularly savoury, like Isaac's savoury meat, like feeding at some noble feast : where a good appetite, and a right palate, feed and savour, still savour the delicacies and varieties successively, every thing is savoury. There are some things savoury, as nature yields them; others, and in great variety, as art reduces and orders them ; and, accordingly, there are very admirable diversities of savoury things, which have their degrees of savouriness. What great varieties are there made by art, from the meanest food to the highest delicacies ! yet in the gospel feast of fat things full of marrow and wine on the lees well refined, in the feast of all heavenly varieties, meditation hath more unspeakably rare dainties, than all that nature or art can yield. " Eye hath not seen, nor ear heard, neither have entered into the heart of man, the things which God hath prepared for them that love him," 1 Cor. ii. 9. Not the greatest of the greatest princes, not Solomon's most glorious feast, not Ahasuerus' royal feast, not any of the Persian or Roman emperors so much spoken of in histories, could occasion a feeding with such high savouriness, as may be had in the rich and precious things meditation hath to feed the soul with. Therefore, O let meditation be still most

savoury, let every spiritual thing be very savoury ; as
there are more varieties of objects, and higher degrees
of excellency in them, endeavour a suitable, and extensive, and an increasing savouring : as men at a feast
pass from the first dishes to the after dainties, with a
more eager feeding and better relishing.   This is the
first thing.

2. Meditation should be sweet.   This I further
add, in that the Spirit of God is pleased to honour this
pious expression of the holy prophet, (by recording it
for us,) who after a most heavenly torrent of elegancy
in expressing the surmounting excellences of God in
the wonderful ways of his workings and governings,
says there in Psa. civ. 34, " My meditation of him
shall be sweet."   How sweet must meditation be upon
infinite sweetness, and from whom all other sweetness,
creature sweetness, word and ordinance sweetness, de-
rives itself !

" How sweet are thy words unto my taste ! yea,
sweeter than honey to my mouth," Psa. cxix. 103.
This must be chiefly by meditation : it is that which
presses and sucks out the rare sweetness in the precepts, so holy and righteous ; in the promises, so
precious ; in the encouragements, so high ; and in all
the excellent things in the so perfect word of Christ.
He not only asserts the sweetness he found in meditation, but is transported with high admiration.
And when he could not speak of it to the height and
fulness, then (which is our usual manner) when we
are at a loss for expression in words of comprehensiveness, to wrap up ourselves in the elegancy and
terms of an interrogation and admiration ; yet not
contented with this way, for fuller representing his
experimented sweetness, he takes up a comparison,
says sweeter than honey, which in that pure air of

that blessed land of Canaan, was the most surpassing
sweet honey in the world. Yea, in Psa. xix. 10,
" Sweeter than honey," and the distilling of the honey-
comb, which is the sweetest of all others: but this
was in holy meditation, that made the honey melt in
his mouth, and give down its sweetness. Meditation
that drives the hive, drains the honey, and drops in
the delicious sweetness into the musing spirit. Lord,
teach us the way of this heavenly art, and make this
honey drop, and the heavenly manna of Divine truths
fall richly into our hearts.

3. Meditation may and should be attended with a
heavenly and spiritual satiety: " My soul shall be
satisfied as with marrow and fatness ; when I remember thee upon my bed, and meditate on thee in the
night watches," Psa. lxiii. 5, 6. His rare hours in-
troduced and made returns of heavenly satisfaction.

The largeness and excellency of it he sets out by a
very suitable expression, satisfied as with marrow and
fatness, which to the stomach yields the best satisfaction,
the speediest and sweetest, the most large and lasting.
No food satiates better than marrow and fatness. So
Isa. xxv. 6. The gospel feast is " a feast of fat
things full of marrow." There are the fat things of
a perfect righteousness applied, of a full pardon obtained, of reconciliation and peace with God made,
and glorious adoption conferred through Christ, John
i. 12 ; the feast of the feast, together with the satisfaction of the blessed image of Christ, in the beauteous lineaments of holiness and righteousness, light
and life, of all graces and excellences ;. and all drawn
to the life, and wrought up by the Holy Spirit's inhabitation and operation, and arising from believers'
happy union and communion with Jesus Christ and
his fulness. And likewise as a glorious superaddition,

that of assurance of a most happy condition, and of
the unchangeable love of God, and that blessed hope
of eternal life, which strews sugar, drops unspeakable
sweetness and satisfaction, upon and into the holy
heart, 1 Pet. i. 8.   These and sundry others are the
fat things full of marrow, and make up the feast ; and
are from the actings and industries of this happy way
of meditation.   As therefore the heart is hungry and
thirsty, in continual lingerings and longings, and
never quiet, meditation must carry it to this royal
gospel feast, and thereby meet with a blessed satisfaction, not being contented with the sight of the feast
and the delicacies of it, without attaining some happy
satiety.

The prophet Isaiah mentions one dreaming of eating, but when he awakes his soul is hungry.   If we
look not well to it, meditation may be but such an un-
profitable thinking, as when we have ended it, we may
miss of this satisfaction, find our souls empty.   It
must be still so managed, that it prove a help and
cure to my soul's inordinate lingerings, and improve
to a spiritual satisfaction.

Plutarch in his Morals tells of one Pythos, who,
finding a rich mine of gold, and out of his eager desire to have the treasure in the mine, was so continually attending at the mine, that he neglected coming home to his meals.   To confute his covetous
industry, his wife one day (instead of providing him
food) prepared nothing but golden dishes, with several
sorts of meats cast into the forms of sundry things
edible, but all of gold ; whereby he could observe a
curiosity of invention, but was disappointed of feeding and satiety.   We must not in our meditation content ourselves with feeding the eye for curiosity, but
endeavour feeding the soul unto satiety, heavenly

satiety. Ah, let my spirit mind more a fulness of
satisfaction, than newness of notion; carry it from
head work to heart work, from bare speculation to
rare and ravishing satisfaction.

4. Admiration. Let me, to set the crown on the
head of the duty, add one thing over and above, let
meditation be carried up to admiration; not only should
we be affected, but transported, rapt up, and delighted with the beauties and transcendencies of heavenly
things, act meditation to admiration, endeavour the
highest pitch, coming the nearest to the highest patterns, the patterns of saints and angels in heaven,
whose actings are the purest, highest ecstasies and admirations. Thus were these so excellent artists in
meditation, David a high actor of admiration in meditation, as often we see it in the Psalms, as in Psa.
viii. 1, 9. "Oh how great is thy goodness!" Psa.
xxxi. 19. "O Lord, how manifold are thy works!"
Psa. civ. 24. And in other places David's meditation and admiration were as his harp well tuned and
excellently played on, in rarest airs, and highest
strains; as the precious gold and the curious burnish-
ing, or the richest stone and the most exquisite
polishing and setting of it. So blessed Paul, who
was a great artist in musing, acted high in admiration; his soul was very warm and flaming up in it: it
was as a bird with a strong and long wing, that soars
and towers up aloft, and gets out of sight.

Thus sundry of the ancients, as holy Augustine,
Bernard, and others of those, who have recorded their
rare hours of meditations and transportings of admiration, liftings out of themselves, and liftings up to
heaven. A precious minister of Christ often in his
life-time would wish he might die in the heavenly exercise of singing a psalm, in which he used to be

transported in meditation and admiration : at length he had, in singing a psalm, his holy wish, dying in the performance ; whereby he was rapt up (after his rapture in the duty) into heaven, changing his place, but not his work. Another, a man eminently learned and heavenly, riding with a friend in his coach, fell into a rare contemplation and discourse of the glory of heaven, and the beatifical vision, and within a short time he was suddenly taken from this earth, to take his possession of that glory he had so before in contemplation.

Chap. XVIII.—*Of the Ends of Meditation.*

MEDITATION we described to be an institution of Christ, and duty of a Christian, wherein the mind acts upon spiritual things, or other things in a spiritual manner, by a due considering of them, and this to holy ends or spiritual uses only : now the ends of meditation are three.

1. Such as refer to the most high God.
2. Such as respect ourselves.
3. Such as relate to others.

1. Such as refer to the most high God.   Meditation is to be the motion of the heavenly spirit heavenward ; to carry it up to heaven and keep it a time there : a looking of the eye of the mind, and a lifting up of the heart, a making a stay, and taking a spiritual solace in heaven with God.

All duties we perform must be done to the living God, " to serve the living God," Heb. ix. 14.   If otherwise, our duties are but dead works, loathsome as dead carcasses. A living work must have for its supreme end the living God. God that is the first and best, must have the first aim and levelling to.

They say in philosophy, the last end must have the first intending : the first looking at, as the first ground and mover to any work. And as they say in optics, in treating about the nature of seeing of objects, that which first irradiates, sends forth that which through the medium first conveys itself to the eye : this is first visible, and that is light. The first thing the eye of meditation should fix upon, is that which is the light of lights, and that is God, who is all light, beauty, and glory. Meditation should be chiefly acted to see God, and to aim at glorifying of God above all ; " Whatsoever ye do, do all to the glory of God," 1 Cor. x. 31.

The Gentiles, wise men, and great philosophers, because their speculations were not acted to the glory of God, were vain imaginations : see Rom. i.

Whatsoever the aim be, if the glory of God be not the real scope, nay, if it be not the master mark, the work is miscarried ; and but a ravelling out of time, a losing of labour. Meditation must make sure of the right method and order of aiming at the glory of God, like the sun in the heavens that outshines all other lights below and above, and that which is to be seen before, and above all others ; so this must be eyed and aimed at likewise, far before all other.

Three things to be eyed : 1. The infinite glories and resplendencies of the eternal and all-sufficient God. 2. The infinite distances and heights he is in above us. 3. The infinite obligations that ever lie upon us, to exalt him beyond all.

As in the making of our whole man, whereby he is

total owner of us, and proprietor in us.   And in our
preserving, whereby we are yet more highly bound.
And in the provision for our eternal happiness, which
is far beyond all the former.

Therefore there is an absolute necessity of this method and order, of still first aiming every duty, and
acting at this grand mark; and then to make it the
striving and pressing hard of our spirits to it.   Oh that
in my thinkings, in the ascendings of my thoughts,
this glory of the great God may ever still ascend! for
no thoughts nor actings can truly ascend, if they go
not up to the blessed God and this glory of God: if
God goes not up higher in our thinkings, they then
go not higher than self, and which is but indeed
downward, and not upward at all.   Nay, it is a worse
descent than that also, it is destruction and hell-ward
whatsoever is self-ward, and is not to the advancing
of the great God.   Meditation is not only to be acted
to God as a duty, but as this duty, in its peculiarity
and propriety, as being a peculiar straight line to God,
as a singular way for our taking aim, this high aim, at
exalting the praises of God.

Thus did that rare marksman, holy David, as it is
admirably conspicuous in the Psalms.   In Psa. ciii. 1,
2, in the very entrance he lays a strict, a repeated
command upon his soul and all that is within him, to
bless, and bless, and praise God: yea, not only lays
his meditation level to the mark, but raises up his
spirit to take the purest, the fullest aim; this both by
a selecting and improving of spiritual reasons, the
strongest he could find, and the most quickening motives he could apply, all that his heart might carry
up (in a heavenly flame) the highest praises of God.
Thus you shall see him very frequently acting his

meditation up with the greatest fervour to this exalting highly of God.

Meditation is a peculiar visit made to the great God; a mind, a thought visit, wherein, as to a great friend, the soul, as it were, comes and saith to God, Lord, I come to see thee, I now come purposely to see thee, to spend some fit portion of time with thee, and I come for that high honour and observance I am infinitely obliged to tender to thee. Every meditation is giving a fresh visit, and thereby a new tender of highest honour we owe to this best of friends.

The next end is, our highly pleasing of God, which by meditation we are to intend: God will be both obeyed and pleased with our respecting and acting of every appointed way; meditation is the best way, the most pleasing way of thinking. We are to "walk worthy of the Lord to all pleasing," Col. i. 10. Therefore this must be performed to an intended pleasing, a due serious thinking, a pondering and dwelling of the thoughts upon heavenly things, and chiefly upon the infinite beauties and excellences of God, who is the perfect thought and heart knower, the exquisite searcher and observer of soul actings. And then most, when purposely pleasing is designed: this must very highly please him, when we especially design pleasing, with our most wishly eyeings of him, yea, to intend the doing our best to please him; and this, oh how should it greatly also please us! David, in Psa. xix. 14, prays for pleasing God, "Let the words of my mouth, and the meditation of my heart, be accceptable in thy sight, O Lord, my strength, and my Redeemer." So it is not only to be prayed for, but made the holy aim of meditation with our utmost care. What industries do the favourites to great princes use to please them, especially that their thoughts offered in counsels may be acceptable! Thus, how did Philotas act, who was the favourite of Alexander the Great; and Mæcenas, the favourite of Augustus; and so divers among ourselves! But how near goes it to them if their counsels please not! as with Ahithophel, when his counsel pleased not Absalom; and on the contrary with Hushai, when his counsel pleased. So when Haman's counsel was rejected; and how contrary with Mordecai, when his counsels were adopted! Pleasing of a prince is a great encouragement; but pleasing of a God is a sweet soul contentment; it is most worthy striving after. Oh how unspeakably sweet will the finding and feeling of this prove in thy heart, when meditation is performed purposely to please thy God; when it runs in a pure stream, when thy spirit, reflecting on its actings in meditating, makes discovery of this holy aim of high pleasing the most high God! As the Scripture commands pleasing, the saints are peculiarly commended and greatly honoured for it. As with wise and well-bred people, (obliging and pleasing in good things,) great pleasing is a great praise. As Abel, Enoch, and others, from this character of pleasing God. It is a heavenly ambition to earnestly design pleasing; as in all others, so in this walking with God in meditation.

G

CHAP. XIX.—*Meditation respecting Ourselves.*

As there should be such aims relating to the great God, so meditation must have its advantageous aims respecting ourselves.

1. The grand scope and end of our own happiness.
2. All other subservient and excellent ends.

1. The grand end of our own happiness, and working out our own salvation, is the next spiritual end that meditation as a mighty engine should set on going to effect. It should be sure to be ordered up, and duly aimed at ; acted according to the aptitude and fitness of any way in it, to further this important end : musing and right meditation hath a most rare tendency and helpfulness, as to the working out salvation. As it is a sanctified means on God's part, so it must be an earnestly employed help on our part. We must ever so meditate that it may help on salvation ; we must mean it and level it sure, not any way deceive ourselves, but take the best and surest aim. Salvation challenges the best eyeing, the fullest, steadiest, strongest aiming of every way and help. Soul happiness must not have slender aims ; we cannot have aimings too serious and intense.

Let my aimings here have the keenest edge of seriousness, be elevated the highest, made the firmest and the most extensive. Let them take in universally whatsoever may most excite to and quicken in this high operation, proportionate it to this working out salvation, the so great gospel salvation.

Thus did the prodigal, (who represents the returning sinner,) when sensible first of his unspeakable misery ; and thence, apprehensive of the great obtainable felicity, the so glorious gospel salvation ; never did he so act any thinking, make such warm work of it, as now.   In like manner the jailer, Acts xvi. having such a dreadful awakening from sense of a lost condition : oh what a pondering of salvation was that, from a heart so warmed and edged ! when extremity of misery hath the deepest sense, meditation of salvation and recovery hath the highest seriousness.   What can have such a thinking, as when one thinks for life, and that eternal !

Let meditation take in those considerations that are most awakening, that unspeakable misery comes upon us by sins so innumerable ; as contracting on the person such horrid guilt, and conveying into the heart such hellish filth.   Every sin, with the aggravations, contracting a debt to Divine justice, and that entered into God's debt book, which we never can pay or get paid without a surety, but must bring destruction in eternal fire.   Then weigh the great uncertainty of life, and how certain death casts every one upon an eternal state unavoidably, upon inconceivable eternity.   Then must be weighed the mighty enemies, and multitudes of hinderances, lying in the way of escaping.   Next come the considerations that are the most highly encouraging to strive to enter in at the strait gate, such as the Scripture's fulness supplies.   Oh how great and prevalent are those in the gospel, to make wise and warm us, to strengthen and heighten meditation ! As eternal life, which in the believing heart is already begun, with sure promise of carrying it on to perfection, by our yet co-working with the Holy Spirit of Christ, working in all his, which we must do continually : ' Work out your own salvation," &c. Phil. ii. 12.   What may I say of conjunction with God, by union with Christ, by faith of communion with

Christ, in justification and pardon of sin, a most glorious righteousness, reconciliation, adoption, with a sure title to heaven, and the glorious graces of Christ, his image, holiness, wisdom, life, power, peace passing understanding, joy unspeakable, with establishment, growth in grace, victory over all enemies!

Ah, what wishful lookings should we exercise daily at this so great salvation, and the transcendencies and perfections of it ; and at last such an outlet of all evils, such an inlet of all good, such a crown of glory, with all the inconceivable excellences of it, and the perfect fruition and vision of God for ever!

I shall yet add one thing more, and that which is (after all momentous considerations besides) the greatest, of strongest influence and efficacy, that is the vastness, inconceivable vastness of eternity : not eternity merely in the abstract, only considered in itself, but in reference to misery or felicity. I say, to all other inducements add eternity; hang on this great weight of eternity of misery and felicity. Endeavour with thy utmost art and industry, by all resemblances, to have the liveliest and most operative representations of it.

Breathe thy soul often by healthful exercise here ; breathe thy soul frequently up this hill of eternity. Whatsoever thou meditatest on, let still this be one object entertained in thy serious thoughts, this vast eternity : let this have its due time.

Holy meditation hath, besides the former, several other excellent ends to be aimed at and improved to. As artificers do with their gold, beat it out sometimes to its utmost ductility and extensiveness ; improve this gold of precious heavenly objects, beat them out to the utmost by this hammer, this art of divine meditation.

The art of meditation will, like Solomon's temple overlaid with gold, overlay thy heart with Christ's pure gold, and make it rich and glorious.

Ah, therefore, Christian, act up thy meditation to these precious ends, and chiefly lay a mighty stress upon that so momentous thing, eternity of soul misery or felicity.

CHAP. XX.—*Of the particular Ends of Meditation in respect of Ourselves.*

THERE are various ends of meditation respecting ourselves : I shall mention, among others, these seven, relating to our own spiritual advantage.

1. As a principal improver of saving knowledge.

2. To make our knowledge clear and distinct.

3. To found a rich treasury of truths, and make them sure.

4. To be an introducer of habitual wisdom, an acquired habit of wisdom, to the first given wisdom, in heart renovation.

5. For a kindler of heavenly fire and flame in the heart.

6. For a mighty corroborater of holy purpose.

7. To be a constant quickener of the Christian course.

1. Meditation is a principal improver of saving and heavenly knowledge. To set as it were more lights on the golden table in the temple of the holy heart, to replenish the golden candlestick with more and better lights, and glorious burning lamps, to yield

clearer light in the dark heart. I am wiser than my enemies, for thy commandments are ever with me; that is, in meditation continually, as, Thy law is my meditation continually, or " all the day ;" " I have more understanding than all my teachers : for thy testimonies are my meditation ;" and, " I understand more than the ancients," Psa. cxix. 97—100. Here is an assertion in a kind of gradation of the success-fulness of his holy meditation, namely, understand-ing, wisdom, and excelling in them : wiser than his enemies, yea, than his teachers, yea, than the an-cients, that have had longest time, largest opportuni-ties, for greatest knowledge and highest wisdom.

Meditation is the ground, inlet, and improver of knowledge. It is not the great and much reading makes the scholar, but studying and pondering what is read. It is not reading much that makes the knowing Christian, but meditating on what is read : reading without meditation is like swallowing much meat without due chewing ; that makes a lean man, so this makes a lean mind. Many read and hear much, but understand little, because they bring them-selves so little under this ordinance of meditation. If thou wouldst be right excellent in knowledge, be rich in it, and of a higher stature in wisdom than others, as David was ; strive to write after his rare copy in abundant meditating.

2. Meditation is to make knowledge clear and distinct. The apostle, in Phil. i. 9, mentions love, its abounding in knowledge and judgment, and in other places we have mention of discerning and judg-ing. As to matter of learning in arts and sciences, they have the most clear and distinct heads, have their notions most methodical, distinct, and most mellow, who muse most ; on the contrary, those are

the weak and easy scholars that muse least. Divers Christians have their heads full of raw, confused things, a company of broken ends, notions of small use to themselves or others, for want of due digestion in meditation. Gold ore, without refining and sound hammering, is of little use ; want of refining keeps the metal base, want of hammering makes it brittle, it will not be burnished up to a full and perfect brightness, it will not obtain a just firmness : you cannot have so rich plate or utensils, no vessels of it for your special use. The minds of too many Christians lie strewed over with precious truths, but neither clear nor distinct : they are like houses or closets where the rich things, furnitures and rarities, lie covered over with dust, or want brightening ; or are so dissevered, lie so scattered and out of place, that scarce any thing is for any present use. So there may be multitudes of notions and truths in the mind, but they are obscure and confused ; a dust covers them, a curtain is drawn too far over them ; they are of little use, because meditation is little used. Meditation is that, and must be that, which methodizes them, that sets them in order : meditation brightens them, and helps to make them clear, and give them a lustre. Clearness and distinctness will not be had without giving down-weight in due meditation. And without a clear and distinct apprehension of things, they are of little light to the Christian ; of less influence as to others' instigation and encouragement. A scholar that hath his notions raw and obscure can make (at the best) but a bungler. An artificer, any tradesman that hath not his art but imperfectly, will make of it but a mean way to live and subsist : he that understands his way in religion, will prove the wise, warm, and fruitful Christian.

3. Meditation is to be a chief help to the repository

and treasury of truths, to lay and lock up store of precious and useful truths more sure, to fix the lights of truth firm, make them stand fast in the mind. Serious meditation is a great advantage to memory, the soul's treasury; that lays up precious truths in the close conveyances of the understanding, and locks the doors fast. Such as meditate most, will have the surest memory for things heavenly.

Holy David, to lay up and hide the word in his heart, Psa. cxix. 11, did it, as by other, so by the way of meditation: as in the 15th verse, by meditation, and in ver. 97, continually. As truths came to him, so made he them sure by meditating: his treasury and stock grew richer, and were kept the safer. As in scholars, not the multitude of books, or great reading, will make a treasury of precious notions, and make them sure for use, but the due afforded allowance to the clearing and fixing of them by meditation. Christians that meditate will be rich in knowledge, and keep it sure.

CHAP. XXI.—*Of the next Particular, the fourth End, to produce habitual Wisdom.*

THE next particular end of meditation, is to produce an habitual wisdom in the mind of a Christian. To be a moulder and former of the spirit into habitual wisdom, to superinduce upon the first fundamental, (that infused wisdom given in renovation and heart change,) I say to the first saving wisdom, to superadd and introduce an habitual wisdom, (acquired, as they call it,) such a wisdom as makes a Christian more knowingly and wisely skilful and ready for his way and work; to be beyond a mere learner, to prove an artist for working out his own salvation.

There is an infused knowledge, and an infused wisdom; a wisdom stamped upon and given into the mind in its first renovation and conversion, for then a man ceases from being a stark fool for salvation, as the Scripture makes all in the state of nature, Prov. i. 22. But by conversion and change of heart, and by union with Christ first, and then communion with him, as the wisdom of his members; by this they become wise, by an infused wisdom, whereby they are wise indeed, wise to salvation; wise whereby the right and chief end and happiness is discerned, and the right way and means to that end is discovered, and both thereupon designed and intended. But this is but a lower measure at first, a seed, a grain of mustard-seed, as the Lord compares the state of grace begun in the heart, Matt. xiii. 32.

But beside the former infused wisdom, there is requisite an acquired wisdom, a superaddition to the other. This is a noble help, and an improver of the first; that as to the eye of reason and natural wisdom, learning and experience and exercise brings in an habitual wisdom, enlarging the natural. As it is with a scholar, or an apprentice to a trade, first his tutor or master infuses principles for the wisdom or skill of his profession or trade, whereby he can a little begin to act or work, make trial, though but in an imperfect manner; but then by minding and musing of his instructions, and by exercise, he comes at length to an acquired habit, to act and work knowingly and with facility, because he hath a new wisdom to understand his way. But without minding and musing he would

never have had the way, the art or trade intended.
Meditation (beside others) is a singular help to
habitual wisdom, to attain the art and trade of Christianity. " The wisdom of the prudent is to understand
his way," Prov. xiv. 8. And Eph. v. 17, " Be ye
not unwise, but understanding what the will of the
Lord is." Though they were excellent Christians,
by the large measure of wisdom they at their first
conversion received, yet he calls upon them to seek
for more, to improve the wisdom infused to further
wisdom, to a spirit of wisdom, to an acquired habitual
wisdom, to be artists in their way, and excel in it.
Nothing doth so mould the mind into habitual wisdom, as meditation ; nothing so improves and enlarges
spiritual understanding, makes to understand our way
and rule of walking, as meditation, as serious and repeated thinkings.

In natural, or any civil affairs, wisdom in and
about them is not obtained by bare thinkings, slight,
short, and transient thoughts, or by seldom, and now
and then in a fit to think and away, but by serious
thoughts, weighings, and ponderings, yea, by frequencies and constancies of thoughts and mindings. This
way of thinking makes a man wise in his way, trade,
or in any business. It is impossible to be wise with
this acquired habit of wisdom, without taking time,
making a stand, an abode of thoughts, and those
serious also.

If we are hasty, short, give not due allowance of
time, and down-weight of thoughts, serious thoughts,
we shall not come up to habitual wisdom ; nor shall
we act as wise Christians are required to do, if habitual
wisdom be wanting. No man can act wisely, or in
height or eminency of wisdom, except he act by a
perfect principle, as the angels and saints in heaven

do, or as a perfect artist, that hath a perfect skill and hand at some art or work. Most good Christians, though they have true, saving wisdom for the substance, yet have little, very little, wisdom to understand their way, little of this acquired habitual wisdom. This is the reason of their being so frequently to seek, so at a set, and at a loss, not knowing what to do. The want now of this wisdom, is from want of meditation, serious and frequent musing to frame and mould the mind into habitual wisdom, and so increasing in wisdom daily.

That a Christian may be an artist, and have his trade, have head and hand adapted and ready for it, this must be by habit, through custom and use. There are these four special things, excellent advantages in a habit among others. 1. It lays in ability for doing. 2. It induces facility in doing. 3. It produces delight and complacency with doing. 4. It holds up evenness and constancy in doing.

A scholar or an apprentice put upon employment for learning an art or mystery, at the first wants the ability to act as an artist, a logician, a philosopher, or the like ; and so the facility, pleasure, and constancy cannot be come at, because they are the higher steps or stories built upon the first, that of ability. But when by time he hath accustomed himself in a way, he comes to an habitual knowledge and skill, and that habit brings ability to do ; and with ability goes facility, easiness to act in the art or way ; then with facility is pleasure and delight attending ; what we do with ease is pleasing. Then what produces pleasure, brings also constancy, and doing with evenness and equality. Oh how desirable is this wisdom in Christianity, how highly is it to be contended for, to have this wisdom, this art of going to heaven, of living to the living

God, to arrive at a doing with an improved wisdom, a wisdom of superadded ability, with a happy facility of acting, a sweet delight in acting heavenward, and a beauteous, a glorious evenness and constancy; so as not to be and remain still weak in our trade of godliness, not to be to seek so often, as not knowing our way in divers cases, not to drive so hardly on, not to be so dull and heavy, nor yet so unevenly and brokenly to carry on our work, but with all the forenamed advantages, to be daily still experienced to higher encouragements !

This is a grand end of meditation, to work up to habitual wisdom, to help a Christian to excel in this soul beauty of an exquisite artist and operator for heaven and eternity.

Chap. XXII.—*Of the fifth End of Meditation, to kindle and inflame the Affections.*

MEDITATION hath not only its excellent ends and uses, relating to the understanding and mind, but also is of singular use relating to the affections. Meditation is that which keeps alive the fire on the altar, and helps to make it burn : it is that which both gathers the sticks, the fuel, and materials for keeping the fire from going out, and that which kindles them, blows upon them, and makes them burn and flame up to heaven.

In the Levitical law, the fire upon the altar must never go out, but it was kept burning by the priests' continual minding it : if they had not minded that fire continually, it would have gone out. The fire in the holiest heart must be kept in, kept burning continually by meditation and constant mindings. Meditation is a great heart warmer; it renews and increases spiritual heats, drives away dulness and dead-heartedness, brings a new life, strength, and vigour into the spirit, when it faints and flags.

They say of the loadstone, (that wonder in nature,) when either by carelessness in keeping it, or by some accident, it loses its virtue, yet by laying it some good space of time in the filings of steel, it will again recover its virtues ; when the spirit of a Christian, by not looking well to it, loses of its heavenly heat and liveliness, the way of recovery is by laying it asteep in this so warming and quickening meditation. Oh how burning and flaming may we often observe the spirit of the holy psalmist David, in his acting of meditation ! As Psa. xxxix. 3, " My heart was hot within me, while I was musing the fire" kindled or " burned :" musing made him hot, yea, burning hot at the heart. Thus often in the beginning of a psalm we find his heart low and discouraged, but as this musing was acted and heightened, his spirit grew hotter, and at last flies all on a flame, flies up to a very high pitch of heavenly heat. Oh how do all the conscientious practisers of meditation, ever and anon experience these happy heavenly heats and heart enlargements ! Oh if all the saints' so glorious heart quickenings were gathered together, what a rich chain of pearls, pearls of rare experiences, would they make up of the heart-warming efficacies of meditation !

Meditation is a mighty engine to kindle cooling hearts, and make them flame in fervency. The rule of effecting a business, especially entangled in

H

difficulties, is by removing the obstacles first, and then applying furtherances.   Meditation is instrumental to heart warmings and quickenings :   1. By making a grand inquest into the occasions of heart coolings, and helping to remove them.   2. By stirring up to the efficacious means of warmth and quickening.   It is a rule among the schoolmen, that every negative is founded in an affirmative ; that is, every not doing is founded in some positive act of doing something else. And as to the like purpose, we say in philosophy, the intention of one thing is the disintending of another : meditation makes an inquiry, and thereby a discovery of that which hinders spiritual heat.   The extinguishing of fire and heat in nature, is either by casting on much water, or smothering it ; by either throwing on much incombustible matter, or hindering the air's openness, and its free coming to it, which chokes it, or by withdrawing the fuel upon which it feeds.

(1.) Meditation finds heart coolings to proceed from a giving way to and the present prevailing of some corruption or lust, that like water quenches the fire.   They say that some rich spirits and rare extractions, if taken in some acid or sour liquor, the sour liquor turns the edge of those spirits, and frustrates their operation : as cold, clammy humours at the head of the nerves or sinews, stop the course of the animal spirits, and occasion the numb or dead palsy ; or as some cold poison taken in, quenches the vivifying heat and spirits, endangers, if not induces, death ; so a corruption or sin let out and given way unto, chills, and cools, and quenches the heart heat, and the longer yielded to, the cooler will the affections grow.

A sin given way unto, damps the heart-warming ordinances, quenches the heart-warming spirit, obstructs thy communion with a heart-quickening Christ. " Whoredom and wine and new wine take away the heart," Hos. iv. 11: what is there spoken of a more total taking away the heart in evil men, is true of a gradual taking away the heart, the heat and liveliness, in godly men.

(2.) Meditation on due inquiry finds heart coolings to arise from Christians smothering their heat with heaping up businesses and troubles upon themselves, launching too far into the seas of worldly affairs and over-carings.   The thorny ground had the word choked by cares and affairs of this life: what cares and business doth to the word, it doth to the heart's warmth.   If thou canst entangle thyself in the matters of the world, thou wilt cool apace.   The farther a man travels from the sun northward, the cooler he is : turn your face from heaven to the world, go far, and you come to not only cool, but freeze. Or as the woman in Roman history, that out of a design to enrich herself, contracted with the enemy to betray the castle for that which the soldiers had on their left arm (meaning their golden bracelets); but the soldiers, instead of their bracelets, threw their shields on her, whereby she, instead of being enriched, was smothered.   To engage in a throng is the way to be smothered : the world will smother thee if thou engagest too far ; it will still cool thy heart heat, make thee of a warm and lively, a cool, dead-hearted Christian.   There is a fish called the torpedo, if you touch it with your bare leg, or hand, it presently benumbs the limb that touched it.   Touch with thy heart upon the world, it will leave it numb ; there is no such way to keep in thy heat, as to keep out the world, avoid the danger of a crowd of business and cares.

(3.) Meditation, upon searching, discovers the decay of heat is from decay in heart-warming ordinances, where the Sun of righteousness shines warm upon thee, whereby the soul heat is both preserved and increased. Abatings of heavenly heat arise from drawing away the fuel of heavenly duties, or thy own remissness and negligence in them. If a man shall cast away his clothes, leave his food, and decline the means of preserving heat and life, he must needs grow cold, if he be not quickly killed. If a man reads not, meditates not, prays not, hears not, or is negligent and formal herein, he must needs, like a dying man, grow cold. It much depends upon the lively performance of holy duties, that you keep heart warm, or that you decay in your fervour by carelessness in the means : meditation will mind you of this, and put you upon mending it in time. The angel of the church of Ephesus, forsook or left his first love, his heart heat ; and Christ intimates, he had left off his first works, Rev. ii. 4, 5.

2. Meditation is instrumental to spiritual vivacity and warmth, by helping to apply the things that recover and promote heat and liveliness.

(1.) Meditation mightily helps here, by being a great instrument of searching out, applying, and working home the Scripture's heart-warming considerations, such as the quickening Spirit, the Inditer of the Scriptures, that knows what things are most proper and proportionate for recovering or increasing heat, what he hath left upon record to use in this case. As consideration is the first mover in the soul, so warm considerations are the first warmers. Oh what a latitude and fulness hath meditation to fetch heart-warming considerations from ! If the eye looks up to the heavens, what abundance of heavenly bodies for conveyance of light and heat it soon discovers! But if the eye of meditation looks into the Scriptures, what a prospect of various rare and glorious passages is there to be found of considerations! like abundance of richest spirits, highest cordials, and preparations of all sorts, in artists' shops and closets. Oh what heart-warming considerations can meditation fetch and apply from the infinitely blessed God, his infinite excellences, eternal love, sweetness unspeakable, of the sense of his favour, and the like! Oh what heart-warming considerations from Jesus Christ, to behold him and view him all over, in all he is in his inexpressible glories! in all he hath done, whereby he hath outdone all that ever was or shall be done! What warming considerations in respect of the Holy Spirit, the grand and mighty applier of redemption, by his habitation and operation! What in respect of the word, the precepts, promises, threatenings, and examples in it of sundry sorts, all for our help and comfort! What of the covenant of grace, so sure and sweet! What in respect of ourselves, soul's state, and all the great concerns of it in salvation! Meditation can never want heart-warming considerations, can bring stores of arguments of all sorts, and blow upon them, to make the heart kindle and flame, although it was chill and dead, and never so low brought.

(2.) This engine of heavenly meditation produces heart warmth and vivacity, by taking thee out of the shade and cool, and leading into the sunshine of heart-warming ordinances, wherein the Sun of righteousness arises, and shines warm, and his quickening Spirit breathes warm upon thee. As a cure of cooling and decaying love, Christ counsels the angel of that church of Ephesus, first to repent, and then to do

his first works, Rev. ii. 4, 5.   Negligence in holy
duties, omission of them, or remissness in them, in-
troduced a cooling of his love ; therefore what was
lost by not doing, must be recovered by such a doing
as the first was ; that his first works-done again, might
be a rekindler of his first love: disuse of exercise
abates the natural heat and vigour, but returning to it
will again recover it.   Meditation, when it finds the
failure and defect, will provoke and engage to the just
remedy and relief.

CHAP. XXIII.—*The End of Meditation in Reference to the Will.*

MEDITATION, as it is to be a helper to warm the
affections, so for a means to strengthen and fix the
holy purposes and resolutions of the will.   It is not
a wavering and weak purpose, or a feeble resolution,
will serve for a foundation for building so high as
heaven, for carrying on so great and hard a work as
soul saving.   The Scripture mentions cleaving to
the Lord with " purpose of heart," Acts xi. 23.
Holy David often in the Psalms tells us of his will,
his purpose of heart, Psa. cxix., and his heart was
fixed, Psa. cviii. 1.   Meditation is singularly instrumental here,

1. Of fixing and deeper rooting of the grand general
purpose of pleasing and glorifying God, and working
out our own salvation.

2. It is greatly instrumental for corroboration, and
for strengthening the lesser roots of derivative pur-

poses, that spring from the grand purpose, that are the particular abettors and helpers of the main and general forementioned purpose.   In every holy heart there is planted at first conversion, that fundamental and noble purpose of pleasing and glorifying God in all things without exception : this purpose also must be often renewed, have its reiterations for corroboration. There must be also derivative and subservient purposes, particular purposes, in reference to advancing the main purpose, and the soul's chief end and intendment, purposes for particular soul concerns, particular duties either respecting mortification of particular corruptions, and particular self-denials, or that respect particular graces and duties, in the seasons required for them.   Every particular duty and soul concern, must have the hand of a peculiar purpose lent it to assist it.   Right undertaking, as it must have the mind acted in wisdom to direct it, so it must have the will acted in purpose, deliberate purpose, to effect or endeavour it.   Grace in the will must work it into a due purposing for the particular occasion of every particular incumbent duty, purpose of heart to ground performance.

The Scriptures give frequent instances of both general and particular purposes this way practised. First of the general and grand purpose ; thus David very often in the Psalms declares, " I will keep thy statutes," Psa. cxix. 8 ; there is a general purpose superadded to the first purpose that he did when he first gave up his heart in conversion to his God. Thus in the 69th verse of this psalm, " I will keep thy precepts with my whole heart ;" there is another general purpose.   And Psa. cxvi. 9, " I will walk before the Lord in the land of the living ;" there is another of his added general purposes for serving God.

" Thou art my portion, O Lord : I have said I will keep thy words," Psa. cxix. 57. There he tells you what he had done in the time past ; he had said, as in the former he saith, what he would do for the future. So in the 106th verse, he tells you what a purpose he had taken, such as had a confirmation of an oath, or, as some express it, had, as it were, the strength or force of an oath ; yea, here tells you what he did in time past, and what he will do for the future : " I have sworn," there is the time past ; " and will per- form," there is purpose for the future : a recalling of his old purpose, and a renewing of a fresh purpose to back the old. So others of the saints in Scripture are to be observed, to accustom themselves frequently to strengthen the first general purpose, with the additions of frequent following purposes.

Also for particular purposes, for particular coming occasions, we have frequent instances of holy men's practices. In reference to avoiding sin, " I will set no wicked thing before mine eyes," Psa. ci. 3. In reference to taking heed to our ways and words, " I said, I will take heed to my ways, that I sin not with my tongue," Psa. xxxix. 1. In reference to trusting on God in difficulties, waiting upon God, worshipping God, praying, praising, and all sorts of duties and graces, love, joy, hope, courage, constancy, and the like.

Purposes and resolutions, general and particular, and the frequent use of them. Linking purpose to purpose : strong purposes are still necessary for every Christian that will work out salvation ; yet all must be done in the strength of Christ, else they will not hold, but wear out and snap asunder.

Now meditation is greatly instrumental herein. 1. Instrumental to make our purposes wise : we must ponder and consider before we purpose; rash purposes and more sudden, without due bottoming in a previous meditating, will prove but miscarryings and abortions.   They are like foolish building on the sand, they soon fail: a purpose the more deliberate, the more durable.   2. Meditation helps to make purposes strong and firm: we have need of strong purposes for the great things of eternal life: we have strong opposition from corruption within, and temptation without. Meditation helps mightily to strengthen resolution.   It repairs to your spiritual magazine, and thence fetches forth strong spiritual arguments to raise strong resolutions and purposes.   Arguments out of the rich stores of Scripture, of all sorts and natures, to relieve the weakness of the will in purposing.   Meditation acts a divine reasoning, disputes you into a purposing, when it shows you have so much for it, and nothing at all against it.   Also meditation selects and sharpens arguments, sets home, and improves them upon the conscience, that you must yield, must resolve, and firmly, strongly, in such matters as none can be higher.

Oh how many strong and unanswerable arguments can meditation come furnished with, to dispute against carnal unresolvedness, to plead for your acting strong resolutions for any part of an enjoined duty !   What weight can it put into the balance to cast the scale for God's and your soul's interest !   I need not name the heads of arguments, such as the indispensable necessity of the precept and means, the great sinfulness of unwillingness, the excellency of the thing, with the sweetness, comfort, confidence, and advantages attending it : but this I shall add, the excellency of a Christian lies chiefly in his will ; and the excellency of that will is in the height of its purpose and

resolution, freest purpose and choice, firmest resolution and determination for the work he came into the
world to do.   And the great assistant, on our part,
of holy resolution, is holy meditation, applying fit
reasons to stir up resolution, and instigating to all
those ways that produce and cherish it.   And this
latter is another particular whereby meditation is a
relief and fortifier of good resolutions and purposes.

Meditation, I say, is a great strengthener and
stablisher of holy purposes, both as it is a directive,
and instigative ; as teaching us what are the ways to
help us in purposing, and as instigating and provoking
to the ordinances and means, that will water the plants
of holy purposes, make them root deep, and shoot up
high, flourish and bear fruit.   If our purposes are
weak ; if our hearts in purposings are apt to slip out
of joint ; no sooner set, but as soon slipt, or ready to
dislocate and be out of joint ; what remedy then have
we but consideration or falling to meditate, to make a
true inquiry first of the right and proportionate ways
of healing this will malady, this heart infirmity?   And
then meditation instigates to a due use of discovered
helps, of infirm and inconstant resolutions, draws you
to and through the whole circle of means, provokes
you to try every remedy to cure these abortive purposes.   It directs and leads you to all the ordinances
of help, to the promises that make over help, to a
Christ and all his fulness of help, to the Holy Spirit
for his applying effectually of help, to stirring up faith,
to acting recumbencies and restings on Christ in the
promises, to stirring up ourselves, to humble ourselves
for our failings in our purposes, and to strive against
them, watch our heart's slipperiness, and to labour
keeping our resolutions and purposes better.   In
nature's order, doing is upon resolving, resolving upon

considering ; so in grace, performing is upon purposing, purposing arises from pondering and meditating. The saints in Scripture that acted the highest
resolutions, exercised the deepest meditations, as we
see in the man after God's own heart. Fits and
flashes of fancy never produce firm purposings ; but
such resolutions that lie longest asteep in due preceding meditation, have the deepest tincture and
holding colour. Longer I have been upon this particular, as a point more material, because the art of
raising and fixing, heightening and improving, holy
resolutions, is such a happy fruit of divine meditation
ordered to that blessed end.

CHAP. XXIV.—*Of Meditation as a grand Sup-
porter of the Christian Course.*

MEDITATION is for a constant keeper-up and sup-
porter of the Christian course, as to the evenness of
this golden thread, without decays, sinkings, stands,
and interruptions. Also as to improvements and
goings-on to perfection. And as to conflictings with
enemies and oppositions.

This was holy Paul's practice, by still taking in
the highest provoking considerations, minding and
due pondering of them ; it made him to labour so
abundantly, to press so hard to the mark, forgetting
the things behind, and looking to the things before,
Phil. iii. 13, 14. He meditated on the prize of the
high calling, kept his eye on the crown of righteousness ; he kept his eye alway on the stores and varieties
of gospel encouragements.

A Christian of the greatest consideration will ever keep up best his evenness and constancy. New, fresh meditations are new soul feedings, new meals, which add new strength and vigour ; they make a Christian like Elijah, when he had eaten, to travel with new strength to Horeb, the Mount of God.

We should not move like the sloth, but contrarily, like the bird of paradise, that is seen generally flying, and in a very expedite motion. Divers for running the blessed race of godliness, go creeping slowly, making little haste or progress ; certainly they meditate little. The swiftest of foot in Christ's way are the frequent. serious meditators : meditating makes the birds of paradise, the Christians of the perpetual motion.

Chap. XXV.—Of the End or Use of Meditation in reference to Others.

The third and last end or use of meditation named, was in respect of others. As the former ends were in reference first to God, then towards ourselves ; so this we come now unto, is in respect of others.

Meditation in reference to others, to persons of all sorts, is to fill the treasure of the heart with good things, and to fit the good man, out of the good treasure of his heart, to bring them forth to furnish others, and be serviceable to their spiritual condition. " The good man out of the good treasure of his heart bringeth forth that which is good," Luke vi. 45. He first lays in a good treasure, stores himself with the riches of heavenly treasure, and then brings it out : it is not a work merely of fancy and imagination, but

chiefly of meditation and consideration.   Imagination
takes in varieties of things in a promiscuous manner,
without differencing or distinguishing them.   Imagination makes a collection, meditation makes a selec-
tion and adjudication.   Meditation observes what
precious things are offered us, and lays them up, and
discerns what are not precious, and lays them by ;
yea, by meditation there is not only an old store laid
in, but there will be also an adding of new.   It is
this rare art of meditation that both founds and fills
the treasury with old and new.   Fancy and imagination, as it is in divers, may fill the mind with trash,
but not with treasure ; with things that glister, but are
not gold.

It is this meditation that makes discerning betwixt
the precious and the vile, that takes up on searching
the treasure found and discerned, and lays it up in
the treasury of a good heart.   And this is first for
the good man's own store and supply ; but then it is
also to enable him to bring forth, for others' use and
help, to bring forth in first discourse, what is spiritual
and savoury for the nature, and that likewise is seasonable and suitable for the occasion offered ; to bring
and show forth the apples of gold in their pictures of
silver, as Solomon saith of a word spoken in season,
Prov. xxv. 11.   Likewise, to hold forth things that
are exemplary as to a fruitfulness in walking, to bring
forth the good things of light to shine out, light of
precious edifying truths, and light of rich and rare
experiences, and to bring out the good things of a
heavenly, quickening, comforting, and encouraging
nature.   Meditation, as it is the great way of gathering up things that are useful, and filling the heart
treasury ; so it is to be the way of direction to open it,
and bringing forth in discourse the good things stored

up. And by this imparting them to others, we our-selves have a double advantage often following. 1. A clearer and more distinct apprehension ; as silver and gold brighten by use, not by laying up. 2. A warmer and livelier affection; and when they come forth warmer by discoursing, they are the apter to warm others and make their hearts burn within them.

This then is one end, one great and excellent end of this so excellent way of meditation : that as face answereth to face in water, so heart may answer heart in warmth. When things have been well warmed in the forge and furnace first of meditation, and then in our communication, fire may kindle fire, and one warm heart may occasion another. Discourse that is the mere product and fruit of fancy and memory, and hath not some rise and tincture of warm meditation, some discovery of heart heat, is like flashes of lightning, or the shining of the moon ; they make a show, but warm not ; nobody is warmer by the one, no heart is warmer by the other.

PART II.

CHAP. I.—*Of the several Kinds or Ways of Meditation.*

WE now, from the divers ends of meditation, proceed to the several kinds or ways of it.

Meditation is either that which is more set and solemn, or that which is more sudden and short. That which is more set and solemn, is either the more ordinary and daily, or that which is extraordinary, upon some more peculiar occasions, both which the Scriptures hold forth in the recorded precepts and precedents therein.

1. The necessity of daily meditation. The first way of solemn meditation, is that which should be daily : that as private praying and other duties are a Christian's daily ways of exercising himself in godliness and walking with God ; so holy meditation is one golden path in the great road to heaven, one way of breathing his soul daily up the hill of eternity, and meeting with God in the mount.

The holy prophet makes it a character of the blessed man, that he meditates in the law of God day and night, Psa. i. 2: where we have held forth the grace, and the degree of that grace : the grace, he doth meditate ; the degree, day and night. Thus much hereby must then be implied, that as it is to be performed often, so it cannot well be performed by the rule in this Scripture passage, if every day in course there be not something done in this way, either more or less :

I 2

certainly we cannot give God and our soul's concerns too much measure.

In Psalm cxix. David tells us his daily practice, to meditate both in the day and night. Now his example, being a king and under such varieties of important affairs; so many and so great as none can have more: and if he had still such cares, troubles, and dangers attending, might not these have excused some abatement of his constancy? but it did not. This therefore leaves all sorts of persons without excuse, none being able to allege that which he could, or more urgencies of daily occasions. There is no doubt, that as it is a work which lies upon every one, so sure as the day returns and the fresh businesses of it; so this meditating of right doth challenge for itself some fit season and portion of the day, being one of the great businesses for the soul's help.

As no Christian can plead exemption from this daily incumbency, this daily soul affair; so no good, prudent Christian can conceive but he may find out in the revolution of the day, some at least fit opportunity for serious meditation. Or if not in the day time, (the time of action and avocation,) yet in the night upon the bed, the time of rest and freedom. What was said of that great warrior Hannibal, making his way into Italy over the high, rocky mountains, the Alps, with fire and vinegar, " Hannibal will either find a way, or make one;" and is said of love, " It will creep if it cannot go;" a good heart will find or make its way over mountains of difficulties and business, to have communion with Jesus Christ, Cant. iii. 1—3.

Ah, it is most sad if I can allow so many hours in the night for rest and sleep, so many in the day for businiess and emergencies, so many for eating and drinking, so many for company and discourse, yea, so much time for pleasure, play, for trivial things next to nothing, it may be for things worse than nothing, for sins and lusts, and that no part of the twenty-four hours must be afforded for serious thinking, thinking of things ten thousand times more momentous and important to us than the sum total of matters that sweep away and swallow up precious time so much. The good Christian cannot but at least close with the eternal obligation of this duty; and the wise and fruitful Christian cannot but yield some compliance with the practice of it, and let this come in for its due share in the time of the day, as one important business to be despatched, and that must still contribute to the right making of it up, and improvement of it. After some evidence of the equity of this daily duty, I come to speak to the nature and way of this meditation. This being of all other sorts the principal, which therefore challenges a more distinct and careful handling.

If Christians very well understand not this way, or fall very short of the due manner and order of it, the work is neither so pleasant nor successful as it might be and should be, and, questionless, is to Christians such as are the great artists herein, such as have been well practised and experienced in it. I shall therefore now endeavour to show the nature of it, and something of a method of due proceeding in it.

In general, it is that daily exercise whereby we single out purposely some spiritual or useful matters, to act the searchings and ponderings, which according to our ability and opportunity of the day we can exercise for our spiritual advantage.

The mind is a spring always running in thinkings, a wheel always turning, a forge always framing, a wing ever moving; it is the most active, busy, nimble thing in all the world, therefore hath the greatest need to be well looked unto, to be kept, as Solomon saith, " Keep thy heart with all diligence," Prov. iv. 23, to be guided with the best skill and care, with the steadiest and stiffest rein; like a horse of highest mettle, ready to run away with his rider; it will run wildly away, and carry the soul into vanity, folly, and self-mischieving.   Meditation is a spiritual rein and curb, and the peculiar designed way to reduce, rectify, and order it.

To bring the heart's thinking power into the highest subserviency, the greatest usefulness to the main, to the soul's grand interest, there is a great necessity upon every good heart of daily and much meditating.

Chap. II.— *Of the Manner and Way of daily Meditation.*

Every Christian is to awake with God in the morning : as David when he awoke was ever with God, Psa. cxxxix. 18, at his awaking times in the night, by thinking of God; so chiefly when he awoke last, when the night was past, with all the dangers of it, and the day dawned, then the morning-star of meditation arose in his heart.   The first work in the morning is to awake with God, and the noble thinking faculty, which upon awaking will instantly awake, and begin to stir, begin to act: let it be awakened into this sweet way of self-entertainment, by engaging of it in holy meditation.   Look we that the heart be first of all seasoned, sweetened, and perfumed with heavenly thoughts.

Begin with serious reflections upon the great goodness and tender mercies of God in our preservations from Satan's malice and mischiefs; what affrightments, in noises and appearances, in violence and harms, would he exercise, if he were let loose upon us! What other harms from wicked men, usually taking the advantage of the dark and still night, when all are at rest, besides harms from accidental occasions that we are liable to! There is also the great mercy of beds to lie on, rest without tossings, ease without torments, sleep without holding our eyes in awaking, having our sleep sweet, awaking with refreshing, having our formerly weary bodies and decayed spirits revived and cheered, and we ourselves under a new adaptation and fitness for the succeeding day's occasions. There should be also a stand and abode of thoughts upon any thing in the night which is more signal and remarkable, that comes down from heaven as a brighter beam of favour to take the eye with, that is let down as a more peculiar hand to take up our thoughts to heaven by, that is sent as a more special love-token, stamped with more legible characters of the care and kindness of a God towards us.

When the night's past mercies have had some due reflections and musings, had a down-weight of improvement endeavoured for warming and enlarging the heart toward our good God; if then it conveniently may be, nothing to the contrary interposing, and that justly may hinder, the next thing then for the way of our thoughts should be to look forward to the day coming on, and the spiritual concernments of it; or if it then cannot at the present be, yet so soon as we can to set to and engage in this so useful meditation.

Chap. III.—*Rules about Meditation.*

The more particular rules we may use for this daily meditation, are these following.

1. Meditation of setting up the master mark, the glorifying of the most high God.

2. Next unto it, meditation of eternal happiness in the enjoying of God.

3. Meditating then after it of the sure and adequate means for attaining them both.

And these are therefore to be meditated upon.

Meditating on, 1. Jesus Christ, the only way to the Father by his work of redemption.

Meditating on, 2. The Holy Spirit, the great applier of Christ and his redemption.

Meditating on, 3. The holy ordinances of God, the usual ways of the Spirit's coming to apply Christ by.

Meditating on, 4. The word of God, chiefly the promises of the gospel: these on God's part.

Meditating, 5. On our part, by our use of the ordinances, and the word and promises, and that faith and holiness whereby we come to union and communion with God, glorify him, and obtain salvation ; faith as the instrument of receiving Christ, and both faith and holiness, or the graces of Christ, as our principles of life and power, to live unto God, and growing up to perfection against all opposition.

1. The first thing according to the rule of best wisdom, which lays the surest foundation in any course, is first to take into most serious consideration the supreme and chief end, and to act a fresh setting up before us that master mark and scope of the most high God, and the glorifying of him, to be con-

tinued as we can through the whole course of the
day.

Meditation of this glorifying God, for pure, lively,
and highest advancings of it, this is the soul's best
operation, and runs most parallel to the perfect work
of heaven.   Heaven's higher acting is contemplation
of the most blessed God, for the most transcendent
exaltings of his glory : the rule of Scripture is, to do
all to the glory of God, 1 Cor. x. 31.   And this rule
must therefore have its place and power here ; therefore this daily meditation must take it in, and set it
up.   It must be every one's wisdom to bottom our
day meditation, with the still eyeing of and aiming at
the glorifying of the most high God.   To begin with
the fresh thoughts, and also the warmest frame of
spirit, for furthering the supreme end, the glory of
God, and with it, as fit to be annexed unto it, that
which is wrapped up with it, our own eternal happiness.

In a watch, and divers artificial motions, the evenness and expediteness of the motion is from evener or
unevener, stronger or weaker drawing of the spring,
the first mover.   Thus is it in godliness, a Christian's
motions are answerable to his eyeings more or less of
the main end.   Christians complain of their daily
dead-heartedness and unevenness ; it much arises
from the so little or listless lookings at the main mark.
Paul looked earnestly, and he pressed hard.   In
archery, those who eye the mark most earnestly and
steadily hit the oftenest and fullest.   The wisest Christian is the most earnest, equal eyer of the main
end.   There be many particulars in this head, which
according to prudence and leisure may have their
seasons of ponderings.

The variety will produce delight, and set an edge

upon the spirit, apt to grow heavy and weary; they are such as these: as the considerations of the most high God, in all his infinite glories and perfections: his all-sufficiency, in his knowledge, wisdom, holiness, righteousness, and the rest ; but chiefly in his so infinite and unchangeable love, and riches of free grace: the infinite obligations eternally lying upon us, for glorifying and exalting of him : the infinite excellences and fulness of the second Person, and his infinite love, in undertaking with his Father, to redeem lost sinners : and the infinite love of the third Person, the Holy Spirit, the applier of redemption. Some most serious meditation of God, and glorifying him, to give down into the heart a glowing heat and liveliness for all the following day, is still fit in some measure to be practised.

2. The next should be some serious musing on that next end, our own salvation and eternal happiness, further to be wrought out, to be our day labour, by the opportunity of a new begun day, a day which will bring us nearer to the ocean of eternity.

Chap. IV.—*Of the next End, Salvation.*

Next to the highest God's interest, must be mused seriously upon this great soul interest : If thou art wise, thou art wise for thyself, Prov. ix. 12. Wisdom to salvation, 2 Tim. iii. 15. This, because self is so near and dear, and the immortal soul so unspeakably precious, the heart being once stamped with a spiritual, high, strong self-love, will

have a mighty influence of warmth abiding on the
spirit.

Here two things are to be attended and practised.
1. Meditation of salvation, in a more general notion
and consideration, works little or nothing, but the
pondering of particulars in salvation. It is a rule in
oratory, and so in preaching, that for moving and
drawing the affections, generals and things in a confused manner spoken, hit not, work not, draw not.
It is the distinct seeing and viewing of particulars
which moves and affects to purpose : so meditation to
be effectual must particularize the things comprised,
in some sort, in this happiness and salvation—as that
so blessed freedom from sin in the guilt, in pardon,
and righteousness ; from the dominion of sin, by
power, life, image of Christ, and holiness, and the
glorious privileges of a Christian here, and everlasting
glory hereafter ; and such like.

2. There is another rule among orators, that things
moving the affections, do it either by their greatness
or excellency, or by their presence or nearness : as the
greatness of a person, or the presence of a person ;
or the greatness of a good or evil, or the nearness and
presence of it.

1. The greatness, the surpassing greatness of salvation, as Scripture sets it forth, Heb. ii. That so
unspeakable deliverance from such a height, breadth,
and length of misery by sin ; and that inexpressible
happiness by union with Jesus Christ. The so great
things of this glorious state should fall by our meditation upon the affections, and daily, like fire from
heaven, kindle them greatly.

2. Things move by their presence or nearness : the
remoter the object is from the faculty, as the objects
of the external senses, as seeing, hearing, and the

rest; or the farther a thing is apprehended to be, as any place, or time, or the like; the less it affects: but the presence or propinquity of a thing moves most; as when a poison or dangerous thing is near or present, as an antidote or a help when near, when death or deliverance is at hand, when a friend is present, or the like, this moves most. So the way of meditation here, is by representing salvation as present or near, 2 Cor. vi. 2, escaping hell *as now*, being put into possession of heaven *as now;* if I were *now* dying, and my soul sitting on my lips, ready to take its flight *as now;* if *now* the last trump were sounding; *now* Jesus Christ seen coming to judgment; *now* the sentence of absolution passing. Let me thus season and strengthen meditation by this kind of representation, seeing it as near, as present, now acting, now doing, or now having, and fully possessing this salvation.

CHAP. V.—*Of the Means conducing to this chief End.*

THE next thing in spiritual wisdom, to be the object of daily meditation, is to give (as we can) some allowance of serious thoughts, of that which should be the due and adequate means, conducing to the chief end, of eternal life, with the glorifying of God, as formerly we have mentioned.

1. Christ the way. Therefore the next thing, (being the highest and uppermost of all conducing means to the supreme end,) the next thing, I say, to

be the great object of meditation, must be Jesus
Christ, our way to the Father, and our highest way
of glorifying him: "No man cometh unto the Father," saith Christ, "but by me," John xiv. 6.   Initial coming to God by faith to justification, reconciliation, and union with God, is by Christ: all other
after-comings, and glorifyings of God, are still by
Christ, as also all salvation is treasured up in him:
so it must be the best way for our meditation's method,
to be daily acted in some measure upon our mighty
Saviour, our great and only way to our great and
chief end; so he calls himself the way, John xiv. 6.

Here what a most glorious and delicious object hath
the eye of meditation!

Christ, in Isa. lxv. 1, calls, "Behold me, behold
me!" Ah, what a spirit must that be, that for such an
infinite beauty cannot afford one cast of the eye, one
wishly look in the whole compass of a day; that can
look every way freely, fixedly, and unweariedly, but
Christ-ward!

Ah, when a heart is strongly inflamed with a love
to Christ, the eye will be acted in most wishly lookings upon Christ; as the love grows, the earnest lookings will grow.

Here then the rule is, to meditate in some due
measure on this glorious object, so both infinitely
excellent in himself, and so mighty a Saviour unto us.
His infinite riches and preciousness, in his natures
united, in his offices conferred, in his graces fulness,
perfect performances, most perfect redemption; his
infinite love, pity, willingness to save lost sinners;
the so great free offers of himself, and giving himself
to us, applying his whole redemption to us, by his
mighty operation in us: some singular seriousness
and vigour of meditation cannot but daily be due, as

that first and chief means to the chief end. Christians that least look at Christ, and least distinctly view him, will make the slowest progress; and such as study him most, will have the easiest and most expeditious coming up to the main mark.

CHAP. VI.—*Meditation of the Holy Spirit, the Applier of Christ and his Redemption.*

2. SOME due proportion of thoughts seriousness is proper to be daily acted, in reference to the mighty and only applier of the work of Christ's redemption, the Holy Spirit, and our great daily helper. The Holy Spirit first comes to the soul and person of a Christian, applies Christ to him, brings Christ into him, makes him his temple, and a habitation of God and Christ to dwell in the heart. The Spirit comes, inhabits, sweeps, and cleanses; furnishes the heart with light, that was darkness; with truth, that was error and deceitfulness; with power, that was weakness; life-warmth and qualifications of heavenly graces, that was cold, dead, and altogether sinful; and draws the glorious image of Christ upon the soul. He enlivens, establishes, enlarges, and encourages, and fills the spirit with peace and joy unspeakable. We act from his blowings on the gardens of our hearts, then the spices of graces flow, Cant. iv. 16.

The wheels mentioned in Ezek. x. 17, moved from the spirit in them; so a Christian moves or not, as the Spirit moves or not. Every day, and for every duty in the day, there is need of a new blowing of the

Spirit, that the spices may flow ; new moving, that the wheels may move us.

We must neither grieve, quench, nor resist the Holy Spirit, Eph. iv. 30 ; 1 Thess. v. 19 ; Acts vii. 51; the Spirit who is our helper and applier further of Christ, and receiving of his fulness.

If we would act wisely, the eye of the soul by meditation must daily be pondering the necessity of the Holy Spirit's influences, stirrings-up, strengthenings, and enlargements. When we neglect and slight the Spirit, and so justly want his help, we must needs drive on heavily ; but when we mind him and have his assistance, this wings the soul, and makes it to move strongly and nimbly to the main mark.

If the question were asked, What were the highest thoughts the mind can possibly think ? they would be such as these three following. 1. That thought of the so infinite and all-admired love of God the Father, in giving freely his Son for sinners. 2. That thought of that infinite and all-amazing love of God the Son, in giving so freely himself for his Father's enemies. 3. That thought of God the Holy Spirit's infinite love, astonishing love, in so freely giving himself into such corrupt, hellish hearts, to make them his glorious habitation, his palace and solace, to be the mighty heart helper and comforter. This Spirit then must not be grieved by the least neglect, but highly and constantly both honoured and cherished, with our utmost thought preciousness and earnestness ; that so thinkings may work up to liveliest lookings for him, lookings to listenings for his knockings at the door of our hearts, listenings for ready lettings of him in ; and being let in, we may give him the highest and freest entertainments, with yieldings of the fullest obedience unto him.

It is reported, that formerly, sometimes travellers sailing by the coasts of Arabia the happy, have had by the winds blowing off the land, such rare rich perfumes of the precious spices, that (without the experience of it) it is hardly credible. Sometimes the Holy Spirit so blows on the garden of a Christian's heart, that the spices in such sort perfume it with raptures of peace and joy that are inexpressible, and then it runs apace to the main mark.

Then it must be best to enter on the work of the day, by an early and earnest eyeing of this glorious helper, the Holy Spirit, who is sooner ready to lend us his helping hand, than we are ready for it.

Chap. VII.—*Of the next Particulars, the incumbent Duties of the Day.*

3. The ordinances of Christ are the next general things meditation may fix on. The ordinances are our ways of communion with God, the ways whereby God conveys himself to us, the King of heaven's highways of spiritual commerce and trade. The roads and paths wherein the Holy Spirit walks, and comes to apply himself to us; and our ways in which we are to go forth and meet him, apply ourselves to him, fix a heavenly intercourse and acquaintance with him.

The winds blow from all the quarters of heaven, and the Holy Spirit breathes and blows from all his heavenly ordinances: we may therein look for the breathings of the Spirit, but we must not look for the Holy Spirit out of his own ways.

The prerogative of the Spirit is, not to be abso-lutely tied to ordinances; our liberty is not to be loosed from them. We are tied to the ways of Christ, which are our warrantable ways for communion, and waiting his Spirit's comings and assistings.

The eye of meditation should act daily in such fresh and vigorous lookings on the ordinances, as may more highly commend them, raise their value, represent them more lovely, reduce us to more evenness in performance, by finding them more easy and sweet in continued use, and exercising ourselves in them; and induce still higher admiration, by our experiencing their help and efficacies. The ordinances of Christ have their high ratification in the Holy Scriptures for their power and efficacy. The saints in all ages have given their great confirmation, set their seal to each of them, by millions of encouraging experiences.

When ordinances are more precious, they are the more efficacious: oh let our meditation's daily scope be, to make them more precious, that they may prove more efficacious. Like that eminent pattern, that great meditater David; that high progress he made in meditating of the ways of God, set their value higher, and made his heart warmer. He meditated and he valued more, admired more, and he acted more eminently, and arrived at last at that pitch, which hath left him on record in the highest rank of saints that ever lived. The ordinances therefore are most worthy our daily musing on, as for their own excellency, as the King of heaven's high institutions; so, as the Holy Spirit's walks, wherein he comes to meet us, and have communion with us, and apply Christ more unto us.

CHAP. VIII.—*Of Meditation on the Word of God, and the Promises, whereby the Spirit first is given, and after works.*

THE word of God is that sure wisdom revealed unto us by God, to lead us by his counsel to glory ; that only infallible rule given us to walk by : it is the golden sceptre of Christ, for the subjects of his kingdom to come and touch the top ; the dear purchase of Jesus Christ for the only rule of his redeemed; the breathing and dictate of the Holy Spirit ; the high product, and that clearest shining forth of the brightest beams of infinite wisdom, truth, holiness, righteousness, mercy, free grace, love, power, and all glories and perfections of the Author, for the blessed ends it is bestowed.

It is the excellent instrument in the hand of the Spirit, whereby he effects his great soul-saving work ; whereby he brings about that work of wonder, the applying of lost sinners to an all-sufficient Saviour first, by effectual calling, and then applies Christ more and more, building them up more in him unto perfection. If I look for the Spirit's operation, I must look for and apply myself to the help of that rare instrument by which he operates. Think what an engine it is, what most admired, glorious work he hath effected by it, upon millions of blind eyes, hard hearts, persons impotent, crippled in their souls, dead in sins and trespasses, at a dreadful distance from God, haters and enemies of him, and all things leading to him ; enlightening them, healing them, and reconciling them to himself and his word and ways.

CHAP. IX.   BY DIVINE MEDITATION.   103

Chap. IX.—*Of Meditation of the Spirit's drawing to Christ by the Promises.*

As it is the instrument in the Spirit's hand, and without which it would do nothing, could not awaken,
humble, and convert the soul; so it cannot either
convert and bring in, or confirm and build up, without
that most signal sweetest part, the precious promises;
and the promises would do nothing out of the hand
of the Holy Spirit, and his efficacious managing of
them.

The grounds and encouragements of all our draw-
ings near to God through Christ by his Spirit in his
ordinances, are the promises of the gospel, and the
covenant of grace.   Sinners must not draw nigh to
God, without his warrant and command first given.
But a command will not be yielded to, unless there
be the encouragement of a promise of an acceptance
and help, in both the first and all other after-ap-
proaches to God, Psa. cxix. 49; Gen. xxxii. 9;
Exod. xxxiv. 6; Numb. xiv. 18.

And the promises must be managed and ordered
by the Holy Spirit, else they will have no vigour or
efficacy, as to either the first application of Christ, or
to any further and fuller application of him.   The
Spirit is called the Spirit of promise, as given by the
word of promise, Eph. i. 13.   " Received ye the
the Spirit by the works of the law, or by the hearing
of faith ? " Gal. iii. 2.   The gospel (that is by the promises of it) is called " the ministration of the Spirit,"
2 Cor. iii. 38; which is not only of the extraordinary
gifts of the Spirit, but the saving operations of it,
from its inhabitation.

It is called the Spirit of promise, as conveying and working all to us and in us by the promise. Christ and his grace is not offered by God, nor received by a Christian, by any man, (I mean grown-up person,) but by the offer of him in a promise : there is no immediate acting upon Christ, for a first or after and fuller receiving of him, but by the medium, the way of an intervening promise. God holds forth, and faith sees it, and takes Christ offered in the promise. " To him give all the prophets witness, that through his name whosoever believeth in him shall receive remission of sins," Acts x. 43. As the Spirit's humbling is by his whetting and setting home by his art the threatenings of wrath and death eternal ; so the comforts of the Spirit are by his setting home the promises of salvation : and further supplies of grace are by the promises through the co-operating of the Holy Spirit, bringing us to receive further of Christ's fulness by the promises, that are " Yea and Amen in him," 2 Cor. i. 20. But all this further operation of the Spirit, and receiving more of the grace of Christ, is by meditation and pondering of the promises.

Fresh receivings from Christ must be founded in fresh meditation of the promises. The more intense and earnest the ponderings of the promises of growth and increase are, the larger will your desires, the more earnest your endeavours, be after more of Christ. Christians are sometimes in great haste to believe strongly, but cannot reach it, because they meditate on the promises slenderly. They make the best work of it who dwell and act most upon the promises, that still meditate from promise to promise. By the promises we are made partakers of the Divine nature, 2 Pet. i. 4. " Cleanse ourselves from all filthiness of the flesh and spirit, perfecting holiness in the fear of God," 2 Cor. vii. 1.

There are great varieties of precious promises for justification, sanctification, and the rest. There is a transcendent truth, goodness, and freeness in the promises, great and rich supplies made over to believers by them ; but they will not nourish the soul, without our due mindings and daily meditatings on them : meditation must press out the juice and sweetness, gather the rare honey that is upon these flowers of precious promises. If bones be full of marrow, it must be gotten out by pains and knocking : the promises, so full of marrow and sweetness, must yield it forth by meditation. Lay sound weight of meditation on them, to press out the spirit and virtue in them.

If, therefore, a Christian would daily have his recourse to Christ, if he daily would touch Christ, so as to have virtue go out of him, for healing and help in any kind ; bring your eye to the hand of the Spirit, and to the promise, which he must be expected to work your coming to Christ by, and fresh receivings of grace from. Meditate well, that you may speed well : let the promises mellow in thy heart by meditation, that thou mayst find how sweet they are.

CHAP. X.—*Of the next thing Meditation may best take in, which is that on my part I am to perform.*

5. IF I would perform in the day what is incumbent on me to be rightly done, I must meditate of the

way where the Holy Spirit may meet and help me. Meditate I must of my necessary putting my hand to the work of Christ, and bearing his burden, and the need I have of the Spirit's lending his hand to help me, who helps our infirmities : I must eye the rule of the word, by which the Spirit teaches me, and the precious promises whereby he encourages me.

And in that all my conversation in the day must be holy and heavenly, comfortable and fruitful, I must meditate of stirring up the grace given me, to act by the help of the Spirit upon Christ, and to him, for working out my own salvation, and the glorifying of God thereby.

This must be (if·I consider) the living the life of faith more peculiarly, and exercising of, likewise, every holy grace the work of the day requires : therefore, next, my meditation may be upon the graces that in the duties of the day are to be exercised for to be improved.

Without the exercising of these graces all the conversation is carnal, not spiritual, all duties are but dead and loathsome to God. I must think how my daily course must be a living to the living God; a living peculiarly to him that died for me, and rose again ; and a living to the blessed Spirit, that dwells and works in me, and is my mighty helper.

Likewise, I must consider it must be a living very exemplarily towards all men, especially the godly, that my light may shine before them, to provoke and profit them all I can.

1. Particularly, I must meditate of living the life of precious and glorious faith, the grace of graces ; faith as to the whole word of God, all the precepts, promises, threatenings, and recorded examples ; acting more peculiarly faith in the promises, and by the pro-

mises on Jesus Christ, acting more on his all-sufficiency to save, and for receiving fresh strength and
supplies for the duties and occasions of the day ensuing.
Likewise, through Christ I should think of my access
to the Father, of trusting to God's all-sufficiency, his
wisdom, truth, righteousness, holiness, goodness,
mercy, love, free grace, and all his infinite perfections;
with his providence, preserving and governing all
things, to the least; and toward my own self in particular, in a most excellent, wise, holy, and righteous
manner, to the salvation of his people, destruction of
his enemies, and his own glory.

2. I may meditate (at least sometimes) of the other
soul beauties, of heavenly graces; as of that grand
rare grace of love, holy love; that which is the fulfilling of the law, the great producer and feeder of all
obedience.

Love, which daily as a fire must be blown up, and
made to burn afresh in the heart, and enliven the
daily course : ah, what a Christian may do, by keeping
his heart hot and burning in love !

Joy. Meditating of living the life of heavenly peace
and joy, rejoicing in the Lord alway : not living the
life of sadness and pensiveness, most unbecoming an
heir of eternal glory.

Hope.   Meditate also I may of heavenly hope,
which makes not ashamed, Rom. v. 5.   An anchor
sure and firm to ride out all storms, Heb. vi. 19. And
of all the graces, as of holy fear, humility, meekness,
patience, contentedness, zeal, courage, constancy, all
the chain of graces, mentioned in 2 Pet. i. 5—7, and
other places.

The whole day's actings should be considered
so as not to be a complication of vanities, follies,
and careless walkings, but a showing forth, and

shining in the glorious beams of heavenly graces and excellences.

3. Meditate daily I should of the spiritual dangers I am surrounded with by spiritual enemies : that principal and arch enemy the flesh, that sin which is connatural to me, dwells in me, Rom. vii. 17, and so easily besets me, Heb. xii. 1, that is alway present and too prevalent ; the fountain and forge of all other sins ; the heart touch-wood and tinder for temptation ; the ground out of which all the corrupt and poisonous weeds of lust grow up ; and that ground and foundation of the deepest tincture and grain colour of all soul-defiling habits, and customary sins, that so enslave and lead a sinner captive.

Also of that so potent adversary Satan, his subtlety and depths, vigilancy, and unwearied diligence, whet-ted by implacable and improving malice, 1 Pet. v. 8.

Also the world, that bait for Satan's hook, and great engine whereby he acts, by the many sweet allurements on the one hand, and determents on the other hand.

These I must every day watch and war with.

Therefore, I must daily consider my helpers, God the Father, Son, and Holy Spirit. The armour of God I must put on for every part, and my fighting in the strength of Christ, by whom I may be made more than conqueror, Eph. vi. 13 ; Rom. viii. 37.

And for the last general, there must be meditation of the unspeakable preciousness of time, running on without possibility of a stand, or least stay ; with the frailty of life, Psa. xxxix. 4, with the uncertainty of it, and the certainty of death, and unavoidableness of that which will cast me upon eternity.

These are the more general things, among which my meditation may take its walks, and upon which

my seriousness may daily sit down and make its
spiritual advantage.

CHAP. XI.—*Of some Particulars to be added to
the former Generals.*

THERE are some things in particular I may add, which
may help to direct and quicken a Christian in his daily
course.

1. For the Scripture I daily read, or hear, to endeavour some thoughts which may help to higher
quickenings, and heart enlargings, by further fresh
ponderings of the surpassing excellences and mighty
efficacies of the Scripture ; to think of a required higher
rising estimation, more inflamed affections of love, joy,
hope, longing, and the rest, seen and so observably
conspicuous in the saints in Scripture ; to light our
candle by their flame : and the more rooted resolution
I should take up and engage in, to be more (by my
looking into the glass of the word) transformed into
the image of it, 2 Cor. iii. 18.

Of faith in the word. I should further think of
that faith I am necessarily to act, in the truth, and
certainty, and usefulness of the word I now am to be
exercised in; and of my mixing of faith more abundantly with it, Heb. iv. 2 : as to any doctrine, precept, promise, threatening, or examples, and whatever
is there related for my use.

Of wisdom. I should think also of the wisdom
which that I read requires, in selecting that out is most

conducible, is my proper portion, and best fitting my soul's condition.   As Samuel at his feast set forth something peculiar for Saul, 1 Sam. ix. 23, 24. Joseph caused to be prepared for his brother Benjamin, Gen. xliii. 34.   God will now be seen, if wisdom be used to hold forth a peculiar prepared portion.   Some eye-salve to anoint mine eyes, Rev. iii. 18, some rich balm to heal some sore, some corrosive to eat out some proud flesh, some cordial for a strengthener and cheerer, some piece of spiritual treasure to enrich me, some rare jewel for ornament wanting to me; something there is now in my hand, for my now spiritual advantage, if I can see it ; and see it I may, by that which must be the auxiliary and constant assistant of my reading, if I would meet with a due profiting, which is my conscientious and careful pondering, weighing, and weighing this pure gold, stored up in Christ's rich treasury to make me rich.

Reading brings me meat, meditation brings forth the sweetness.   Reading brings the coals to the wood, meditation makes the flame.   Reading brings me the sword of the word, meditation whets it.   Reading barely, proves pouring water into a sieve ; meditation is putting gold into a treasury ; the former lets the water out, the latter locks the gold up.

Oh let me read much, but let me also meditate much, that meditation and reading may be commensurate ; my soul's digestion proportioned to its reception, its taking in by reading : let me read and meditate, that I may not have a meagre, lean soul, like them that have an eager appetite, and a weak digestion ; but that it may be fat and well-liking by this good digestion of due meditation.

2. Some lively and vigorous meditation should be

daily performed, in reference to private prayer ; I say for assistance and furtherance of secret closet prayer, that so important and sweet soul exercise.

Consider that importancy and concernment, that the main stress both of the whole work, and likewise of the heart's after-warmth and life in the day, lies greatly on it.   Also its heavenly sweetness, that it is the chief way of our private familiarity with God. Also its excellency, that it is our only way of private speaking unto the great God, of having the high honour and favour of whispering in his ear, access in private to his throne, and the chief way of procuring his private signet and seal of blessed assurance of happiness.   The way it is of the soul's freshest, freest, and most elevated actings ; such as ofttimes praying in company must not, cannot bear, and the way of strong, high exercise of sundry graces.

It sends private embassies daily to the King of heaven by faith.   It carries up daily the soul to heaven in a chariot of fire by love ; and leaves continually an agent in the court of heaven by hope.

It is the great heart warmer by privacy, giving the greater advantage of importunity, without any check from the presence of others.   The great heart humbler, melter down, and refiner, instrumentally, by actings of sound and kindly repentance ; making the dross and base mixtures of corruptions and lusts to pass away, and the heart become purer.   It is the peculiar advantage to learn and act the rare art and secret of wrestling with God, and returning with the high encouragements of holy overcomings of him.   It is the way of the rarest hours, highest soul raptures, richest pourings in of comforts, and most happy experiencings of the descendings down of heaven in purest, sweetest, largest soul satieties.

Therefore for richest furnishing us with fittest matter for a best heart frame to perform this daily duty, performing it in the most spiritual and effectual manner, for doing it, as to outdo former, all former doings, we must look to lay the foundation deeper and larger in better and more suited thinkings and meditatings; think to the utmost, to pray to the best. The same word in the Hebrew signifies, as divers of the learned say, both meditation and prayer. First it signifies meditation, and then by a metonomy of the cause for the effect, it signifies prayer. To show what prayers should be still presented to the great God, such as have some due weight of meditation, which are made out and made up of meditation, or have at least the best seriousness we can. That great man of prayer, the psalmist David, ordinarily calls his prayer his meditation ; and peculiarly his prayer in the morning (the foundation of the following day's work) his meditation, Psa. v. 1, 2, in that excellent and warm beginning of that psalm. Prayer and meditation, like Hippocrates' twins, were born, lived, and died together; so meditation and prayer rise, and warm, and grow fervent, or cool, fall, and decay together : prayer cherishes meditation, meditation feeds prayer. Oh let my spirit be still warmed, inflamed, and melted down in meditation, that it may run and flow and flame in this heavenly devotion, and both issue in my daily wiser and warmer working out salvation.

3. My serious and curious mindings must make sure to single out, and set in full view, that or those things I particularly want, and are most proper and necessary for the soul's present state. There is no godly man but hath ever something which concerns him most. Some corruption stirring that must be

subdued, some temptation to be encountered, some
grace to be endeavoured, some comfort or help sup-
plied.   It may be many things may be the present,
if not urgent concerns.

CHAP. XII.—*Meditation of daily Self-denial.*

IN the next place, let me meditate of what I want as
to self-denial and mortification, evidenced by the
weeds of corruptions coming up in my spirit, Mark
viii. 34, or ready ever and anon to arise and get
ground, and all still upon that grand interest of self,
or the relics of the roots or stumps of it.   This which
hath not been spoken to, this self-interest, the taking
of it down in my heart, is one of the greatest concernments meditation daily should fix upon.   Self is
the great hinge the carnal heart hangs and turns upon :
there the centre is self, the circumference self, all the
lines are drawn from self and to self.   Self is the
great rival and competitor with the infinitely surpassing God, and contends for superiority with him, yea,
self sits in the throne, wears the crown, holds the
sceptre, and self is the sinner's all in all.

1. All positive actings in sensualities, pride, and
covetousness, and other evils, are but to satisfy self.

2. All negative ways and omittings of good are
but to gratify self, to ease slothful self, loth to be put
to stir, unwilling to labour, toil, or strive, least of all
to lose, smart, and suffer.

Self claps the great strong bias on the soul, is the
spreading, prevailing poison in it, and impoisons it all

over.   Self is highest in the estimation, nothing
passes at so high a rate, not God himself.   Self is
highest in the affection, nothing so near as self.   Self
is highest in the purpose and intention, nothing so
aimed at as self.   Self in the conversation, it hath
the endeavours and earnestness.   It is like the most
dangerous seizing, deep-rooting, and spreading poison,
of greatest virulency and prevalency : thus it is in a
natural heart.   In a holy heart, though the most
high God, by the power of grace, be now highest,
really chief, yet that remaining part of self, the pieces
left behind, oft as it were do jostle him, frequently
jostle him, to get his place and sit uppermost ; for
what do sins, when our minds, wisdom, desires, and
wills, and our ways, when they thwart and cross his
mind, wisdom, will, and ways, but as it were jostle
him, and strive to be uppermost ?

Hereby self sometimes (out of carelessness) seems
to have regained the throne, and repossessed itself of
the sovereignty lost.

In the best heart there is so much of this bitter
root springing out, so much of this soul bane, so
much of this touch-wood, tinder, powder, to presently
take, and instantly blow up, so much of this idol, this
Dagon set so near the ark, that it hath need of the
greatest daily mindings and ponderings ; as the greatest
enemy that hath gained the greatest advantage of us,
it lies still in our bosoms.   It is like the worm that
breeds and feeds of the body's own flesh : this of all
others is the greatest idol ; I say, self is the greatest
idol that ever was or will be.   There is no image of
jealousy like it in the eye of a God, therefore no one
thing requires a more daily minding, for a daily
watchfulness ; mindings for the effectual help and
relief against all particular lusts, which are but the

lesser branches of the great root of self, the scouts and foragers sent forth from the head-quarter of self.

This self it is that is the great correspondent and confederate with Satan : if self were not the ground within, of his attempts from without, he could do nothing. The mathematician boastingly said, Tell me but where I may place my engine, and I will shake the earth. Satan knowing where to place his engine, knows how to shake us and worst us, if we watch him not, and this self.

I must mind it most, and trust it least; labour the most peremptory and constant denyings of it, and as my highest wisdom, to mortify particular lusts that are all fed from this great root, and likewise to keep off Satan from this advantage ground.

CHAP. XIII.—*Of some other Particulars which may be sometimes meditated upon in the Day.*

1. A PARTICULAR sin. It will be my wisdom to consider that sin or corruption which troubles me most, which out of this spring of self and sinful interest is more apt to ooze out of my heart, and make a breach in the banks that Christ by his grace hath made there. That particular evil which is so strong, stirring, and striving, to carry me down the stream and keep me under : " I was upright," saith the prophet, " before him, and I kept myself from mine iniquity," Psa. xviii. 23; that sin which had been of peculiar prevalence, and would be so again ; the sin that had special edge and eagerness, too oft appearing and endeavouring it,

attempting to make its escape from his watch, his heart keeping, and appear in act and power.

There is some corruption or evil in every spirit, which like some rank weed in the garden is still putting up, or ready to put forth ; like some leak in a vessel, ready to run out by it. This needs a special minding and considering suitable to its dangerousness, as that which will be a thorn in the foot, hinder our going, work disquiet, dash our confidence before God, and weaken our hands from our work.

I must peculiarly consider this daily, that it get not at any time ground of me, but that I gain upon it more, that I watch it, fight it, look that this gangrene spread not, run not up to my heart, but that I stop and kill it. Minding it duly will provoke to endeavour a right course for the just cure and sound healing of it.

Meditation may be also of what other evils are busy in my bosom, what are stirring most, what are getting any ground, and what are losing it.

2. What graces I want, or have most need of, to enable me more to lift up the name of Christ, sweeten my spirit with peace, ease my course, and render me more serviceable to others.

Every day I should well attend to what gospel ornaments and jewels I ought to put on and wear before others, to make my conversation shine, Col. iii. 12 ; 2 Pet. i. 5—7.

Christians must consider their putting on, and wearing the rich ornaments and jewels of heavenly graces, to shine gloriously in them, and take the eyes of all that behold them with the discoveries of the soul-inward beauties of faith, love, hope, joy, fear, humility, meekness, patience, contentedness, heavenly-mindedness, and rest, to the glory of Christ, in whose beams of beauty and glory they ever should shine.

3. When holy David in his course of meditation, after matters of his private concernment, closes so ordinarily the whole meditation, with that grand interest of Zion, the church's case ; may not this be then a rule to our meditation, for a high demonstration of our public-spiritedness, our constant mindings of that superlative and transcendent interest of God in this world, the glory of his great name in the kingdom of Jesus Christ, and the people given to him, their peace, prosperity, and glory, and the disappointments of all their enemies' designs, which also is an article in their heavenly jointure ?

Some other particulars might further be mentioned to be taken in by meditation ; such as matters of our callings and daily converse in varieties of companies and friends, and how to be right Christians in them, excel in improving them to their proper uses and ends, for the glory of God.

4. Meditation for review of the work of the day. In the close of the day there should be that meditation of review, or that overlooking of matters in the foregoing day, to make a happy closing it up, by a fresh humbling ourselves, and returning to God, and acting new recumbencies on his free, rich grace in Christ, by the precious promises, to sweeten our lying down.

5. And in the night season, that great time with David and others of the saints, when I awake, let me be ever with God, and "my meditation of him sweet," Psa. civ. 34.

CHAP. XIV.—*Of the Sabbath and Lord's Day.*

THERE now remains but one thing more to be added
to what hath been said concerning daily meditation,
namely, the meditation relating to that eminent day of
God, first the seventh day of the week, now in the
New Testament times changed to, and called the first
day of the week, and the Lord's day.

1. As to the rise, nature, ends, and advantages of
the sabbath in the Old Testament, and the Lord's day
in the New, it is the best day that ever the world saw,
or shall be seen on this side heaven.

2. It was and is that day wherein the infinite glories
and excellences of a God have shined brighter and
warmer on the spirits of men, than in any other days
beside ; namely, his infinite wisdom, power, love, goodness, mercy, and riches of free grace.

3. The sabbath, as some judge, had its rise so early
as in Paradise, or when man was in state of innocency :
it must then be of very great antiquity, and a rarity
of great worth.   And,

4. Then it must be that only holy day which man
in state of innocency had ; and possibly, if he had
stood, should ever have had afterward.

5. After the first institution it had the most glorious and tremendous promulgation and sanction, such
a delivery and ratification, as no other law (except
those that were spoken at the same time) ever had,
namely, by God's so wonderful and most astonishing
appearance on Mount Sinai, in the sight of six hundred thousand persons.   There it was one of the ten
words spoken by God's own mouth, by God first
spoken in the ears of all that so prepared and awaken-

ed numerous multitude, and after in the mount was written with the finger of God, written on the first table of stone, before the six commandments of the second table. This commandment thus written, was with the others reserved in the golden ark or chest, made purposely by Moses from God's command to keep the tables, and then by God's appointment was to be preserved in the glorious tabernacle made by Moses, and there it was to be with highest honour preferred to be kept in the holy of holies.

6. Though some yield it not, yet a vast majority judge the sabbath had its change, from the seventh to the first day of the week, by the Lord of the sabbath, Christ himself, or at least by his apostles from his authority.

7. However it be changed, yet it is looked upon as grounded on that so amazing part of our redemption, Christ's so glorious resurrection on the third day after his passion.

8. The sabbath formerly was the Old Testament church's fixed time to behold as in a mirror the glory of God the Creator, his eternal Godhead, power, wisdom, goodness, and most glorious excellences, in the so admirable frame of heaven and earth, and the so various and curious pieces in it, all most exquisitely wrought and finished. It was the peculiar time for setting up the ladder of the creatures by contemplation to climb from earth to heaven with. But now changed into the first day of the week, it is the Christian church's time for beholding, as in a mirror, the glory more peculiarly of God the Redeemer; now not in his humiliation, but in his appearing and begun exaltation in that his glorious resurrection from the dead, that his concerned people might joy with highest and most heavenly rejoicing, for this rising of the

Sun of righteousness, to be under the warmest and most vivifying beams of his infinite love.

9. Let me meditate of this day, as the time afforded for largest spiritual advantages, no day being so eminent for me and my soul as this day.

10. Let me meditate of this day as that happy season, wherein the ordinances of Christ do run in a fuller, higher, and stronger current. More is offered me on this great soul-mart day than on other common market-days, other week-day opportunities; it is the day whereby in some respects I have far better ordinances, the public; in communion with Christ, in the midst, among those that are gathered together in his name. And then by the public I have better advantages for the private, to perform them better. Private duties having a better time and better helps, I must thereby be minded of my better performance.

11. It is the eminent day of meeting with God in his upper walks of more solemn ordinances.

12. The day of days for our best speaking with our God, and of highest familiarity with him.

13. It is the great time of our hearing from God, and having him most eminently to speak to us. There are no hearings from God like this day's hearings, no such voice, no such efficacy can be expected as on this day.

14. It is the day wherein God sits out, and is most to be seen; the great day of seeing God's goings in the sanctuary, seeing his power and his glory, Psa. lxiii. 2. No such day for this as the Lord's own day.

15. A day of feeding more on " the feast of fat things full of marrow," Isa. xxv. 6. Of being brought into the King's banqueting-house, having the banner of Christ's love spread more amply over us, than at

other times, it being the day wherein the highest flamings-up of his unspeakable love appeared, in that he not only died, but rose again from the dead, without which all his other labour and sufferings had been lost, and our souls been also lost.

16. It is a day dropped down from heaven, may serve to give a taste of the sabbath and day kept there, and to set a copy for us here to write after, in our holy restings and actings, attended with heavenly refreshings. God that made all things, when he had finished his work, he then rested on the seventh day, and with his example of resting, gave the precept of sanctifying the seventh day to the church of the Old Testament. And the Lord of the sabbath, Christ Jesus, resting from his work, and rising the first day of the week, gives the example, and with the example the precept of resting and keeping holy the first day of the week, to the church of the New Testament, as some think, which therefore they say is called the Lord's day, Rev. i. 10, as the ordinance of the supper is called the Lord's supper, as instituted by him.

17. It is the day of resting the body from labour, of respiting the mind from worldly thoughts and cares, and of refreshing the spirit with heavenly manna, which rains down now on this day more plentifully; and with water of life, that runs more abundantly in the pure channels of holy ordinances.

18. Meditated on it should be, as the season of the best reciprocations, mutual actings between earth and heaven, wherein the soul hath the advantage of acting higher and more vigorously, to glorify and please God, and wherein God commands the blessing more, and affords assistances more usually than on any other days, as experience proves.

19. It is a time to come from sweeter and fuller

M

communion with God in Christ, (whose blessed day it is,) to come with our faces shining and hearts flaming, made better to be on earth, fitter to live in heaven: and hereupon,

20. To leave upon the spirit a more eager longing fully to enjoy the Lord of the sabbath, and have time turned wholly into eternity.

These or such-like meditations may be suitable and quickening for improving the great opportunity of this day of Christ, and we cannot think too much or too seriously for this great occasion.

Chap. XV.—*Of Occasional Meditation, and that which is more extraordinary.*

Solemn occasional meditation comes now to be considered, which is the soul's taking of time for, and acting meditation on some particular selected subject, either out of the word of God, or among the works of God, or something providentially falling out, or something concerning ourselves, any thing offering fit occasion for fruitful meditation.

They may be chiefly referred to these two heads.

1. Either such things as purposely we (out of varieties of subjects before us) do single out for meditation, to help and quicken us in godliness.

2. Or some new, fresh thing which the hand of God's providence holdeth forth, for our particular observing and improving.

1. That which we ourselves, out of varieties of subjects, may or do single out for our spiritual advantage.

Here the scope and compass our eye hath to make its choice of and fix upon is very large.   The eye in meditation hath before it the fullest, fairest prospect can come in view: here is a breadth, length, depth, height, a compass and circumference, that in point of lawful liberty, you may look from earth to heaven, yea, through the whole world, in all its vastness, and varieties of objects in it; and beyond them all, unto him that is so infinitely above them all, God himself, in all his so inconceivable exaltations and perfections.   Oh how narrow then must that spirit be, which shall be straitened and at a loss for matter to employ and busy its seriousness about! that hath so large a field to walk in, and so great varieties, as the vast world, heaven and earth, and all things in them; and the infinite God, with so many infinite excellences as are in him; and yet to seek how to meditate! Ah how barren, low, and poor must that spirit be which is enriched with so great provisions for mind and thought entertainment, and for time's improvement, and yet cannot fruitfully employ itself on some one thing or other that presents itself to us, and invites our seeing and pondering of it!

Although meditation hath so great a latitude and liberty; a liberty to travel farther, and see more by far than all the great travellers that have been in the world; yet spiritual wisdom teacheth us to endeavour the most advantageous way of engaging our thinking power in meditation.   For the wisdom of this way we now are upon, it needs must lie in that manner and order as most may conduce to the great and main end of glorifying God, and our own salvation.   It is most true, that in point of liberty it is my Christian privilege to take and set before me any profitable subject to fix my thoughts upon, when no particular occasion

M 2

of meditation doth otherwise oblige me : I say, when no particular contrary obligation is upon me, I may choose to meditate either on this or that useful subject as I please.

I have the whole creation for my eye-walk, my meditation, and spirit's recreation ; yea, and farther than the whole world extends: I may go to contemplate him that is the highest ; if I please, like David and other saints of God, I may with my eye walk and look among the works of God, the so excellent and unimitable pieces of his most admirable framing ; on all the so stately fabric of the world, any of the rare built stories, lower or higher, any of the rich furnitures or exquisite things contained in it.

First I may view the lower story wherein I am ; fix upon the precious things the earth hath within, the riches of minerals and precious metals, silver, gold, and the so useful other sorts ; the riches of all sorts of precious stones, diamonds, carbuncles, rubies, emeralds, and all the rest.

I may view the innumerable exquisite things upon the earth, from the moss and imperfect plants, to the grass made for the cattle, to all things growing in the whole garden of nature, and more peculiarly made for the service of man ; among all the herbs, flowers, shrubs, and trees of all sorts, and see in them the so fair characters of the infinite power, wisdom, and goodness of the great Creator, written most legibly on them.

I may meditate on all sorts of living creatures, from the least and lowest mite or insect, all creeping things, with all beasts and birds that go upon the earth, wild or tame.

Consider I may their several natures, features, and shapes, beauties, and excellences ; and withal, the serviceableness and usefulness of them, to that poor clod of earth, man, for whom they are.

I may look to the waters, fountains, rivers, and vast seas, with the innumerable things and creatures about and in them, fowls, fishes, and these of so many kinds, forms, and shapes; all of them the demonstrations of the infinite glories of that unimitable Artist the great God. My meditation also may, with the psalmist, take in the eternal and mighty hills and mountains, with the rocks, sands, and bulwarks made against the raging seas, " that they turn not again to cover the earth," Psa. civ. 9.

I may go up to the higher stories of this fabric of the world, to the waters above, to the clouds and their bottlings-up of waters in them, and that so great wonder in nature, the invisible and so powerful wind, which carries the clouds from place to place, whereby they at length open, fall down, and water the thirsty earth with dews and showers; they also serve to purge and purify the air we breathe in.

I may eye other sorts of meteors or exhalations, and things appearing in the air, as those fiery and dreadful sometimes impressions, making us to wonder; the falling stars, fiery dartings of some, and fixing, standing brightnesses of others, of several shapes.   To all these I may add that voice of God, the fearful thunder, and the concomitant coruscations and lightnings; lightnings also sometimes alone ; all these are mighty and stupendous operations of the great God.

Higher yet I may go, to another higher story, that of the starry heaven ; contemplate the so innumerable stars of several glories, and wonderful motions and influences, with the beauteous moon to shine by night, and her changings, increasings, and decreasings, and hidings; and that eye of the world, the most glorious

sun, all so admirably meditated upon by the psalmist,
Psa. viii. 3 ; xix. 1 ; civ. 19 ; cxxxvi. 7—9.

I may go yet one step higher, to that third heaven,
the palace of God, where also Christ is in his human
nature exalted, and appearing in highest glory. It
is also the native place of the glorious angels, and the
place of happy reception, entertainment, and habitation
of " the spirits of just men made perfect," Heb. xii.
23. But of this more particularly hereafter.

But among all, I may more peculiarly muse, and
in musing greatly wonder, at that one thing, namely,
man, Psa. viii. ; the making of him in so great excellency, and all things in the world for his use and
service ; all for a little speck of dust, with a little
spark in it of an immortal soul. Oh what is man,
that a God should be so mindful of him, and do so
for him ! But oh what must man then be, that so
little minds God ! and what must that man be, that
does not, that cannot, or rather will not find mind
employment, how to engage and act that rare endowment the thinking power, in the rich and ample provisions purposely made for objects of mind entertainment ! All this being then my eye-scope, and having
so great varieties of eye-walks, so large a latitude to
exercise my thinkings, so profitably to act this holy
duty of meditation, I am left wholly (if I neglect it)
without any excuse ; if I still daily let my thoughts
run and ravel out in vanities and impertinencies, and
can fix no where usefully for my spiritual good.

But in that multitudes of things may produce
confusion, prudence must direct to find out the best
method and order, that so I may meditate with more
ease, pleasure, and advantage. My best wisdom
therefore is to consider of the fittest way, if not in itself, yet at least for my particular ability and times.

1. As either to meditate of some portion or passage of Holy Scripture, some precept, promise, threatening, direction, encouragement, or example, or some grace, virtue, vice, or sin : and for more delight and help, meditate I may by setting one contrary against another ; as one promise being singled, or some of the promises, I may turn upon the threatenings. If I meditate upon a reward and blessing given to any, turn I may to the punishment and evils that have been inflicted, or are threatened ; reward on obedience, and punishment on disobedience.

2. Meditate I may over the heads and chief points of religion in order, as I can set them ; or as some short bodies of divinity and catechisms comprise them.

3. Or something of the works of the great God, as creation, that so amazing and utterly inconceivable work, set out as it is in Genesis the first, and in other scriptures : or providence, God's so strange and admirable preservation and governing of all things in the world, from the greatest to the least in it, and about it, every motion, mutation, and disposing of it to a sure end, his own highest glory.

4. Or something particularly of my own spiritual condition, for my more peculiar benefit.   As,

(1.) Something which may make me wiser to salvation, and add to my treasure of spiritual truths.

(2.) Something which may make me warmer, and increase my heat of holy affection.

(3.) Or something which may strengthen and fix my soul's great purpose of walking with God, and render me a more highly resolved person for heaven.

(4.) I should, as a grand business, the affair of chief concernment, meditate frequently and most seriously about the case of my soul, how in very deed it is, 2 Cor. xiii. 5, both without any self-flattery on the one hand, or self-injury on the other hand, Psa. xxxvi. 2.   Neither making myself and state better than it is, nor worse than it is.   That I may not on any mistake be confident, presuming fondly, nor diffident, desponding and discouraged weakly.

(5.) I must frequently meditate of the evil and most deceitful heart, that arch-cheater I continually carry in my bosom, and therefore am never to be secure, but alway awakened for fear of its falseness and deceits: meditate therefore of that so excellent scripture, " The heart is deceitful above all things, and desperately wicked ; who can know it ? " Jer. xvii. 9.   Therefore I shall more largely speak to it.

CHAP. XVI.—*Meditation should often be of the Heart's great Deceitfulness.*

MEDITATION should be very frequent of the heart's great deceitfulness.   The right and best way of this meditation lieth in these four particular paths.

1. In pondering the infallible certainty of it, and particulars in it.

2. Pondering the sad condition every one is under by it.

3. Weighing the sad attendants and consequences.

4. The way of deliverance and relief.

1. It is best here to begin with the meditation of the infallible certainty of this so superabounding heart deceitfulness.

(1.) This first is to be minded, as that which is asserted so by a God, for whom it is impossible to lie,

Heb. vi. 18, being infinitely wise, holy, righteous, and good; he affirms it, and that before and to the very faces of all persons. He hath written, recorded it in his Scripture of truth; he hath commanded all persons to read what he hath there recorded; he hath preserved miraculously these records against all haters and opposers, men and devils; and among other ends, that men may have a glass, a perfect, undeceiving glass, to show them what they never would or could see or believe, if God had not held this glass to them, and made the true and lively representation of the heart's deceitfulness above all things by it.

(2.) These Scripture assertions of the heart's deceitfulness, are from that God, who is the only both heart framer and heart searcher and knower, Psa. xxxiii. 15, having his eye, omniscient eye also, every moment and least particle of time upon it, and every where, in every chamber and corner, every part of it; therefore he must needs know exactly all the heart's deceitfulness, and desperate wickedness. As he made the whole frame of the soul, and all the faculties, the springs and wheels of that exquisite frame; so he knows all the foulness and soil of sin which hath fallen in, and which it hath gathered; all its motions irregular, all its stops and stands, all its commissions and omissions, all its defects of principles, all its corrupt principles. Therefore knowing both the natural powers of the soul, with all superadded corrupt principles evilly inclining, aims and interests biassing and leading, he keeping also such an eye ever upon it, for of the things in the whole world, there is no one thing the eye of God looks so upon as spirits and hearts, he must know the deceitfulness of it, by being the only Maker, and likewise the continual observer of it; and therefore if he affirms how deceitful the heart is, it must be so.

(3.) But besides, there can be nothing in the heart
to alter and change it, to restore and raise it from this
bad state, but he knows it ; his eye is ever upon the
heart, he keeps alway an awakened eye, that is still
watching it, narrowly viewing it ; he is the heart continual searcher and trier.　He tries the heart and the
reins, Psa. vii. 9.

(4.) He must also be Judge of the secrets of men's
hearts, Rom. ii. 16.　God shall judge the secrets of
men's hearts, therefore all deceitfulness of it ; therefore he must know it, and it must be true. " The judgment of God is according to truth," Rom. ii. 2, and
the word of truth whereby he will judge.

(5.) Take in also the recorded demonstrations of
it, such as God discovered, foretold, and after came to
pass, setting a seal to this infallible truth.

Hazael was by revelation from God told of the
evil he should do by Elisha, and with much seeming
abhorrence disclaimed it, yet instantly is confuted, and
had his mouth stopped, 2 Kings viii. 12, 13.　The
apostles were told of their forsaking Christ, and Peter
of his denying of him, which he would not believe,
Mark xiv. 29—31, yet within a very little time appeared : Scripture records of the heart's great deceitfulness are left us to conclude and confirm us herein.
But oh how hard is it to see, to believe against ourselves ! our own great frequencies of experiences, the
very instances out of the nurseries of our own hearts ;
the evil plants that put forth fresh continually of their
fruits' deceitfulness, prove it to our faces, if we make
observations of them as we ought to do.　Oh there is
not one day, if we are watchful, but is full of sad
instances from morning to night.　At all times we
may find our hearts ready to commit cheats upon ourselves ; and in soul concerns, as to our spiritual estates,
oh what grand deceits are we too apt to have therein !

As particularly, in respect of God, how ready to think erroneously of him, as to his omniscience, truth, holiness, righteousness, mercy, free grace, power, and providence, and such like! As the self-condemned drunkard says, " I shall have peace, though I add drunkenness to thirst," Deut. xxix. 19. And he in Psa. l. 21, " Thou thoughtest I was altogether such an one as thyself:" so the best are, out of predominant corruption, very ready to commit great mistakes and deceits, in respect of their own sins, graces, the things of God, and things of the world; there is no end of naming: excellent treatises are written of this heart's deceitfulness.

2. Meditation should proceed to the unspeakable sadness of this heart temper, every one should cry out with the holy apostle, " O wretched man that I am! who shall deliver me from the body of this death," Rom. vii. 24, out of the hands of this deceiver so great and so near, gotten so far within me, and that will be a cursed inmate so long as this house of the body stands, and will not out utterly whatsoever hard usage it finds? Oh how sad is it to have such a self-betraying companion so deeply rooted within me! to have in my own bosom such a continual forge and fountain, acting and running in so violent tides, high spring tides, ever and anon carrying me down to that I must so sadly bewail and smart under!

3. The attendants and consequences of this heart deceitfulness should greatly be pondered, as to be so fooled by myself, by trusting myself. " He that trust-eth in his own heart is a fool," Prov. xxviii. 26. May I not trust my own heart, without having such a character and brand upon me? Oh then what a fool have I been, and that millions of millions of times! Oh how great a fool exceeding often, in suffering so

notorious cheats to be put upon me ! such a lust or corruption to clap a bias on my heart, and fool lead me ! lead me so far, so deep into the dirt, so far from home, from heaven, from God, from peace, comfort, hope, and heart of returning ! How many and many ways have I been a fool ! yea, and still am daily most unwise : he that is so easily and ordinarily unwise must be a fool to purpose. Whosoever shall be but twice or thrice cheated by the same person, and not beware, will be accounted no wise man ; but for a sinner to be not twice or thrice cheated, but thousands of times by the same deceitful heart, cheated with the saddest, saddest imaginable deceits, must be unwise indeed. Oh how sad is it that we cannot by all experiences take heed of this deceitful heart !

I can take heed of every one better than myself; it may be I scarce will trust any body in worldly affairs, but myself, that is worse than any without me, that I will trust, and so be deceived : O let me often think what trusting my own heart is, and needs must come unto.

I had need think well of the foolish builder, Matt. vii. 26, that built his house upon the sand, grounded his hopes of salvation on a false foundation ; and of the wise builder, who built his house on a rock, by real building, by precious faith on Christ. And let me likewise meditate often on the ten virgins, the foolish deceived with a lamp of outward profession only, and the wise that with their lamps provided the oil of grace, a heart, right renovation.

4. The way of deliverance and relief.

(1.) Meditate on the heart knower. Against heart deceitfulness, let me as the sure way look up continually to the only perfect heart knower, to beg most earnestly his help, to show me my heart's deceitfulness.

(2.) On Christ my wisdom. Let me mind this well, that Christ only must be my wisdom, 1 Cor. i. 30, my teacher, whom I must apply and rest on peculiarly for his wisdom and teachings daily, to extricate and carry me out of the labyrinths and many secret windings of my so deceitful spirit.

(3.) On the Spirit my helper. And must consider the mighty helper, the Holy Spirit, to help me against my self-deceivings, Rom. viii. 26. He " helpeth our infirmities," and he helps against this infirmity of being so ready to be cheated. Christ, by his Spirit, can and will deliver me if I trust upon him; he hath given me his word.

(4.) The word. I must meditate on the word; there are the sure rules and ways revealed, to show how to undeceive myself. The word is " a discerner of the thoughts and intents of the heart," Heb. iv. 12; if I make it my exercise to meditate in the word of Christ, he by his Spirit with the word will teach and help me, if I obey it.

CHAP. XVII.—*Of divers other things for solemn and set Meditation.*

(6.) SOLEMN and serious meditation, a very great and diligent consideration, I should often act in reference to that arch enemy without, namely, the devil, who, though he be an enemy without, yet gains and maintains all he can. a correspondency with corruption within me.

Satan I must consider as fallen from God, and so

from his primitive station and happiness, into damnation and hell, fallen out implacably with God, and for his sake with his best creature on earth, man. Out of his implacable hatred, his aim is to drown men in the same perdition and hell with himself. He seeks whom he may devour, 1 Pet. v. 8; he hath his deceits, depths, methods, and arts of both tempting and troubling, Rev. ii. 24 ; and these acted with the purest enmity, keenest malice, utmost vigilance, and unwearied diligence, 2 Cor. ii. 11.

He hath the higher ground of us by far, as being a spirit, and of the highest rank of creatures, as to his nature and essence, and is thereby most wise and strong and agile. He is immortal, never can die, nor in any sort decay, as we and other creatures decay in strength, senses, and exercising of our soul's faculties, understanding, memory, and others: as he is never dying, nor in the least decaying, so he hath been, is, and ever will be, to the world's end, trying and tempting. Trying and practising upon the innumerable sorts of persons, of all sexes, all ages, (that are capable in the least degree to be tempted,) of all ranks, conditions, relations, in all places whatsoever, through the vast inhabited earth, Job i. 7.

He also enlarges his experiences, puts still fresh on his file ; improves continually his arts of deceiving ; and doth he not grow more bold, raging, and busy, as his time grows shorter ? Rev. xii. 12.

Pondered well it should be, that it is not one single devil to tempt us, but there are legions, very many of them ; and they are all one huge army of devils, under one great head, " The devil and his angels," Matt. xxv. 41 ; Rev. xii. 7. His angels are his assistants, which constantly and exactly comply and co-operate with him. The devils never are divided, do not jar and act against each other, but are all of one interest, of destroying souls, and accordingly do harmoniously contend. Often in Scripture mention is made of Satan and the devil, as if he were a single one ; but this may be to show their unanimity and unity.

The Scripture hath sufficiently warned us, and related his attempts and prevailings; as first upon Adam and Eve in their state of innocency and perfection ; yet he then, (though they knew not only their own happiness, but all their posterity's, though never so numerous, lay at the stake,) he then by his artifices and subtlety prevailed. After that, upon the second man that ever was, upon the deceived parents' first-born Cain ; therefore in 1 John iii. 12, Cain is said to be of the wicked one. And Satan has thus continued to tempt sundry other wicked men all along the current of time.

Yea, he often hath prevailed upon the very best saints that ever the world had ; Job, David, Peter, and others, Job iii. ; 1 Chron. xxi. 1 ; Matt. xxvi. 69—75. He forbears none ; therefore it is very much to be considered, and how he is to be watched and warred with ; and the armour of proof is to be duly minded, and the putting of it on, Eph. vi. 13.

He that hath conquered him, the Lord Jesus, and that hath conquered him for his members ; this glorious conquest must be meditated upon, as the strongest cordial in the case ; and way of taking it, the promise, with the way of acting by the promise, praying and other ordinances given for our help, this need be often a great meditation.

(7.) That enemy the world should have its due meditation ; its allurements on the one side, its oppositions on the other : I must meditate on the diversities of baits, the latitudes of pleasures, heights of honour, heaps of wealth, 1 John ii. 15 ; friends, relations, company, converse, cares, business, and all my lets, diversions, entanglements, of all the evils; in troubles, forcings, frauds, plottings, and all ways of insnaring and ruining me. Also the world, in so many respects being suited either to my natural inclination, or my customary readiness for closing with it ; or otherwise to my fears and cowardice, softness and fickleness, weakness, and weariness to withstand or overcome it. Yet I must consider how the saints have overcome the world, by acting, as Moses and others, their self-denial, looking to the recompence of reward, looking to him that is invisible, and especially to Jesus, " the Author and Finisher of our faith;" and by faith and patience both enduring and gloriously overcoming.

(8.) Sometimes I may very fruitfully meditate on the wants and weakness of my grace begun in some measure, 2 Pet. i. 5 ; its often ebbings and flowings, its stops and stands. A little progress at the best my so carnal heart makes. Also of the extreme need I have of continual stirring up and exercising faith, love, hope, fear, and other graces, thereby to grow stronger, and put forth vigorously on all occasions ; minding also the helps I have in Christ's holy ordinances, encouragements in the precious promises, and supplies by the blessed Spirit's operations out of the so great fulness of Christ.

(9.) Often I should apply my seriousness to that so concerning particular, the continual and fast running out of the golden sands of my time, and special seasons for working out of my salvation. " The time is short," saith the apostle, 1 Cor. vii. 29. " Behold, thou hast made my days as an hand-breadth," Psa. xxxix. 5. Seasons past can never be recalled, seasons present cannot be stopped from running out. Opportunity is the greatest talent, as the saying is, as that whereby we employ all other talents.   Therefore we are so often earnestly called upon for redeeming time, as Eph. v. 16, " Redeeming the time." " Whatsoever thy hand findeth to do, do it with thy might, for there is no work, nor device, nor knowledge, nor wisdom, in the grave, whither thou goest," Eccl. ix. 10.   Though time and seasons, as the course of the heavens, may be made to stop, if the sun, as in Joshua's time, should miraculously stand still, Josh. x. 13, or as in Hezekiah's time go back, Isa. xxxviii. 8, yet men's particular time then did not go back, or stand still ; so our particular time of life cannot go back or stand still, Job ix. 25, and xiv. 1, 2, and ver. 5. Life every moment shortens, and is melting down into its appointed period.   Life is a thing of the greatest contingency and uncertainty, there is no insurance office that can secure its continuance. It passes swiftly, without pause or stop ; this the Scripture both minds us greatly of, and furnishes us with rare precedents of the saints' serious and moving meditations about it. O let me then look on them and do likewise ! let me use and improve the patterns purposely there recorded, to help and quicken my forgetful, dead spirit.

Chap. XVIII.—*Meditation of Death.*

The uncertainty of life last mentioned, leads me to the subject next akin to it, that so considerable and consequential point of mortality, death and dissolution.

Oh that here I could be the highest artist to speak
most fitly and movingly to this subject death, or at
least to do something which might prove effectual to
some such proper and proportionate way of directing
and quickening this so necessary and useful meditation!
This is the great momentous and most highly concerning thing, the end and winding up of life, and all
affairs and matters relating to it, and that which determines my condition for all eternity in woe or happiness. Let me therefore endeavour the best I can
at all times to improve my thinkings of it.

1. Let me first begin with the meritorious cause
of it; that which heathens knew not, nature saw
not, philosophy and learning could not find out nor
reach; only Holy Scripture tells me, and shows it to
be that most black inlet sin. Death entered into the
world by sin, Rom. v. 12; and ver. 17, " By one
man's offence death reigned," not only entered, but
reigned, hath mastered, and will master all sinners.
Sin, that greatest evil in the world; sin, the only contrariety to the living God, that gave life to man at first,
and ever since; sin, that only injury to the blessed God,
bred and brought death, the greatest misery to man
here; sin that provoked God to pass the sentence;
sin occasioning the vindictive cause, the justice of
God, to let in death, death with the consequences of
it, that would follow without a Mediator, that Adam
knew not of: death so considered, is the way of the
very deepest revenge a God can take.

But then this black part of it, bodily death, without
that blacker train of hell and eternity in it, is that
which must challenge a very great proportion of
ponderings.

2. Let me look at, not only the rise of it, and the
bare wrath occasioning the inflicting it, but that so

fixed and irreversible sentence, that, like the law of the Medes and Persians, cannot be broken. It is appointed for all : the universality of sin hath given death a universal sting, Heb. ix. 27 ; and the statute of heaven hath impowered death's extensiveness over all, and set a seal of irrevocableness to it as to all men. Therefore it is appointed, I must think, particularly for me ; whatever I am, or do, or can in utmost possibility do. I must not once think of making an escape from it.

Yea, let me consider, as I must die, so the very year, month, day, hour, and moment is immutably fixed, and can never be altered, Job xiv. 5 ; the place also where, the means whereby, the manner how, all circumstances about it are unchangeably determined.

3. But how material is that particular of the uncertainty of the time and manner to me! That is a reservation and secret kept in the Lord's own breast, not possibly to be exactly known before, without it be revealed, as Christ of the great day of judgment saith, " Of that day and hour knoweth no man," Matt. xxiv. 36.   And ver. 42, " Ye know not what hour your Lord doth come."   And 44, " In such an hour as ye think not the Son of man cometh." So the two latter may be applied to this of death, when he calls for an account of our stewardships and talents, and passes particular and personal judgment.

3. Let me pass next to the meditation, serious pondering of the nature of it, and that great dreadfulness of that most terrible of terribles, that " king of terrors," Job xviii. 14.   Here, that I may duly look on it, let me look up for a God to teach me, as to number my days, Psa. xc. 12, so to be wise to consider my latter end, to do that hard work, overcome that difficulty of looking death-ward.   Nature abhors

the thinking of it, corruption all it can opposes it; but grace must bring and fix earnestly and often the eye upon it, familiarize death to me: let me then eye my dissolution, the parting of the two nearest, dearest friends, the soul's taking its sad farewell of its former dwelling; its going, going in an instant out of the body, and then that which death doth as an enemy to all former life concerns; and as an entrance upon an eternal condition.

(1.) As an enemy to all enjoyments how sweet so-ever: pleasures all now quenched, honours now all dashed, riches and estate now all lost, power now utterly ceased.

(2.) An enemy to all relations, friends, acquaint-ance: now must I shake hands with all nearest and dearest, the sweetest and most helpful relations.

(3.) An enemy to all employments, necessary or pleasurable, no work, no business, no invention after it.

(4.) An enemy to all opportunities and means of grace; never to read the Bible more, never to hear one sermon more, never to receive the Lord's supper more, never to make one prayer, the shortest of one of the fewest words more; and then also when thou art just launching into the length of vast eternity: but now must be prayerless and totally helpless; yea, now thy soul's condition becomes becalmed, and thou canst not obtain one gale of the Holy Spirit to blow upon thee, and help move thee in any measure.

(5.) It is an enemy quickly to the curious frame and so exquisite building of thy body, with all its parts and members, made with such adaptations and suitableness whatever, with all the tempers, qualities, offices, abilities, and actings of it: an enemy likewise to all the senses; seeing, hearing, the two disciplinary, with feeling, tasting, smelling, the so likewise necessary.

(6.) It is an enemy and destroyer of all comeliness and beauty, form and shape. And all these former by being the enemy and destroyer of that thy so sweet and precious life; by making that jewel drop out of the cabinet of the body: or rather driving forth thy immortal and invaluable soul, bringing with it a writ of forcible entrance, coming with an execution, to turn out that old inhabitant of the body, securing it from regaining possession, making it stand empty, and thence exposing the body to rot, ruin, turn to dust, and expose it to oblivion, as if it had never been.

But then upon thy soul's thus leaving thy body, immediately and instantly it is cast upon a state of eternity; of misery if thou wert not in Christ, or felicity if found and dying in him.

When life ends, eternity begins. Oh this all-amazing eternity; this so vast and inconceivable eternity, no way to be expressed or set forth, no way to be understood or known, a glass that is ever running, a chain that is ever lengthening! who can number the sands of this glass, who can reckon the links of this chain of eternity, without stop or period, bound or end? Oh let me be ever musing of this ever! have it so full in my eye, while I have time, this moment of time here, that it may wind up and leave me in possession of most happy eternity.

But to affect my spirit aright, and be wise in the due managing of this meditation of dreadful death, let me look to and ponder the Scripture commands for remembering and considering my latter end, and the arguments strongly inducing to it. How frequently and earnestly is it urged upon all! Oh let me lay the weight and stress of them close to my heart, not suffering it to put by the thoughts of death, how awkward and averse soever my carnal spirit is towards it!

Let me therefore not only muse on the sentence, the peremptory and irrevocable sentence passed upon all in general, and so upon myself in particular, but on it as ready to be executed this hour, yea, this moment, for aught I or any in the world can tell: Ah, let me say to myself, the warrant for my death at this very instant may be sealing, and immediately in a moment put in execution. Ah, therefore, should I not still daily represent and realize to my heart, my own particular coming death; represent it by those frequent examples the hand of death brings; and sets full before my face, to force my observation?

The deaths of both strangers to me, and familiars with me, of near neighbours, dear friends, sweetest relations; bereaving me, it may be, of the father that begat me, the mother that bare me, the children I love, the wife of my bosom, or the husband that was my guide and stay; or some other very comfortable relation, and so the comfort of any such relation ceases. All relations are broken by this bond-breaker, this tie-dissolver, death. When I see these thus called away, and must be my relations no more, should not I hear myself called upon to come away (shortly it may be) after them?

Oh but with these near warnings without me, let me take those nearer warnings upon me, and within me, inevitably still seizing me. Let me take those many successive summons given for my own personal change. Ah, how many are those joggings the hand of death daily gives me, for my awakening into that serious pondering of that death I either seldom or slightly mind! How many strokes may I observe death daily gives at the root of the tree, making, as it were, the chips fly in my face; making me smart by pains, aches, weakness, craziness, failings, and fallings of the spirits and strength, and increase of infirmities, by all declaring he is making at me! and how many pieces of my house of clay may I see crumbling and mouldering away, now one, and then another! after the morning of my age, my sun soon gets up higher, soon it is noon, afternoon, and night with me. How soon is the sun at the height, with any in the bright and warm beams of bodily beauty and strength! but how impossible is it for to say effectually to it, Sun, stand thou still, and go not down for the least moment! How soon appear, one way or other, the tendencies to death in and upon us!

Decay in beauty and comeliness. Sometimes, yea, ordinarily, when we are in the flower, presently the beauty and comeliness begins to blast: the best and fairest face, as to the pure white and red, soon either becomes paler or higher coloured, after grows darker and deader, still one way or other worse. As to the feature and curious shape of face and whole body, soon that likewise changes, either by a contraction in leanness and thinness, or by an extension in corpulency and grossness : both the curious and rare colours and features change, warning us of tendency to the last great coming change. Or sometimes an intimation is given by the grinders of our food, whereby we live, by the decayings still of the teeth; the teeth which are absolutely the hardest and strongest things about us, these so soon decaying, as it is in most, plainly it demonstrates that the softer and weaker things in and about us, and so the whole frame, will go at last. By this, the soon decaying of the hardest pieces, death seems to set his black mark on us,

we have his mark in the mouth ; and by their decayings and rottings we touch as it were these his warnings continually with our tongues, thence to mind us
of what change is coming.　For when the teeth fail,
(the grinders and meat preparers, made to fit meat for
the stomach,) this causes the stomach to act less perfectly; and on its failing in degree, all the depend-
encies must needs fail in their offices.

But if these death's marks begin not so in some,
yet how do we find generally some other marks of
decay set upon us !　If death come not early, yet how
soon upon most doth he set his mark !　most observably on the very top of our houses of clay, bringing
forth grey hairs on the highest part, the head, and
turning them whiter every day ; making the almond
tree to flourish, as Solomon elegantly speaks in Eccl.
xii. 5.　And in how many elegancies doth there the
wise man discover, and represent rarely the decays of
the body in old age ; all as demonstrations of death's
being continually busy about us, both to prepare and
reduce us to his possession !　What varieties of warnings are given us in the impairings of this or that
member, or of several parts of the body, showing a
coming dissolution !　how many mortal diseases, (besides others shaking the houses of our frail bodies,) I
say incurable diseases, whereby we are told that death
hath us now fast in his hand !

If not so, yet what warnings otherwise are given,
in the senses beginning to fail ; as our sight growing
dimmer, hearing duller, and in the rest !　And as
in the parts more common, so in the noble and principal parts, in the liver, heart, head, and others ;
these not performing so perfectly their offices,
whence the spirits, strength, and motion are im-
paired; the flesh wastes, the skin wrinkles.　Memory

and understanding likewise decay, and appearances of death come all the body over : what are all the forementioned and concurrent decays, but a being death-smitten ; a coming out full of the tokens of death ? What are all these successions of decays, but so many added links of that great chain death holds in his hand, and draws us to him by ? all messengers that have the sound of their master's feet, death, behind them.

Oh how exceeding gracious is God in his multiplications and connexions of warnings, who might smite every sinner without any notice of death given !

Therefore, as a piece of highest wisdom, let me strive to represent the possible suddenness of death's sad coming upon me ; and this by all the ways and inducements I can apply. The examples, such as are in Scripture, of Abel's death, Lot's wife, Nadab and Abihu, Uzzah, Amnon, Abner, Ananias and Sapphira, Herod, and others : and in history and experience, of so many and so various ways suddenly snatched away. Not a year, or some small portion of time, but it furnishes with fresh examples. What hath befallen others, may befall me ; I have no security against sudden death ; but wheresoever, and in whatever time, death may seize me.

If I travel, a thief may kill me, my horse may throw and kill me, the coach or carriage I pass in may ruin me ; on the water, I may there be drowned ; on the land, and when I am passing in the streets, some casualty may despatch me ; at home, by some mischance or sudden distemper, something at the table, fire, bed, or other place, within or without doors ; some imposthume, palsy, apoplexy kills, or some venomous inward evil may strike me to the

heart. Multitudes of experiences we continually
have. If not suddenly death seizes, but is a stroke
with warning, either shorter or longer, yet it comes
at last, in the way and at a time or hour I just
know not.

My best way therefore is frequently in my thoughts
to put myself into the condition of a present dying ;
how it must be with me; let me look on myself how
certainly, without flattery, I am prepared to die. If I
have a Christ in my bosom, the love of God assured,
and can die in the Lord, die in faith, and look death
in the face boldly, resign up my soul freely into
Christ's hands, these make for this agony the highest
cordial ; these furnish me with armour of proof
against this enemy.

But let me then look on myself as having no means
further to preserve me, all physic, art, and experiences withdrawing their usual help, friends standing
about me, pitying, lamenting me, but not able to evidence more than their kind wishes, and I myself
perceiving death's summons sent me, as to king
Hezekiah, but without expecting any messenger
after to be sent with better news. Prayers now and
all such means also reversed, and proving labours
lost, I now feeling my decays and hastening away ;
my disquiets and pains increasing, strength failing,
spirits sinking, heat turned into chilness ; cramps,
contractions of nerves and limbs following, breath
shortening, speech faltering, heart pangs and agonies
now multiplying, the whole frame of the body shaking, the hands snatching, eye-strings, as they say,
breaking ; and after many deep heavy sighings and
groanings, the soul comes forth with gaspings, and
sitting upon my quivering lips, upon the last gasp
takes its nimble flight, leaves its old habitation to

rottenness and corruption, and launches forth into an everlasting new condition.

Lord, teach me so to number my days, see how frail I am, Psa. xc. 12 ; xxxix. 4 : let me so often realize this dying to myself, in most serious meditation, put myself into this condition of death's coming, and acting his part, his utmost on me, that I may both familiarize and facilitate this so dreadful and difficult work, that I may be greatly desirous to be dissolved, and be thereby with Christ, which is best of all.   Oh that I may perform this last work best ! which that I may, and make that great enemy my great friend, my losses greatest gain, let me still mind Christ's healing this bitter water, making it sweet, making this death's-day better than the birth's-day ; let my thoughts be on the sting's pulling out, that it cannot hurt, if I am Christ's.

Death is ours if we are Christ's, and for our most high advantages, as being the great outlet of all evil and misery : I now shall sin no more, be tempted and insnared no more, the world shall now be corruption's bait and Satan's hook no more, Satan shall never throw at me any fiery dart more, God will never desert me, hide his face from me more.

All miseries, crosses, losses, poverty, shame, pain, sickness, weakness, weariness, faintness, hunger, thirst, cold, nakedness, labour, toil, cares, fears, sorrows, and disquiets, and whatsoever of this life's evils can be named, are at an eternal end.

And death becomes the great inlet of all good, to flow in most abundantly ; a passage to heaven, to be possessed of a crown of glory, to enjoy the innumerable company of saints and angels, to be with Christ, and seeing God face to face, and fulness of felicity for evermore.

CHAP. XIX.—*Of Judgment after Death.*

ON the sad parting of those two dearest friends soul
and body, comes instantly the doom and sentence,
Heb. ix. 27, the particular judgment of the person,
to pass and be put in execution to an eternal estate,
either of happiness or misery, immediately as to the
immortal soul, and afterward at the general resurrection
of body and soul in conjunction.

This therefore little foregoing day of judgment,
upon which, by the body's mortality and necessity of
dying, and the soul's immortality and necessity of
not dying, every person comes to be fixed in eternal
misery or happiness unavoidably, is a point of most
high consequence, to be well considered, deeply
weighed, often dwelt upon in our most prudent improvements of retiredness.

A very great frequency and repetition of our best
thoughts and serious ponderings, must be the tribute
of this concern, this vertical point, this judgment
which casts the scales, and makes full weight for
misery or felicity for ever; for as the tree falls, so it
lies; as death leaves, judgment, this particular judgment, finds us, dooms us irreversibly; there is no
bringing a writ of error, no appeal to be made, no
pardon now the Judge will give, no petition he will
receive, no stay of proceedings can in the least be
granted or looked for on any ground.

This to every particular person in some respect is
his great day of judgment, this disposes and de-
spatches, this secures and keeps me for the great
general assize and judgment; this is the foundation,
that will be the superstructure; this is secret, that is

solemn; this for a private execution, that for one in open view of all. But this judgment particular strikes the first stroke of utter undoing, or lends the first hand of help to an eternal saving, and without which the great judgment doth not proceed.

Ah, then, well may I afford this judgment a great frequency, largeness, and seriousness of thoughts, which launches the ship of my soul into the ocean of eternity, which lets my soul, either presently to sink into the bottomless pit, purposely sends it thither, casts it into the lake of everlasting fire, or sends it into Abraham's bosom, into the harbour of eternal happiness, and enters this jewel into the cabinet of heaven. Oh how unspeakably considerable is this particular judgment! The very moment of my death, that is uncertain, and the very next moment after death comes certain judgment, irresistibly and irre-coverably, and determines our state of eternity.

CHAP. XX.—*Of the general Judgment-day.*

BUT then particular judgment foregoing, this is but the foundation and introduction of the following.

The private and partial execution on the soul separate from the body, shall have a public and most solemn both manifestation and consummation with it.

1. This day, among other ends, is reserved for the so great and glorious manifestation of the infinite holiness and righteousness, grace and mercy, wrath and severity, and other attributes of God; never in

this world having their so full discovery, as now by
the intendment and most wise contrivance of a God
they shall have, before angels and saints, devils and
wicked men.

The judgment-day is called the " day of the revelation of the righteous judgment of God," Rom. ii.
5 ; of that righteousness, that so great and glorious
attribute so little understood, less considered, so much
questioned and cavilled at, the highest declaration and
fullest revelation that ever was, shall be then made
and seen by all.   So the rest of God's attributes
shall obtain their meridian height, and shine forth in
their most perfect resplendencies.   Therefore it needs
must be a very great day, when it is so intended,
purposely, to be the greatest day that ever was or
can be.

2. It is also purposely constituted for the highest
glory of Jesus Christ, that he may both be admired
of saints and angels, and magnified in the sight of all
wicked men and devils.

Therefore he now is to appear in the highest glory,
splendour, and power : and he being made now the
visible Judge, this must be most glorious, in that it
is the consummating work of his mediatorial kingdom, preceding immediately his delivering up his
kingdom to God the Father, as the apostle tells us,
1 Cor. xv. 24.   For the method and most fruitful
way of this so very necessary meditation, I conceive it
may be,

1. To begin with those scriptures that most clearly
and distinctly present us with the infallible certainty
of this grand point.

2. To gather up the remarkable particulars of it in
Scripture, as to the nature, manner, and the things
that both accompany and follow it.

3. How to manage it, to our being best moved and stirred up by it.

1. For the infallible certainty of this judgment-day, let me look out those scriptures in the Old and New Testament that speak perspicuously of it, and then labour by meditation and prayer to sink deep into my heart, to lay them so strongly to infuse as to leave a deep abiding tincture upon it.

To be put into a full possession and assurance of faith, in this so high soul concernment.

Enoch, the seventh from Adam, that so walked with God, and that was first translated, prophesied of the Lord's coming to judgment, Jude 14. Job, who is supposed by the learned to have lived when the Israelites were in Egypt, and before Moses' time, in chap. xix. 25—27, has a most clear and full assertion of his Redeemer's being the last day on the earth, and seeing him then, &c. Solomon, Eccl. xii. 14, " God shall bring every thing into judgment," every secret thing, good or evil. They that sleep in the dust shall arise, some to shame, others to life, Dan. xii. 2.

In the New Testament, out of Christ's the Judge's own mouth, Matt. xxv. 31—46, this doctrine is most fully, with the particulars and manner of it, described, and in the other Gospels often.

So the apostle of the Gentiles. At Athens, the great university of the world, he tells them God had appointed a day to judge the world in righteousness, and by the man Jesus, " whom he hath ordained," Acts xvii. 31. Rom. ii. 16, In that day that God shall judge the secrets of men's hearts. So, " We must all appear before the judgment-seat of Christ," &c. 2 Cor. v. 10. Again, Christ shall come in flaming fire, to render vengeance to all that know not God, and obey not the gospel, 2 Thess. i. 7—10.

The apostle John says, " I saw the dead stand before God, and judged according to their works," &c. Rev. xx. 12—15.

The varieties of places in Scripture, are like many candles lighted in one place, like multitudes of lights in the heavens, all to give light to us below, that we might have clearest discoveries, firmest faith, strongest instigations to yield full compliance and obedience, with greatest readiness, pleasure, and sweetness.

Oh I must answer for having the Scriptures, the varieties, perspicuities, convincing reasons, and persuading endeavours of the Spirit of God towards me in them and by them. The more in the Scripture is done for me, the more will be required of me.

2. The particulars remarkable to be gathered together of this day, as the nature, manner, &c.

(1.) I must meditate of the Person, the so great and glorious Person that shall be Judge, which is God himself, as the Scripture often tells us; as Eccl. xii. 14; Rom. ii. 16, as was mentioned before, God shall judge, &c. Though this be greatly considerable, under which our faith must be concluded; and this alone well pondered may greatly awaken, awe, and provoke us to all fulness of regard and care: yet the word tells us further, it is God, by Jesus Christ; so in Acts xvii. 19, " God hath appointed a day, in the which he will judge the world in righteousness, by that man whom he hath ordained." " He hath committed all judgment unto the Son," John v. 22. It is not committed to the holiest man that ever lived, nor to any mighty angel, it is too high an honour, too great a work, for any created nature, only fit for him that is God and man. For, by being God, there is both an omniscient and omnipotent, an infinitely holy, righteous, good, and merciful Judge ; and by being man, there is to all men's eyes a visible Judge, that the Scriptures may be fulfilled. And this for the saints' surpassing joy, but the greater daunting and terror of the wicked, let in by the eyes both of the one and other : all must be judged by a Judge their eyes shall behold.

(2.) For the time of his coming, it cannot, will not be known : " Ye know not what hour your Lord doth come," Matt. xxiv. 42.

(3.) For the suddenness and secrecy of his coming: The Lord will come as a thief in the night, 2 Pet. iii. 10. " In such an hour as ye think not the Son of man cometh," Matt. xxiv. 44.

(4.) For the place whence he sets out and comes: " The Lord himself shall descend from heaven," 1 Thess. iv. 16.

(5.) It will be in power and great glory, such as never was, and never the like again shall be : never did the Sun of righteousness ascend to and shine in such a meridian, such a transcendent height of glory. " Looking for the glorious appearing," Tit. ii. 13.

(6.) For the company and retinue, it is all the whole court of heaven come to wait on their King of glory. All the glorified saints and angels leave heaven empty, to make up his train, thousand of thousands giving their attendance. " With ten thousand of his saints," Jude 15. Comes with his mighty angels, 2 Thess. i. 7. Cometh, and all his holy angels with him, Matt. xxv. 31. Oh what an unspeakably glorious attendance this is !

(7.) For the dreadfulness of his coming. Christ is revealed coming in flaming fire, 2 Thess. i. 7. " The

heavens shall pass away with a great noise, and the
elements shall melt with fervent heat, the earth also
and the works that are therein shall be burned up,"
2 Pet. iii. 10.

(8.) As a preparative to the judgment, Christ de-
scends from heaven, 1. With a shout (never was there
such a shout made in all the time the world stood).
2. With the voice of the archangel, and the trump
of God : the voice and trump at Mount Sinai, where
six hundred thousand might hear, that was a glorious
and most dreadful voice and sound, but nothing like
this. Never such a voice, that which will make the
whole world ring, and the dead rise out of their graves,
and with the same bodies, the same numerical bodies,
that lived here. 3. Those that are alive shall be
changed in a moment, in the twinkling of an eye, on
the sound of the trump, 1 Cor. xv. 52. 4. " The
dead in Christ shall rise first, be caught up together
with them in the clouds, to meet the Lord in the air,"
1 Thess. iv. 16, 17. Oh blessed and most joyful
meeting of the saints that were on earth, now raised,
changed, and caught up to meet and see the Lord
Jesus their Saviour, and now the glorious Judge,
coming to consummate their happiness in soul and
body together, to die no more, and to meet with all the
saints and angels come from heaven, and to be for ever
with the Lord, never to be from him again. 5. But
others that were wicked and now raised, with the
other black troop that were in hell, and now have
their souls united to their bodies, shall be brought before Christ the Judge, (according to the opinion of
some,) sitting on a high throne in the air, the saints
and angels all attending about him.

(9.) For the manner of these proceedings, alluding
to the manner of men's judicatures, as Rev. xx. 1. All

persons small and great are brought, and stand before God, that is, Christ, God and man. 2. The books are opened, the book of God's omniscience, and the books of men's hearts and consciences, not in an imperfect state of ignorance and forgetfulness, but fully prepared for their work of answering at the tribunal and bar of Christ. 3. It is a judging men according to their works, for that hath been done in the body, good or evil, Eccl. xii. 14. And a judging every secret thing of men's hearts, Rom. ii. 16. Some conceive, that seeing there will be the " revelation of the righteous judgment of God," Rom. ii. 5, therefore it will have a long time, to judge the cause of every person, in all particulars, that so the righteousness of the judgment and sentence of Christ, with the execution of it, may fully appear, and none to have any least objection against it. But others think there will not be so particular a discovery and trial of all things relating to the saints, but a more general one. However, Christians must be diligent to be found of Christ, " without spot and blameless," as 2 Pet. iii. 14.

(10.) When the cases of all have been tried and made to appear, the sheep having been separate from the goats, and set at Christ's right hand, the goats on the left; the sentence then passes, that most comfortable sentence for the sheep, the righteous, (now so judged by the heart-knowing and most just Judge,) " Come, ye blessed of my Father, inherit the kingdom prepared for you." And that terrible sentence on the goats, now openly convicted, " Depart, ye cursed, into everlasting fire, prepared for the devil and his angels," Matt. xxv. 34, 41. To which the saints and angels all give their full approbation, as also to the doom upon the devils.

(11.) Upon which the most righteous execution

follows, of both the sentences ; for the righteous, and against the wicked ones.

To make all this obtain a more efficacious impression daily on my spirit, let me strive to represent this day as now come, that I hear the trump sound, see the dead rise, the living all changed in a moment; looking up I see Christ coming in the clouds, with great glory, angels and saints all attending him, Christ placed on the throne of judgment; all persons collected before him, and myself among the rest ; my case tried, my works, words, thoughts, and all my secrets judged, and my state for all eternity determined ; and now when the world is all on fire, the wicked sent into that everlasting destruction, the righteous going with Christ into heaven and everlasting happiness, what my own particular condition is like to be.

If I can come before Christ, the all-knowing Judge, with confidence and exceeding joy, I shall be absolved, and hear that joyful sentence, " Come, thou blessed of my Father, inherit the kingdom prepared for thee."

CHAP. XXI.—*Of Meditation of Hell, and Death eternal therein.*

THE very naming of death is dreadful, death eternal is much more dreadful, but a being in hell, the worst place possible, is most dreadful of all.   Hell, though in the mere mentioning it makes such a jar upon the spirit of any ; though the least touching on it but by a glancing thought, the least touch be like the needle's sharp point to the apple of the eye, so acute a pain and smart; yet must the eye of the soul, by meditation, not only touch it, but take it close to it, but dwell upon it.

Death natural, but in the very thought, hath a very high attending regret; we cannot endure to look death-ward; but oh how greatly unwilling to look in the least this sad way, destruction-ward, hell-ward, toward death eternal! The first is tasting gall, but the second is a drinking poison; the one hath a deep attending reluctancy, the other a double-dyed antipathy. It is the harshest task for a sinner, it is a hard for a saint, to fix willingly, and dwell in meditation, on so sad and dreadful a subject as hell is: yet is it that which must be done, and by a holy, wise spirit may be both confidently and advantageously done. The best Christian on earth will lose nothing by sometimes looking into hell, and fixing the thoughts there. No man ever yet fled from hell, but first fixed his thoughts in some proportion on it: no man will fly fast enough from this pit of perdition, this lake of fire, if he do not oft look towards it, and keep his eye upon it. Hell and death eternal are set down in Scripture for both evil and good men's flying; but this cannot be compassed without frequencies of earnest ponderings and meditatings.

For a right proceeding in this meditation,

1. Let me first look to that which is my infallible rule, the testimony of that God who founded hell and laid the corner-stone of it; who first threatened and prepared this prison, this pit of destruction; who knows all the large dimensions of it, all things in and about it, and cannot, and will not, in the least deceive us in it. He hath given us his word to tell us, and that under his own hand, in great numbers

and varieties of passages, that we cannot rationally
conceive he would so do, mention and give it so
many times under his own hand, were there no such
thing, no local hell, and second death eternal.

My way therefore, as a good Christian, is to look
up, gather Scripture passages ; passage after passage,
all over the book of God, as I find this asserted in
them. Oh, shall my life's time ravel out without any
redeeming it, as to this particular, of giving due
down-weight of thoughts, frequent serious thoughts,
as opportunity can be had, of death eternal in
hell ?

I must not only say, there is a hell ; I must not
only take it for granted, as most persons do ; but I
must be concluded under the Scripture authority ;
see it and say it, upon due persuasion, upon clear
demonstration, demonstration on conclusive argu-
mentation, arguments chosen as so many arrows taken
out of Christ's quiver, the Scriptures, levelled right,
flying round up to the mark, and hitting full my un-
believing and recoiling averse spirit, making it fall
down under this weighty truth, reducing it, through
Christ's help, to a firm and operative belief ; yea, so to
assent to and ponder this so high concern, as to work
off all my usual wonted easiness and slightness of
thinkings on this particular. And to arrive at a contrary habitual seriousness, and earnestness of mindings, frequent thinkings ; yea, let my spirit not rest,
till I am reduced to, and improve, under the powerful
and prevailing provocations of it, to whatever so great
a thing calls for from me.

That I may daily more answer the intendments of
a God, in relating this hell so plainly and plentifully
in his word for my due notice of it. My way must
be a course of serious pondering the Scriptures,

passage after passage, wherein the second death and hell is set forth, in the several books.

As in Isa. xxx. 33, " Tophet is ordained of old ; yea, for the king it is prepared ; he hath made it deep and large : the pile thereof is fire and much wood ; the breath of the Lord, like a stream of brimstone, doth kindle it." An elegant description in an allusion : so those many clear passages of Christ's own mouth set down so plainly, as words can utter.

' In the very first sermon of Christ's on the mount, he mentions hell-fire, and casting into hell, three several times, Matt. v. 22, 29, 30. " Brought down to hell," Matt. xi. 23. The rich man is said to be in hell, Luke xvi. 23. It is called a prison, 1 Pet. iii. 19 ; prisons being the worst of places, made for securing and punishing. A bottomless pit, Rev. xx. 1. A place of torment, Luke xvi. 23. " Their worm dieth not," Mark ix. 44, alluding to that worm that breeds in and feeds on the body, is lying gnawing, and cannot be cured. Their fire goes not out : fire is the most quick and active, the most tormenting and torturing element. It is brimstone that is the fuel, which is a most combustible, noisome, and suffocating matter.

It is called utter darkness : darkness is a most dreadful and disconsolating thing, as that of Egypt. For the company, it is only wicked persons perfect in sin, and most wretched devils, the worst of creatures : " Depart, ye cursed, into everlasting fire, prepared for the devil and his angels," Matt. xxv. 41.

Oh how hot and scorching must that fire be, that purposely is prepared for utmost torment ! Not like Nebuchadnezzar's furnace, seven times hotter, but seventy times hotter, that which is inconceivable.

In Scripture, hell, or the state of misery, is expressed by the terms of second death. Death, one death in any kind, is very dreadful, above all other things; but after dying a first death, then to come and die a second death, and this not so easy as dying any bodily death millions of times over! If a malefactor should die the most cruel death, and then be made to live again, and then die that death a second time, yea, thousands and thousands of times over, oh how sad were the case of that person, that must be so under the both fears of that death first, and then the torments and pains! But what is all this to this second death, being under the fulness of infinite wrath, and that for ever!

The inflicter of this misery is no less than an infinitely wise, holy, sin-hating, and an omnipotent God; acting in the purest and fiercest wrath, endeavouring the fullest revenge the damned creature is capable of, and for which it purposely is made a vessel of wrath, and that vessel is prepared to receive and hold this wrath.

1. Prepared by being widened, extended, as it were, to receive the fulness of wrath. As the saints shall have their spirits elevated and extended to the utmost, to be made fit to receive the fulness of glory and happiness; so the damned have their spirits widened and enlarged, their understandings and hearts in the utmost extensiveness, that they be brimful of wrath.

2. Prepared by being purposely strengthened to the utmost, as vessels are made strong to hold the strongest wine or liquor, to hold and keep in that wrath poured into them.

Were hell but to have the least torment in the least member, or sensible part, as in the toe, finger, or the like for ever; or but one torment in a noble part, head, liver, heart, or a complication of many sad diseases for ever; how intolerably sad were this state! but to have all possible trouble and torment both in body and soul, set on by a God for ever, oh how unspeakably sad is this!

All the forenamed, this imprisonment, this tormenting, this worm, this fire, the weepings, the wailings, the gnashing of teeth, is not for an hour, a day, a month, a year, an age, nor a thousand years or ages, or what can be reckoned by millions of millions, but for ever : no rest for ever, no ease for ever, no hope of any deliverance, or degree of it, for ever; but sorrow, torment, and terror, sinking in despair and hopelessness for ever, ever, ever.

Oh, then, to improve this meditation, and make it operative upon my spirit, let me first look upon hell begun, in that terror and horror the wicked, instantly upon their raising up from the dead, and changed, are seized with.   The hot burning coals of hell are thrown into their bosom, fill them up, and lie burning and scorching, as they are both bringing to the judgment-seat, and are standing before Christ at the bar, all the time of their arraignment.   Never did any poor guilty prisoner stand in such a fear as this fear, and were so amazed. .

Next observe the then unspeakable shame.   Then all the time of their arraignment, and especially on the pronouncing of that dreadful sentence which will be passed and executed.   Oh what must be the unspeakable shame, mixed with the continuing and increasing sad horror! Dan. xii. 2.   Oh what must be that shame, when all things possible concur to load and cover them with shame! never was there, nor can be, such a shame poured upon any.   A shame in the greatest concourse that ever was, or can be ; all

the saints and angels, yea, all the wicked and the
devils, every particular ashamed, also before all their
own company, in this so desperate state.   And especially a transcendent shame, in respect of the infinitely
glorious Judge, the Lord Jesus, despised and sinned
so against by so many.

Ah, what must be the shame of wicked men, to
stand uncovered, with open faces, to see the so dreadful Judge looking the arraigned person full in the
face, looking with the most stern countenance upon
their uncovered faces; to have all their sins ripped
up, every one adding still to the shame! but then
when the dreadful sentence passes, oh what the
shame will further then be !

And yet far more, when the sentence is executed,
they driven away, and all devils and men thrust into
the dungeon of darkness, what an everlasting shame
will that be !   Now, oh now to think of all their inexpressible losses, of such losses as never were seen ;
loss of God himself, his face and communion with
him, Father, Son, and Spirit ; loss of the company
of all the saints and angels, lost heaven, and all its
glory lost, and all that happiness that arises from all ;
such a state as is so good and glorious, to that utmost possibility as the creature can have ; and for
that so all-sweetening and satiating eternity : and
then, which greatly aggravates the misery, as Christ
himself expresses it, " There shall be weeping and
gnashing of teeth, when ye shall see Abraham, and
Isaac, and Jacob, and all the prophets, in the kingdom of God, and you yourselves thrust out," Luke
xiii. 28.   So to see all the saints, to see all the
godly patriarchs, Abraham, Isaac, Jacob, and all the
other.   To see Moses, Samuel, David, and all the
holy prophets, to see all the blessed apostles, Peter,

John, Paul, and all the disciples of Christ, with all
the glorious martyrs and confessors in all times ;
and all the innumerable company of saints, in both
former, present, and after ages ; all these known in
their times, but neglected, scorned, opposed, persecuted, and destroyed ; yet all these to be taken up
with Christ into heaven : but as other sinners, so
thy woeful self, dying without a Christ, shut out,
and have heaven gates shut up, locked and barred
against thee for ever ; and withal also, ah, locked
up fast in the dungeon of darkness, and filled up
full in soul and body, with unspeakable torment
never to end.

And to realize this more, and make it more effectual on thee that art saved, after the judgment is
ended, sentence of condemnation passed, let me
imagine myself looking after this herd of goats, all
driving down headlong to the lake of fire and brimstone, seeing them taken hold of, and haled to the
prison of hell, and immediately shut in, presently
seized with wrath and torment, filled brimful up
with unspeakable woe and torture.

Then could I but go near, lay my ear to the door
of this prison, and listen earnestly, oh what would
be the dolours, the groanings, cryings, roarings,
yellings, shriekings, that so many, and many thousands, all together tortured, would be heard to make !
The noise of a few prisoners condemning, of passengers
in a ship drowning, of men in battle killing and dying, makes a most hideous impression, makes a man's
ears to tingle, and his heart to ache and tremble :
but oh what is, or can be, like unto this hideous
noise and cry, of so many innumerable millions, of all
sorts and sexes, men and women, under such intolerable torments ! Oh, but might I have liberty and

security to make an ocular observation, with my eyes
to see the gates of that horrid place open, to see
the lake of fire and brimstone flaming, to look in
and see the tormented in their so woeful condition,
most sad postures and behaviours ; all the multitudes
and throngs of persons, and the persons in particular
I desire to see and view ! There I might see that
first murderer Cain, appearing in his chains and
tortures ; and on my demanding who he was, he an-
swers, I am that cursed one, that killed my righteous
brother Abel ; here, here I have been already so many
thousands of years, and here I must remain to be tormented for ever.

In another place appears another, it may be wicked
Saul, that persecutor of holy David ; in another
Ahithophel, or Haman, Herod, Judas, and abundance of such strewed all over this prison ; sinners of
all sorts, idolaters, superstitious, profane, swearers,
cursers, profaners of the day of God, with disobedient
to parents, murderers, adulterers, thieves, liars, covetous, and all others of several sexes, ranks, and conditions.

If I might ask, and be answered upon inquiry, by
the persons I see there, would not one come and say,
I am such a one, another say, I am such, and so
others ? would not one come and show me, there in
such a place are those that were drowned by the
deluge ; there are the people of Sodom burnt with
fire and brimstone ; there are Pharaoh and the Egyptians, those drowned in the Red Sea ; there are such
and such enemies and persecutors of Christ and his
church of old ; there are the heathen persecutors, and
the antichristian enemies ; there such apostates, such
hypocrites, such loose Christians ; in this place such
a man or such a woman you knew, and in that place

another; there you see them, and in the same sad case with myself?

But should I ask of their several conditions, and what they continually feel, oh what doleful relations would they give in, of the scorchings of that fire, of the gnawing of that never-dying worm, of their deepest sorrows, highest fears; and above all, of their overwhelming and unspeakable despair! Prov. xviii. 14. Here when God suffers but a spark to fly out of the furnace of hell, and fall into a sinner's bosom, as Judas, Matt. xxvii. 5, oh how intolerable doth it prove! but when the whole pile of hell's fuel and fire shall be laid and fastened on sinners by the hand of an almighty God, oh what must that torment and that despair amount unto, and then when under infallible certainty of a lengthening out to all eternity!

O let every one meditate often and most seriously of this so dreadful state; not be shy of looking this way, of looking into this lake of fire, and realizing all the so dreadful things comprehended in it: not contenting thyself with thy yieldings and giving it for granted, and never ponder, never labour to any purpose to be rightly affected, stirred up to take a sure course for escaping it. But let this "terror of the Lord," 2 Cor. v. 11, awaken, provoke, and persuade every one to fly from this wrath to come; and fly to that Christ, make sure of him, that only can deliver us.

CHAP. XXII.—*Of Heaven and Happiness
eternal.*

THE last thing I shall mention in this part of solemn
and set meditation, is that of heaven, and happiness
eternal therein : hell is not so miserable a state, but
heaven is as transcendently glorious and happy ; the
one being purposely for demonstration of the fulness
of God's hatred and wrath, the other for the highest
manifestation of the riches of mercy and free grace.
Yea, this being the thing the Lord is so infinitely
pleased and delighted in, must needs have the fullest
and most glorious manifestation that is any way possible for a God to make, and his creatures can be apprehensive and receptive of, and therefore the state of
glory must be glorious indeed : " Eye hath not seen,
nor ear heard, neither have entered into the heart of
man, the things which God hath prepared for them
that love him," 1 Cor. ii. 9. There he is speaking
of things that tend to happiness, the blessings of
grace, peace, joy, and heavenly privileges given in
Christ : but then if happiness only begun be so glorious, oh what is happiness finished up, and consummate !

For our way of proceeding in this meditation, I
conceive it best, by laying a full Scripture ground, in
gathering those choice flowers, springing up thick in
the rich garden stores of the infallible Scriptures, and
are purposely growing there for the hand of faith to
gather, and the eye of our dim, weak sight to be
healed and cleared, to believe and see the glory of
heaven by.

It is not a way of mere general thinkings, or that
of fancy or speculation of our own, but first laying

a Scripture great and firm foundation ; and then after to improve those Scripture assertions, by all the ability and help we can, of reason and inferences of best representations and resemblances, of imagination and invention.   General apprehensions, and grantings of Scripture truths, deceive and destroy many, when they are rested in : general notions of heaven and happiness, granting it there is a heaven and no more, makes many miss of it, miss for want of more distinct apprehensions, well-grounded believing, and due deep sinking of it to the bottom of the heart, there to lie glowing, to warm and kindle the affections, to provoke into a labouring, a mighty striving to win the crown of glory.

The way is (as wisdom in all other cases of con-sequence teaches) to come off every day from general confused thoughts of heaven and happiness, restings on and runnings away with a supposed doing enough. If we still grant there is a heaven and happiness, every day to endeavour distincter and clearer thoughts and knowledge.   Generals will not serve, grantings must not be made the enough of a wise Christian ; he must have an extensive and enlarging clearness, an increasing firmness of faith, in the doctrines, the great points of salvation.   But we having this so prime an article of faith, that which hath wrapt up in it so rich a treasure, and preserves, as it were, that so inestimable jewel of happiness, man's last end ; that which is the great foundation and instigation of all a Christian's strivings and hopes (for he hath no hope in this life for happiness here).   This therefore should not be turned off, nor terminated (as too often is done) with a granting or bare assent ; but still ob-tain of us a fuller, firmer, warmer, and more operative seeing and belief.

Now this cannot be without diligent gathering in, and better still meditating on particular Scriptures, asserting and clearly manifesting this main article, and man's chief end comprised in it.

The Jewish church had this typified in the holy of holies, as Heb. ix. 3, 12, 24, "Christ is not entered into the holy places made with hands, which are the figures of the true, but into heaven itself." This was, that by the visible place faith might be stirred up to eye and view the invisible typified state of glory.

David tells us of it, and was assured to be received up into glory, Psa. lxxiii. 24; that is, into heaven in glory. Of them that sleep in the dust, some shall awake to everlasting life, and shine as the brightness of the firmament, and some as the stars for ever, Dan. xii. 2, 3.

The church of the New Testament, in the writings given by Christ to it, have this doctrine of heaven and happiness abundantly and most clearly set forth. The first mentionings of it are out of the mouth of him that with the Father and Holy Spirit made it. In Christ's first sermon, "Blessed are the poor in spirit: for theirs is the kingdom of heaven," Matt. v. 3. So ver. 10, 12, The persecuted for righteousness' sake, theirs is the kingdom of heaven. Mention is again made of it in verse 20. See also ver. 34, 45, 48; ch. vi. 9, the first passage in the Lord's prayer. At least twelve several times in this first sermon of Christ this heaven is mentioned. And as in the Gospels, so all the New Testament over, you may, many scores of times, find and see it lying, as a most shining and glorious diamond in the mine, or as in a rich cabinet, to be viewed and laboured for. The multitudes of places, well weighed, must needs hold

forth, to all that shut not their eyes wilfully, a local
heaven, a place of happiness and glory.

It is no allegorical heaven, as some have dreamed,
or may ignorantly imagine; when it is asserted in so
many clear passages, which all of them, in our reading or hearings, should have their due weight, weight
of thinkings, and efficacy on us, for firm believing, and
answerable endeavours for not losing, but enjoying it.

For the rank of places, what it hath, the Scripture
tells us it is the third heaven; the first being that
where the clouds are; the second where the glorious
lights, sun, moon, and stars are; this third above
them all, called therefore the highest heaven. This
third and highest heaven is most inconceivably excellent.

The sun, moon, and stars were made, not the first
day, but the fourth day, for furniture of that heaven,
under the highest heaven.

It is the largest and most capacious place, as
that which comprises or surrounds all the inferior
world, and things in that. O here, here is Recha-
both, room enough. In this world, here is crowding,
pushing, crushing of the saints; the wicked world
would quite cast them, every one, out of it, to be left
alone and enjoy all; to be let alone, and have none to
see and shame them any way: but the saints shall all
be brought at last into a large place, where none shall
molest or trouble them.

What a kingdom for territories is this! What a
place for Christ to prepare mansions for his in! What
a place for the all-glorious God and Jesus Christ to
keep a court in highest splendour and magnificence
in! and the Lord Jesus the Saviour, that purchased
this inheritance with his own blood, for him to be
ever viewed, loved, admired, glorified by all his saints

to the highest in! Of all imaginable places, this, this
is the place, this is room, this is a place so large as
the hearts of the saints can wish.

As heaven is the largest for capacity and quantity,
so is it the best place for quality and excellency,
2 Cor. xii. It is called paradise by that blessed Paul
who was taken up thither, to tell upon his return
what a place it was. Paradise mentioned Gen. ii. 8,
it was the best place that ever was on earth; it was
the summary of all necessaries and delicacies for
Adam, in that perfect state, his accommodations, re-
creations, and abundant delight; fit therefore to re-
semble the place of glory by. And so our Lord
Christ thought, when he calls it by this name of paradise; " To-day shalt thou be with me in paradise,"
Luke xxiii. 43. The best place it was made, because
for the best creature on earth.

In other places, it is a place of glory, riches of
glory, a kingdom, a crown of glory, an eternal weight
of glory; a state where there are pleasures for evermore, rivers of pleasures, joys, and fulness of joy.

For every saint the highest entertainments, in all
respects. The ear hath such enrapturing music and
melody, as that best and greatest concert, of all the
innumerable companies of saints and angels, can make.
For the eye, the palace of heaven is unspeakably beyond all places, prospects, and objects that nature and
art could ever yield.

The persons of the saints, as to the numbers so
innumerable, must needs make up the rarest train and
show (as to their sorts and differences) that ever eye
saw. Oh what a rapturous sight must that be to see
Enoch, Noah, Abraham, Isaac, Jacob, and all the
holy patriarchs! Moses, Samuel, David, and all the
holy prophets! Peter, Paul, John, and all the holy

apostles! All the blessed and glorious martyrs of Jesus Christ! All his godly and serviceable, painful and laborious ministers! All the precious saints, kings, and governors, and others that are recorded in the Bible! And not only men, but holy women, Sarah, Hannah, Ruth, Esther, and others in the Old Testament; the blessed Virgin, and Elisabeth, with the women that followed Christ, and ministered unto him, Mary Magdalene, Johanna, Susanna, Lydia, Dorcas, Priscilla among the apostles helping them, all the disciples of Christ which believed in him; with all the eminent godly lights in the church after the apostles, and all the saints in all after-ages to the world's end! And then for all this train, in their sorts and ranks; as to their bodies, to be so all over glorious, to shine as the sun and brightness of the firmament for ever, oh what a show and enrapturing entertainment is here for the eye!

But that which is the top and height, and far surpassing all the other, is that sweetest, most ravishing sight of the most glorious body of Jesus Christ; the highest beauty that ever eye beheld or saw, far outshining all others, as the sun exceeds the stars: ah, here, here will be a sight indeed. Ah, but then to behold him in his highest discoveries of his sweetest, loveliest lookings and smilings on all his saints with him, and upon thee in particular. To see his countenance composed and ordered, purposely to beam forth in fullest manifestations of surpassing sweetness of most intense affections towards his so dearly beloved bride, now present with him to behold him and enjoy perfect communion with him.

And oh what entertainments are there, as to the soul and spirit, for the faculties of understanding, will, and affections! how far transcending those of the senses! as the beatifical vision, seeing God face to face, with all intellectual satisfaction as to all the truths in the word of God, all mysteries, prophecies, and difficulties, and whatsoever may conduce to the glorious happiness of the saints: satisfaction also, as to the works and ways of God, creation and providence, all the riddles and dark things so far made known as is needful.

Likewise as to the will and heart, the beatifical fruition, enjoying of God, Father, Son, and Spirit, and his infinite sweetness, to all possible fulness and perfection.

Likewise all happy communion with saints and angels, to all delight and pleasure. And for all this both body and soul are prepared, strengthened, elevated, and enlarged to the utmost extensiveness.

As all imperfections and sins are utterly removed, so all grace and holiness, light and wisdom, heat and flame of heart communicated, and in a blessed reciprocation, a mutual acting: God, the infinitely all-sufficient, communicating himself to the glorified, to their utmost capacity; and they reacting and putting forth their grace and holiness, to their utmost ability: oh how unspeakably sweet and satisfying must this continual intercourse be!

For the close of all, let me think myself, after a glorious and blessed resurrection and absolution by Christ at the judgment-day, freed utterly from all evil; feeling likewise my complete happiness coming on so fast in my now passage up to the place of glory; and then instantly finding it finished, finished on the first setting my foot, as it were, within the gate of heaven. And now I think what a prepared and furnished place I am in; what company of the saints, angels, and Jesus Christ also I have; what fruition of the most blessed God; what sense of the pleasures, joys, satisfactions, and most rapturous sweetness, under all security, under that which super-added heightens and sweetens all the rest, the charter of inconceivable eternity. Oh then let my frequent and most intense thinkings be, not a looking down to earth, but up to heaven, breathing my soul up the hill to this city of God, in contemplating the glories of it; often let me walk this so pleasant walk. Who will look and pore on a dark dungeon, that hath the sun to behold? who will (that means to hit the mark) look quite beside it? who is it can go to heaven, that thinks most another way? that hath a down-look, as we say; a beast's eye, that hath no muscle of eleva-tion? Ah, such as look most will long most after, labour most for it. O, therefore, let my eye every day be walking to and in this paradise, solace itself in taking a turn still there, be walking in this upper eye-walk by meditation, till I come to see God face to face, till I look myself into this heaven I look on.

CHAP. XXIII.—*Meditation on some things pro-vidential.*

THERE should be meditation on something providen-tial, a matter the hand of Providence acts or orders, holds forth and offers to our viewing and serious thinkings. The great God, as he always is guiding and ordering all things in all places, in heaven, earth, and waters, and among all creatures, especially the reasonable, and chiefly above all in his church, and for his saints, against his and their enemies; as he is guiding with his hand all the concerns of particular persons to the supreme end, his own glory, and likewise infallibly to the salvation of his redeemed: so there is ever and anon something observable, particularly providential; something which, as the hand of Providence holdeth forth, so the heart of prudence and godly wisdom will take up; that purposely it will set itself to see, search, and improve; as it may be something of the church of God abroad, or something of the people of God at home, or in the place particularly we live in: it may be there is some dispensation, to some of our relations or friends, or some matter falls out in our family, or yet nearer, on our person and personal concerns.

There is seldom any space of time but the great Governor of the world is doing some remarkable thing, it may be some admirable and glorious, it may be some amazing and stupendous, it may be some terrible and very dreadful work, if we have our eyes in exercise, and will observe.

Indeed, as to God's goings sometimes, his footsteps cannot be seen, but are very secret and unsearchable, Psa. lxxvii. 19. And there are others of his workings, which are more easy for all to behold and understand.

There are varieties of providences successively following each other, which we should wait and watch for; which we should take, as they come, fresh and warm out of the Lord's hand, and apply them warm to our hearts for a more kindly operation.

Meditate we should upon providences while they

are just new and fresh ; so we shall give them, or rather ourselves, the advantage of a more ready and affectionate pondering, a more profitable minding. If I could still improve in meditation of the promises, and also in a wise, warm, lively meditating of providences ; in the one see better daily the riches of free grace, in the other the glorious governings of a God in wisdom, righteousness, and goodness ; how would my spirit, under the dews of this fruitful meditation, be shooting up ! how would it prosper !   Those are the highest-form Christians, that are arrived here, at the contemplation of the works and great providences of God in the world.

In 1 John ii. 13, he writes to some he calls fathers, others young men, others children.   Some, by children, understand such as are (as to meditation) taken up with the promises, and matters of justification, pardon, and peace ; young men, are such who are gotten further, and exercised about sanctification, and conquering strong corruptions ; fathers, that, beyond both, are taken up and arrived at ponderings and contemplations of the works and ways of God, and his great actings in the world.

So it is sometimes needful to meditate on the providences that are more obliging and engaging, more awakening and inciting, such as are, as it were, the special hand of the Lord touching us, taking hold of us, framing and ordering things for us.   And here there is great reason our meditation should be more serious and curious ; as wherein we may see God's so particular goings and workings toward us, and for us.

Psa. xviii. In that excellent psalm David enumerates and records all God's goings towards him.   Oh then, with the psalmist, let my soul meditate on all the works of God; listen and file up the dispensations of his observable providences towards others and myself. Meditate on his so merciful preservings, directings, prosperings, and all other sorts and ways of providence; that I may admire and exalt him, depend, and trust, and wait upon him, and walk so before him, that his ways may ever be mercy and truth towards me.

CHAP. XXIV.—*Of more short and ejaculatory Meditation.*

BESIDES solemn and set meditation, there is also that which is sudden and short, wherein the soul acts, as one breaking out of a throng or crowd, goes aside from disturbances and diversions, or breaks off from some present and too pressing business, to take breath and respite itself; whereby it makes a stand of thoughts; turns the stream of former thoughts, and, like a bird that was sitting on the ground, rises and mounts up aloft, to sing and sport itself: even so a holy heart, in heavenly-mindedness, will get out of the throng of cares and business, will be often breaking off the thread of earthly thoughts, and interpose some heavenly dart up to heaven, make a short visit thither, refresh itself with some heavenly dainty; take and taste of the manna above, look up to God, to Christ, his Spirit, his grace, his promises, his providences, and gracious orderings; have a running banquet of hea-venly sweetmeats, when it cannot sit down and feed at large by a fuller set meditation.

As there are ejaculatory prayers and wishes, when

there is not opportunity for more solemn enlargements, there should be also sudden and short meditatings, quick interposings of good and holy thoughts ;
then when the urgencies of affairs, encumbrances, diversions, and interruptions by company, hinderances
in any kind, will not admit the opportunity of an
abode of serious thoughts, then sudden dartings up
the soul to heaven may be had, be a refreshment ; as
Jonathan's tasting the honey with the top of his rod,
when being in pursuit of the Philistines he could not
take a full meal. David, who meditated so much, must
needs, in respect of his great occasions, civil, and military,
and domestic, make much use of this short way of meditation, when he often could not go the other larger way.
As he was frequent in his sudden short prayings, so
must he be much in short sudden meditatings, which
were the ground commonly of his prayings. The
Psalms show his frequent using this short way of
meditation and praying : thus Psa. xv., a psalm of
but five verses ; so Psa. cxxvii., a psalm of five verses ;
and Psa. cxxv. the like ; and Psa. cxxiii. hath a
meditation of four verses ; Psa. cxxxi. is a meditation
of three verses ; and Psa. cxvii. is a meditation of but
two verses ; yet the Spirit of God is pleased to have
it recorded. Many other psalms we have very short,
that were his quick meditations, left all for teaching
us to do likewise, looking on his example.

This meditation, though of shorter time, yet, so far
as we can, must have its regulation and governance.

1. It should (so near as we can) have its stamp
and ingredient of holy reverence. All thoughts of
holy things must not be (how sudden soever) acts of
rashness and over-haste, without heed and fear ; the
name of a glorious God is upon every ordinance ; that
must not be taken in vain.

2. It should be the product and issue of holy lingering after God, and communion with him ; from a thirsting for God, to taste a little, when we cannot have fuller draughts of him.

3. It should be the glance of a spiritual eye, looking from love, being enamoured with God and Christ, and heavenly things : not a looking from custom, and a use to satisfy conscience, calling for something may look like a duty; but from the strength and predominancy of the fire of heavenly love : " O how love I thy law ! it is my meditation all the day," Psa. cxix. 97: as other, so this sort of meditation, must have a rise from love.   Love produces longing and looking, it introduces a pleasure in a looking, though but a glancing of the eye, on the surpassing beauty and loveliness of God and Jesus Christ, and the glorious things of heaven.   Ah, how excellent is this frame of spirit, how sweet and pleasant is it to have the eye often on these so rare beauties, from being, as the spouse in the Canticles, both really and deeply in love !

4. It should be aimed and levelled at the right mark, pleasing and glorifying God, and for communion further with him, that he may see how the pulse of our souls beats, how the eye looks, how we act, and how our hearts make still their holy escapes from the crowd, and obstructings of occasions, to give him a friendly, spiritual visit, to let him see the fervour of our love by endeavours so often as we can, to do him homage and honour.   As when we would show our high respect and honour to any person, we make the more frequent visits, when we cannot make long stay; so here when throngs of indispensable occasions hinder the set and larger engagements in meditation, make we it up in shorter visits, in often thinkings : short visits, rightly aimed, bring sweet peace.

Let it not be therefore so hasty, as we observe some children called to go to a place, that run without their errand, to act without aim : right aiming the end lays the foundation of a duty's excellency. Oh let my spirit, if I cannot think and dwell long upon heavenly things, through weakness, let it make up the defect by thinking often. Let the dartings upward be the livelier and thicker, like a golden chain which is very long, though the links be very little. Oh let me trade, drive a quick trade with littles. Light gains make a heavy purse ; little frequent tradings will gain me much here. This short often acting up will make my heart keep still open to heaven ; keep the pathway thither beaten, plain, easy, and so make it pleasant for my spirit to walk in, make this meditation highly sweet, a rare refreshing.

The frequencies of thinkings heavenward will have this threefold advantage, these three excellent fruits.

1. Frequencies of heavenly thoughts will produce and cherish an habitual heavenly-mindedness unto that primitive grace, that habit of regenerating grace (which brings a tendency, and bent of soul, making it incline heavenward) ; it will superadd an habitual heavenly-mindedness, a heart peculiarly and powerfully ready and active heavenward. As an artist, who hath not only reason first to dispose him, fit him for his trade, but the peculiar habit, a head and hand for it to understand and act as an artist.

2. The frequencies of heavenly will thereby be an exclusive and thruster out of earthly thoughts, the right way of a compendious cure. It is not the way so much to stand watching, and striving to drive them away ; to be on the defensive barely ; but to be on the

positive, in acting good thoughts, that will keep out
bad.   As if wine first fills the vessel, there is no
room for water; if a treasury be full of gold, there
is no room for rubbish.

3. This frequent short darting upward will end
with leaving an after-sweetness upon the palate of
the spirit; short, when heavenly, will be sweet, as
every crumb of sugar leaves some sweetness on the
palate; every drop of pure honey, a delicious after-
relish, so this short meditation.

The manna that dewed down upon the Israelites'
camp, lay like small coriander seeds; which they
gathered, ground, and made their bread of, which
had a rare relish. This sort of meditation may
gather still some little seeds of heavenly manna, soul
bread, with new, fresh, delicious sweetness following.
The heavenly-minded person may, as the manner of
some is, go ever with some rich tasted and scented
thing in the mouth.

Whensoever cares and diversions press hard, hang
heavy, draw strongly, greatly disquiet and weary thy
spirit; here is an outlet, an escape, a rare way of in-
terposition and soul-easing diversion, yea, of a short,
though sweet, and heavenly solace. It may be looked
on as a shadow, a resemblance of the blessed apostle's sudden carrying into the third heaven: instantly
thou this way art above, though presently below
again.

This is far surpassing all the sensual and sinful
pleasures in the world. These short tastes, by giving
our worldly occasions the slip, and mounting up to
heaven; these short visits made there, these spiritual,
short applications made to heaven, to the blessed God,
to Jesus Christ for communion with him and the
Father; have more sweet, pure, powerful, and heart-

elevating joy, than is possible to be had in any carnal or earthly things.   They, at the highest, brightest, and sweetest, have something to dim and imbitter them ; " Even in laughter the heart is sorrowful ; and the end of that mirth is heaviness," Prov. xiv. 13. But every way of godliness is a path of pleasantness and sweetness, which none know but such as try it.

CHAP. XXV.—*Of the Grounds and Reasons of this so necessary Duty of Meditation.*

So great and necessary a duty must have its support of strong reasons to conclude it, and help to bear up the spirit better under the weight of it.   Divine and infinite wisdom must needs impose and require nothing without great and sufficient reasons.   I shall therefore endeavour to propose sundry of them in their clearness and strength, as I can in this short intended piece.   The grounds and further demonstrations of this meditation I shall reduce to these four heads.

1. First from the natural order and dependences of the faculties of the reasonable soul ; and the several principles of grace given into those faculties, to enable the soul rightly to exercise itself to godliness.

2. From the transcendent excellency of divine matters, which must have their due and full mindings.

3. From the use and several ends of divine meditation

4. From either the great accruing advantages, or

R

the prejudice upon the due performance or sinful neglect of this required meditation.

1. Ground. From the natural order and dependences of the soul's faculties, and the graces laid into these faculties, for enabling a Christian rightly to exercise godliness. God, as he made man an excellent creature for excellent ends and operations, so he hath made the mind and understanding to be the soul's eye, guide, and director; the first great wheel, the first mover, directing and setting the other faculties of the will and affections in going and doing their several offices.

And because man's nature is corrupted and disabled of itself alone to perform things spiritual and holy in a due manner, without a new heart, a new mind, will and affections all sanctified by new principles given in to them, therefore he must have a new light and knowledge, for his natural darkness, ignorance, and error; a new wisdom, for his natural folly; a new power and goodness of will, for the natural depravity; a new stamp of order, power, and life in the affections, and holiness in all the heart, for the disorder and unruliness. The order in both nature and grace, is, to act from the purpose, intention, and choice of the will, and heat of affections: but first, the will acts from the understanding; that is the golden candlestick which holds the light, and is the spring that brings all motion about, that sets all the wheels of the soul on going: we first must see, and have our guide, before we choose, affect, or act.

The will is a blind faculty, therefore the understanding must guide at first; therefore it must first act by thinking, seeing, and showing what is to be done: in all rational actings, thinking must be first.

And to come nearer to our purpose, in all works

of wisdom, the understanding must act, not hastily, but with heed; not with precipitation, but pondering. All heed and pondering requires time for the mind's bending itself to a thing, searching into it, staying upon it, by musing and meditating. After due consideration comes the conclusive dictate of the understanding, that this or that is to be done ; and before it be done, the will first spontaneously chooses it, and then doing follows upon determining. Things done rationally and rightly, should have not bare, sudden, transient thoughts, but ponderings by time taken, Prov. iv. 26, a fit proportion of time: nothing of moment should be done on a bare present apprehension, unless it hath formerly passed under the test of deliberation ; so wise persons act still. True it is, we do many things in hastes and hurries ; but this is more like brute creatures than men. It is the order God hath set in nature, first of all to consider, then to act.

All wise doing is with a first weighing ; otherwise it is folly and vanity, without comeliness, without profit. As in nature God hath set this order, the mind must first move, and wisdom in the mind will first ponder and weigh ; not act on slight but precedent serious thinkings ; so in religion, in all the matters of it we are to perform, first there must be minding. None must ever in religion say, I mind not what I do. The understanding in spiritual wisdom must ponder and consider all things to be considered ; and the will then must choose, and the affections move by the graces in them orderly; and then the executive power must act, in subordination to the mind guiding, and the will choosing and intending.

As the understanding, will, and affections are as the several natural links of the soul ; so consideration

(the noble act of the understanding) is to produce
and ground the choices and intents of that queen re-
gent, the will, and the orderly motions of her hand-
maids, the several affections; and then must follow
prosecuting and doing that was purposed by the will,
and pondered by the understanding.

As consideration in things natural is fundamental
and necessary to due choosing and doing of all things;
so divine meditation is fundamental and necessary in
some degree to the spiritual actings of the will,
movings rightly of the affections, and a religious
regular performing what was piously purposed, and
piously first pondered and meditated upon.

All the graces that make up the golden chain,
the graces that are the supernatural soul ennoblements,
that are planted and reside in a renewed heart by
way of principle and habit, are planted and laid
into the several faculties of the soul as their relief
and help, to sanctify them and empower them; some
in the mind, and others in the will and affections.
These faculties have all their several golden links of
the chain of graces dispersed among them, and laid
into them; but as the faculties of the soul are all
guided, drawn, and moved by the first mover, the understanding, and the act of considering; so the graces
of the soul, all the golden links of the whole chain
of graces, must move by the first link of the chain,
the light, spiritual wisdom, and actings of it by this
divine meditation. This link must draw first: spiritual wisdom exercised in this holy way of meditation,
must be a constant foundation and rise to all the
duties of godliness.

This should be at the bottom, and a still quickener
to all prayings, readings, hearings, and the rest.
Nothing is well done, that is not first well thought

on : although the duties of godliness are reciprocally helpful, mutually lending a hand each to other ; as reading, hearing, praying, are to meditating, and meditating is to them in different respects ; yet meditation should and must help to make us our firm, even footing, and lively walking in Christ's ways. All things from first to last in our way of religion, and walking by that rule, have their due guidance and managings by this helm and hand of meditation.

God every where in Scripture, when he would have those come right and return that have gone wrong, and such to go on that have well begun, he calls them to consideration and minding their ways : Consider your own ways in your hearts, Hag. i. 5, and again, ver. 7. " Bring it to mind," Isa. xlvi. 8. Put your hearts upon your ways, in the former ; here they must bring their doings upon their hearts, by considering : " He considereth, and turneth," Ezek. xviii. 28. Consideration is the rise of returning. The prodigal's returning was upon his considering, Luke xv. 17 : common wisdom acting in consideration is the soul's helm ; and spiritual wisdom, acting in meditation, is the Christian's helm ; as the word is his compass, and the gales of the Holy Spirit fill his sails, and make him move. We cannot look for a ship to sail well, without the helm's steering well : meditation's helm must steer our course ; our course to the harbour of true happiness must have its rise in due consideration, as the Scripture every where shows.

O let me, Lord, keep up ever this right order and method in my walkings ; let meditation be the spring that carries all the wheels of my spirit right and even ; that still pondering all my paths, my ways may be established.

This then I propound, as a principal ground of the

R 3

necessity of meditation, that dependence of the will, affections, and actings spiritual, on the understanding sanctified, and furnished with light and wisdom for salvation; which wisdom and light is the guide to and stirrer up of the will, affections, and endeavours by the means of divine meditation. This I have the more insisted on, because the great failings of all sorts rise from neglect of this consideration and meditation, because this consideration is no more considered.

All Christians that would have the will purpose, the affections move, the executing power endeavour well, must use the grace of spiritual wisdom; that is the first wheel in the heavenly frame of spirit, and wisdom by the way of meditation, to set on going all the wheels of other graces dispersed through the heart; the graces planted as principles of spiritual life, strength, and motion, and given to animate all operation.

CHAP. XXVI.—*Of the second Ground of this so necessary Duty of Meditation.*

HEAVENLY things should have not only a mere seeing and knowing, but a minding and meditating, from their obliging and challenging excellences. "Have I not written to thee excellent things," saith Solomon, Prov. viii. 6; xxii. 20. The apostle Paul speaks of "the excellency of the knowledge of Christ," Phil. iii. 8. Their so far transcending excellences, their rare objective excellences, give me leave to call

them so ; that is, they are not only excellent things
in themselves, though never known or shown to us,
bu: they are made to be excellent objects for our ob-
ser ation and minding : all made to be minded ; but
sorie of them more peculiarly made and prepared,
ma le great, made high, deep, and large, filled brimful, yea, running over, with both native excellency,
and likewise suitableness for us, suitableness for our
spirits to act and make their chief abode of most
serious thoughts upon, for a spiritual and holy eye
to fix upon, and be pleased in. As in philosophy
they reason, if there be an object of the outward
sense (and that which especially is excellent) ; if
there be odours and rich scents ; if sounds, excellent
sounds ; or if there be rare colour, feature, motion ;
and that so excellent object light, especially such
glorious lights as the several stars, the moon, and the
most glorious sun ; there must be those senses of
smelling, hearing, seeing, which may perceive their
objects, and receive the pleasure and benefit of them,
otherwise they must be all in vain. If there were no
creatures with any senses to perceive these objects of
colour, light, and the rest, to what end were any of them?
  What use would colour or light be of, without any
eye to behold it ? The omniscient God, he cannot
need it : the angels and spirits being without bodies,
they do not need it : creatures blind, and creatures
made without sense ; elements, as earth, water, and
the other ; elementaries, such as stones, metals, trees,
and such like insensitive things ; they need it not ;
neither need any smells, sounds, or tastes, only the
sense is suited to the object, and the object to the
sense : the object is made or manifested and shown
for the sense. So if there be spiritual objects, and
no spiritual eye fitted for them, and if spiritual

objects be held forth and shown, and there were never any eyeing of them, they then in that respect (as to their holding forth) would be in vain ; and the spiritual eye would be in vain, as if the eye had no object to behold, it would be in vain, and as no eye at all.

Therefore doth God in Scripture call so often for a beholding of the things of heaven, because of their excellences purposely shown for that end. " Behold the Lamb of God," John i. 29. " Behold what manner of love the Father hath bestowed upon us, that we should be called the sons of God," 1 John iii. 1.

Therefore when there are such abundance of spiritual and heavenly things, set out in such rare colours and proportions, shining in such high splendour and glory ; when so many most bright and beauteous, when so great and extensive rarities and excellences, beam forth and shine so gloriously in heavenly and spiritual things ; there then needs must be an eye, a spiritual eye, for these so excellent objects, to behold them and be exercised about them.

Yea, when there is such a height, depth, latitude, and length, and vastness every way, of dimensions of excellency shining in them ; and this purposely that they may be viewed and admired, and also improved ; therefore there must be an answerable eyeing and considering. 1. A real sincere acting of minding and meditating, to answer their most real worth. 2. A deep searching of thoughts, to answer their height and depth of excellency. 3. An abode, and dwelling, and enlarging of thoughts, to answer the latitude and extensiveness of excellency in them, that all their glory and excellency, so near as can be, may be known and tasted.

The excellences therefore of spiritual things are for eyeing and pondering, the greatness of their ex-

cellences for great eyeing and. earnest meditating.
Therefore we find that great artist in meditation, the
holy psalmist, so busying his thoughts and meditating in several things ; as about God and his glory,
greatness, holiness, righteousness, truth, mercy, severity, and power, Psa. civ. About the word of God,
in those shining rays of its infallible truth, purity,
perfection, mighty efficacy, and glorious excellences,
Psa. xii. 6 ; xix. 7, 8 ; cxix. And so about the
works and ways of God. The blessed apostle Paul
was so acted in his thoughts about the word of God
and the gospel, Christ and free grace, the fulness of
Christ, Eph. ii. 5, 7 ; 2 Tim. iii. 16, the workings of
his Spirit, and the whole mystery of godliness, 1 Tim.
iii. 16. Thus other saints in Scripture, prophets,
apostles, and divers else. The wise-hearted will have
their eyes thus exercised ; they think bare knowing,
without due meditating, is an undervaluing of spiritual
things.

CHAP. XXVII.—*Of the third Ground of this
Meditation, as to several Ends and Uses.*

THE third great ground of this necessary duty is from
the ends, and the great concernments of them, as to
all sorts of persons.

1. For a sinner's first conversion to God.

Meditation is a duty incumbent on and highly
necessary for persons yet strangers to God, to bring
them home. " Because he considereth, and turneth,"
Ezek. xviii. 28. If they bethink themselves and turn,

1 Kings viii. 47 ; returning of the sinners is upon considering and self-bethinking ; thus the prodigal, in Luke xv. No man is ever truly converted to God, without some consideration of his misery, with his absolute need of Christ and his grace, and flying to him.

Although the efficacious drawing of a sinner be God's work, he awakens, convinces, humbles, and changes the heart; yet not without the sinner's considering, minding, mourning, seeking, and striving. God converts men as reasonable creatures, and conversion is founded on the deepest set reasons, and the strongest working and prevailing arguments in the world. God awakens, and the sinner looks about and considers, he reasons with himself, as the prodigal, and outreasons himself, but by God's mighty working, keeping down the heart's corruption ; and by its quickening the soul with a new, living principle ; and so he resolves and returns to God. If more would muse and consider duly, more, God enabling, would return. When the one is to be done, the other shall be done, men shall come to consider and ponder.

2. For all renewed repenting.

There is great necessity of consideration for our renewing, our returning continually ; for holding up an evenness and constancy of renewed repentance. " I thought on my ways, and turned my feet unto thy testimonies," Psa. cxix. 59. Fresh godly sorrow, self-loathings, serious returnings, must have new fresh considerings of the sinfulness of sin, and laying loads of aggravations on particular new warpings and miscarriages. Especially greater repentings require a deeper and larger foundation in consideration, as David did in Psa. li. that evidences great and deep thoughts of heart.

3. For a vigorous acting of grace.

For vigorous acting any grace, faith, love, hope, fear, humility, patience, and others, as is frequently seen in the saints in Scriptures, what reasons and persuasions they drew out of the depths of considerations, as Job, David, and others!

All the heart graces are stirred and acted in some measure by consideration, either of the command enjoining, the promise encouraging, threatening, awing, examples exciting, arguments in some sort or other inducing and helping.

It is something that works and weighs, is first pondered before the soul acts, or is rightly moved.   A Christian acts not as water or fire, which move by their own inclination ; but as men act in things as men, which is by choice and free election, but upon preceding instigation of reason and consideration.

Grace, though it be a spring of living water, it is not that which runs over of itself: that is for heaven, where the heart will be full and run alone.   It is not like the spring-head of Jordan, that ran of itself, but like Jacob's well, that had always water, but must always be drawn : it must be drawn out by consideration.

Christians mistake and complain often of their hearts, and would have them like a running spring, to run, to act alone : when here in the best, though there be water, as in Jacob's well, yet the well is deep, there must be drawing for every drop, or none will come.   Therefore to make it come, the bucket of consideration must be letting down, and pulling up, and so pouring forth.   What the apostle said to Timothy, " Stir up the gift of God which is in thee," 2 Tim. i. 6, must be said to all, and done by all, that would do any thing.

Some horses, we say, go on mere mettle, without
provocation of whip or spur; others will go well with
some stirring up: so our hearts, if good, will go on
in godliness, but not on mere mettle, but with pro-
vokings of considerations.

There should be endeavoured the best and strongest mindings and reasonings, if we would act graces
vigorously and strongly. There is a necessity that
strong purposes and resolutions, for believing, trusting,
loving, hoping, all acting, all enduring strongly, be
founded on strong mindings and considerings: the
fuller the consideration, the better the actings of
graces; the stronger the spring, the better all the
wheels move.

Chap. XXVIII.—*Of other Ends of this Meditation.*

4. For all duties and holy performances, there is
great necessity of meditation, in some due measure,
for a due, wise, warm, lively, and spiritual acting them,
acting from the right principle of grace within, by the
right rule, eyeing the word, and to the right mark and
end, salvation: real and vigorous performing in this
sort must have some good allowance of pondering
what we are to perform.

This is very conspicuous in holy David, so great a
performer of holy duties, praying, confessing, and
praising; his prayings, and all things in that way, he
calls his meditation. Certainly, those so excellent
psalms of prayings and praisings, were no flashes of a

merely raised fancy, or some hasty runnings over of a hot brain; not an uttering what came next, but the passages so rare, spiritual, and heavenly, and so strongly rational; as they had a touch from heaven in the Spirit's guidance and assistance, so they had a tincture from a wise, holy heart within, laying them asleep in consideration, and acting them with it in highest heeds and mindings, concurring with their utterings. Things so well spoken must be well weighed, especially when they also were to be Scripture records; for holy prophets and Scripture penmen were to use their own natural gifts and their graces in their writings, though the Spirit of God infallibly guided, sometimes raised and elevated them above themselves. Duties of religion ebb and flow, are more lively, spiritual, and heavenly, or more dead, carnal, and such as run lower, according to their fomentings and feedings from the warm spring of meditation; thus in our praying and other duties we may daily experience.

Christians complain they are dead-hearted and cold, slight and hasty in performances; confessions are not accompanied with heart-meltings, shame, and self-loathings; petitions not with fervency, strong cryings, and earnest wrestlings; thanksgivings not with that flame of love, and joy, and high admirings of the so great goodness, and rich, free grace of God in his ways and dispensations toward us; commonly the cause is, the spring of meditation is stopped, the soul runs not in such a current of considerations and quickening reasons as it ought and used to do.

When any part or member of the body fails in heat, sense, or motion, where there is an action or acting hurt or hindered from its natural and usual

s

way, there the principle and feeder of that action
hurt and failing, is hurt and failing itself. As when
failing of sense or motion in a hand or leg, it is benumbed or cannot stir; this is from the cold, clammy
humours lying at and obstructing the heads of those
nerves that did convey motive or sensitive spirits to
that part is benumbed or motionless. Now meditation is a head or rise of motions spiritual, reasons
and arguments are as the nerves that convey and stir
up heat, spirit, and motion into holy performances.
This is one very great cause holy duties are no more
lively and warm; the cure must be in removing the
obstructions, opening the spring-head of meditation,
making that run fresh and full in such considerations
as may warm and quicken. The wisdom of Christians therefore is to take, as we said, that great artist's
way, the holy psalmist, that acted godliness so eminently; and among others upon this eminent acting
still of meditation, he tells how he prayed day and
night, and how he still praised and highly rendered
his thanksgivings and blessings; and he tells you how,
he meditated day and night.

And he tells you his meditation assisted and con-
tributed, as Psa. v. He tells you his prayer was his
meditation, because assisted, quickened, and prepared
by meditation. If Christians would use to meditate
more carefully and constantly, it would help to keep
up better the vigour of prayer; so would it likewise
keep life and warmth in all other holy duties.

No Christians are warmer at the heart, and livelier
in holy services, than those who meditate most; but
never expect the one without the other. Keep this
fountain open and still running; this is the water to
drive the mill, the wind that moves the sails, the
spring in the watch that carries all the wheels, and

keeps them going; I speak as to what is to be done on our part, otherwise God does all in all.

5. Meditation is necessary to be an exclusive and keeper out of evil and vain thoughts, and to dislodge them : naturally all the imaginations of the heart are evil, and only evil continually, Gen. vi. 5.

Vain thoughts lodge and repose, as in a bed, in a carnal heart: " How long shall thy vain thoughts lodge within thee?" Jer. iv. 14. Walking in the vanity of your minds, Eph. iv. 17. The way and walk is in the vanity of the mind. To dislodge these lodgers, and shut them out, is by accustoming and exercising the mind to good thoughts, to be the excluders of bad thoughts. The learned Sir Francis Bacon observes, as the cures of bodily diseases are by applying things contrary to them, so the defects of the mind are helped by contrary studies. Poetry makes men witty, history wise, the mathematics subtle, natural philosophy deep, moral philosophy grave, logic and rhetoric able to contend; these arts help the defects of nature, by working contrary habits proper for the cure of those defects. So in spiritual distempers and defects, there are suitable cures and remedies, by applyings and actings of the contraries: so Rom. viii. 13, If ye mortify the deeds of the body by the Spirit. All sins, particular sins, are mortified by those graces which are contrary to those sins ; so distrust is mortified by holy trusting, passion and wrath by godly meekness, pride by humility, worldly affections by heavenly affections still acted, and so evil thoughts by good, roving, wandering, and wild imaginations by godly consideration and meditation : which accustoming ourselves unto, will work off customary, vain, and wandering thoughts ; a holy principle of meditation, the sinful principle of evil thinkings.

s 2

It is not so much the striving and tugging against corruptions to keep them down, though we must both watch and war against them, but the acting of the contrary grace, that best relieves us : to strive after a bare suppressing of sin and of evil thoughts in particular comes to little.

This is a kind of being only upon the defensive ; for an observing and marking the risings and stirrings of corruption and sins, it may be with a good measure of grief and reluctancy, but this is rather a telling and reckoning the evil thoughts and stirrings, and lying exposed still to fresh assaults, leaving corruptions opportunity to return so often as they will, than to abate and suppress them. It can do little unless we go this way to work. The best and nearest way to dislodge and exclude evil thoughts, is by lodging and acting good thoughts, in this way, this ordinance of meditation, which will keep us. God keeps us, when we keep his and our way ; the way when they come, as we should against evil thoughts act detestation, but withal act diversion ; act not detestation alone, but diversion : let thy heart both turn inwardly against them, and turn also from them, by turning upon something which is both spiritual and seasonable. So soon as the poison of evil thoughts would infect, take the antidote, the best preservative of diversion to and acting of good and holy thoughts ; the art of diversion is better than mere acting still of striving and opposition.

Also, meditation is to be exercised, not only as an exclusive of bad thoughts, but for an introduction of good thoughts, good thoughts in a way, for an arriving at habitual heavenly-mindedness ; for an introduction of heavenly-mindedness, where there was formerly a walking in the vanity of the mind :

All " the thoughts of the heart are evil continually,"
Gen. vi. 5 ; customarily, habitually evil: for, I
say, an introduction to heavenly-mindedness ; and
likewise for an improver of heavenly-mindedness
daily.

In handling the explication of the description of
meditation, when the ends of it were mentioned,
among other ends, this was one ; Meditation must be
performed to be a moulder and framer of habitual
heavenly wisdom, making the spirit of a Christian
habitually wise ; so I add now, meditation is to be
performed, to introduce, and after that, improve an
habitual heavenly-mindedness.

It is not only incumbent on thee to shut out evil
thoughts, and endeavour good thoughts, to take up
the old lodgings of the evil, and so thrust and keep
them out, but thou must by meditation, by constant
using it, seek for habitual heavenly-mindedness.

In all truly gracious hearts, a principle that inclines, that introduces a bent and tendency of soul
heavenward ; but this at the first is a tender bud,
it is but weak and inclines weakly, acts feebly in comparison of after-time, when it is grown and strengthened by exercise ; when we exercise and use to
meditate, this dips and dyes the spirit into the tincture and grain colour of habitual heavenly-mindedness.

Though the first fundamental inclination, and bent
of spirit heavenward, must be sought till it be found,
the carnal earthly-mindedness changed into heavenly ;
yet this, if we were never so assured of it, must not
satisfy ; here no Christian must set up : but to the
now first principle and the fundamental habit obtained, this superadded acquired habit should be this
second grand endeavour and intention, first to have

the spiritual habit, the new fundamental heart tendency, then to have this inclination heightened,
ripened, and corroborated, by habit attained upon frequencies and constancies of practice, and using this
heavenly meditating.   Of David, the excellent example of actings in this highway to heaven, God says,
when he was very young, when Samuel came to anoint
him, he was one whose heart he looked on as being
principled with piety and real holiness; he had a heart
inclined, set for God and things heavenly; but he
acted holiness, exercised himself in it, and in this particular way of meditation, till it ripened and arrived
at habitual meditation, from holding up a constancy
in it.   This may be gathered from the character he
gives of a godly man, and from his own still practice;
In his law doth he meditate day and night, Psa. i. 2.
When a man begins to be godly, hath the principle,
this will incline him to begin this godliness, this meditation.   But then godly wisdom teaches to practise
it, for to use meditating, to get a hand at this rare
work, to come to an habitual heavenly-mindedness.
So David, that was so wise, so excellently wise, as
Psa. cxix. 98, 99, he had acted the fundamental
principle.   He inclined his heart to keep all the commandments alway, Psa. cxix. 112; and he exercised
meditation to habitual heavenly-mindedness; for he
tells us, Psa. cxix. 97; lxiii. 6, he meditated all the
day, meditated in the night-watches; when he still
awoke he was ever with God.   He gets the habitual
heavenly-mindedness, and then it was easy; and by
being found easy, it was withal his delight.   Meditation at first, the burden and yoke of heavenly meditation, lying on the weak shoulders of the new convert, with only his new principle of grace begun, is a
hard and heavy work; though the spirit be willing,

yet to perform it is weak. But when this work is carried on, and daily practised, then by custom and habit (an acquired habit) it is easy; then it is the great soul solace and delight. David's habitual heavenly-mindedness was the rare product and issue of his meditation; he found it so, and therefore followed the faster. Therefore this ought to be a grand intendment: a heavenly-mindedness, when it is habitual, when it is corroborated, and of a young, tender plant is grown to be a tree of strength, and yet is growing more, is a rare excellency, and gloriously sweet attainment: a heavenly-minded man, how excellent is such a one generally in all men's eyes!

This makes a Christian still with God, have his way above, his conversation in heaven, Psa. cxxxix. 18; Phil. iii. 20; to feed on manna, to be filled with peace and joy, overflow and abound in singular fruitfulness towards others.

Out of the abundance of heart heavenliness the mouth speaks, and the whole conversation shines in an exemplary walking. Therefore the heart must be meditating upon heavenly things, that it still may be framing and fixing higher in habitual thinkings. Meditate thyself into heavenly-mindedness, that so blessed and glorious frame. To conclude this third reason: therefore the Scripture holds forth meditation in several sorts. 1. Daily doing it in course. 2. Then occasional meditating as a superaddition. 3. And that of ejaculation, or short and more sudden darting up the thoughts to heaven, to come in as an auxiliary and supply, when the other meditation, more solemn and set, cannot be used; ejaculations may oft interpose in our course. This is a wedge may be driven in, enter the throng and crowd of occasions: when matters lie before us as tough and knotty pieces

of wood, when they will not give way to meditation
at large, but hinder it, this wedge may and will ever
enter, if we apply it, to keep up the constancy of heavenly-mindedness.

Ah, how should my spirit bless abundantly that
God, who hath so fully provided for a lying open of
the way to heaven, that my soul may mount up thither
so frequently, and be either detained above by larger
contemplation, or at least to touch at heaven by ejaculation !

Chap. XXIX.— Of the fourth Ground that sup-
ports this Duty of Meditation.

The fourth and last ground to support this weighty
work of holy meditation, is the consideration of the
great advantages, or disadvantages, arising from the
careful performance or careless neglect of it.   Every
ordinance of Christ hath holy advantages attending it;
those who use them aright, daily experience how
good it is to walk in the King of heaven's highways.

1. The first I shall name, is that so glorious advantage of improving our communion and acquaintance with God, Job xxii. 21 ; 1 John i. 3.   We can
expect no communion, much less can we improve it,
out of the use of holy ordinances, whereby we draw
near to God, and God to us.   Although God himself
be not so tied to these ways, but he may come to us
when and how he pleaseth ; yet we are tied to God's
ordinances, as our ways of acquaintance with him;
and when in a holy manner we draw near to God, he

hath promised to command the blessing to us, Psa. cxxxiii. 3 ; xxiv. 5.   Meditation being then his ordinance, it is a way of communion, a singular way of acting our spirits towards him, of acting our minds and thoughts in a way of reference to him, either more directly or less : sometimes meditation is acted on his infinite excellences, in seeing his infinite beauty and loveliness, admiring and glorifying him ; and by this contemplation we come to an improvement of our knowledge, to understand more of him, an enlargement of affections, encouragement of our wills, choosings of him, and aimings at his glorifying and exalting ; exciting and stirring up the graces of faith, for stronger recumbencies on his all-sufficiency, love to cleave more, humility to stoop and submit more, patience to endure more willingly, and other graces to act higher in their spheres and ranks ; by all in the ways of exercising them, to own him and have him more to be our God.   Meditation helps to move and carry the soul, and all that is of it and in it, towards God; and when we act upon him, open the doors of our hearts to him, Rev. iii. 20.   God comes in and manifests himself in his grace, quickenings, supportings, comforts ; he sups with us, as Rev. iii. 20, and we sup with him; he is pleased and delighted with our graces exercised towards him, and we sup with him in his manifestations of himself to us, in his helpings of us, gladding and cheering our spirits, enrapturing our hearts with the tastes of his love.

CHAP. XXX.—*Of Solace and Spiritual Pleasure,*
another End of Meditation.

2. As it is a way of singular communion with God,
so it is for a heavenly walk, of great soul solace and
delight; a path of pleasantness, to walk, turn, and
recreate thy spirit in; as Solomon, Prov. iii. 17,
" Her ways are ways of pleasantness," all her ways;
all the particular paths in those ways, and therefore
this way; and it is made purposely by Christ, for his
people to walk and turn in : one of the stately, large,
high walks in the King of glory's garden, for thy walk
and sweet refreshings.   Travelling abroad to see sundry countries, towns, cities, and the great varieties of
objects there, is counted a rare sight, a great pleasure
and contentment.

Travelling with the eye of reason, amongst the
great mysteries and rare secrets of nature ; and by
searching, curious, exquisite searching, to make new,
strange discoveries of nature's implanted excellences ;
the makings and framings so admirable, the properties
and efficacies so strange and amazing, in so many sorts
of things.   This travelling in these close walks, these
hidden ways ending in new, rare, and useful experiences, is a very singular pleasure to many, but peculiarly to elevated and refined parts and wits.   But
travelling with a spiritual eye, among spiritual, holy,
and heavenly objects, and to see this whole prospect,
take a view of all the varieties of heavenly beauties
and glories, meeting us in our walk ; this is an enrapturing solace indeed, beyond all others, as far as
diamonds transcend the dirt, or the glorious lights of
heaven do clods of earth or dunghills.

In Psa. cxix. 14—16, the psalmist tells what in meditation walks he met with, more solace than " in all riches," of which he had so great abundance, a kingdom of his own, and the rich spoils of other kingdoms also.

Carnal and sensual persons study sometimes, and act great curiosity, to heighten and enlarge pleasures, and to find out new, rare pleasures not tasted before. Often they are at a loss, and discomposed, for a not having some new pleasures, as being cloyed with the old.   But here is a way for a heavenly spirit, of unwearied walking, of ever tasting larger pleasures ; of ever finding fresh and higher, more pure, more permanent pleasures, such pleasures as enlarge the heart, and then enlarge themselves in it ; such pleasures as come fuller, fresher, sweeter in, and then there fix and dwell.

In John xv. 11, our Saviour tells us of a full joy, and of a remaining joy : who can tell you such happy tidings, where else any such joy is to be both felt and fixed ?   But in such ways where Jesus Christ, the water of life, springs forth and flows, the saints meet with it, drink of it abundantly ; meditate to drink, meditate and drink : they meditate, and in their walking meet with rare, rich things, surpassing sweet. David saith his meditation of God was sweet, Psa. civ. 34 ; certainly it was so, and he means unspeakably sweet : meditation on the word and works of God were abundantly sweet, oh how sweet must meditation of God himself be !

Meditation brings in and gives down sweeter and more surpassing pleasures, than all earthly, carnal things can ; as much beyond them, as manna from heaven is beyond basest bread, meanest fare ; as the wine of Christ's miraculous making, beyond the water it was made of.

Three things especially make pleasures excellent. 1. When the pleasurable things are rich and excellent, as nature yields them, as rare fruits, rich spices, and the like. 2. When they are rare and excellent, as art reduces them, as art meliorates and perfects them. 3. When they have a right and curious, an exquisite receiver and perceiver : as when purest fountain waters are fetched fresh, in a pure, clean vessel, and have a curious taster ; or as the richest grape, by the best art, is made into wine, put into the best cask, and hath best ordering, and then comes to an exquisite palate ; or some excellent flesh or fish is by the best art prepared, and by the exquisitely right and curious taster discerned.

1. Meditation hath those kinds of objects, which in their own nature are most transcendent, purest springs and rivers of water of life, the things most soul-satiating, and unspeakably delighting ; the most glorious God, the unsearchable riches of Christ, the Holy Spirit the great Helper and Comforter, the pure and perfect word, the precious promises, heavenly ordinances, glorious grace, and eternal happiness. These are in themselves most excellent, and therefore the highest ground for our meditation's walk, for solace, and pleasure, and the highest.

2. They have the most excellent means of preparing and fitting them for a right taste ; the art and skill of the blessed Spirit, 2 Pet. i. 21 ; Prov. viii. 9, by his fitting them, and ordering them to the best suitableness for us, both for our minds and hearts, understandings to know them, wills and affections to close with them : they are made plain and perspicu-

ous, persuasive and operative; they have a suitableness conferred by an infinite wisdom of a God that knows how best to deliver them, as he hath done it in the Scriptures.

3. They have the best ways of receiving and perceiving, namely, the highest kind of wisdom, a rectified and elevated understanding, with a stamp and rare principle of spiritual judgment, 1 Cor. ii. 7, and heavenly-mindedness, discerning and savouring of spiritual things, in allowing and approving of them. " He that is spiritual" discerneth, 1 Cor. ii. 15. " Approve things that are excellent," Phil. i. 10.

So the will and affections they receive, and have the excellent principle of relishing and savouring spiritual things, in choosing and complacency, in love and joy: " O how love I thy law ! " Psa. cxix. 97. " Thy testimonies are the joy and rejoicing of my heart," Psa. cxix. 111. This is from the principle of grace, that gives in an ability of relishing the sweet and savoury things of heaven.

But when all these concur, as it is in a holy heart, and in reference to it, the pleasure is most surpassing, far beyond others, where the nature of the pleasures is lower, the preparation lower, and the receiver and faculty of tasting, of either outward or inward sense, or of a mere natural and carnal heart, in its best wisdom and moral excellences, is far lower. Meditation is the rare way to soul solaces and sweetest pleasures, as bringing in the most excellent delicacies, and stirring up the holy heart to act its principles in the mind, will, and affections, of tasting and relishing them, and so to have let in the sweet pleasures and refreshments of them.

The rarest hours, and richest soul banquets, have been prepared and come to usually by this way of meditation : when the spirit goes up to heaven by holy contemplation, heaven comes down to us by rich consolation. Heavenly comforts meet us half way, fill us brimful, and sometimes to such runnings over, as we know not how to bear up under the glorious fulness of them : never doth any sensualist or any sinner, in his way, taste of such pleasures.

It is not possible that sensual and brutish pleasures should be such as intellectual ; nor intellectual in merely sinful spirits, such as spiritual and heavenly meditation, being a spiritual operation acts higher, returns the purest, highest, and most enrapturing pleasures. Let the saints' experience give in evidence; and if sinners try upon heart changing and elevating grace, they then will find, that no sensual, nor any pleasures of most raised fancies, or highest notions, can hold proportion with spiritual pleasures let into the heart, and tasted from this divine meditation.

There are many other high advantages I may add ; as particularly,

(1.) As for brightening and clearing of knowledge ; this was mentioned on a former occasion.

(2.) Meditation serves for improving the judgment ; the most judicious Christians are such as meditate most. Persons of a short spirit, whose thoughts are not full length, not well sized, where thoughts touch as a perfect round thing on a perfect plain ; as lightning passes through the air, and stays no time : not like the sun, that not only shines, but stays, that staying of his light makes the best discoveries of things ; so when things are stayed, and have fuller length of time, this is the way to be a judicious Christian, to attain a spirit of judgment : the shorter you think, the shorter will you be of a judiciousness in the things of heaven.

(3.) Meditation keeps up and improves an awakened and tender conscience, as bringing in more plenty of light, and acting it more upon the spirit, acting stronger reflections, deeper searchings, fuller discoveries in respect of the frame of the spirit within, and the conversation without : they that study themselves most, will be most awakened to greater sensibleness, care, and fear, and set the strongest watches upon their deceitful hearts.

(4.) Meditation makes a Christian keep up his activity and liveliness: the best actings are founded on the heart, put best in frame by raised, elevated, and most spiritualized thoughts. It is greatly conducing to greatest growth : souls, if we would have them fat and flourishing, Psa. xcii., have the garden of graces and the beds of spices flourish and flow forth, must have, as the other helps of heavenly ordinances, so the hand of a constant meditation to water them : he that best orders the first wheel, the first mover, will have all the following move more regularly and exactly.

The spiritual disadvantages must needs be great where holy meditation is neglected and never used, or but seldom or slightly used : the advantages may be the rule of judging the disadvantages; but I shall in particular mention some of the spiritual disadvantages, and then come to the improvement of all that hath been said.

1. The first disadvantage, and that is a prejudice to purpose a total neglect of meditation, or a usual doing it slightly and formally, not seriously and diligently, is a great and principal ground of men's abiding in a state of vanity, a living wholly to no purpose, but utterly beside the grand end that man was made for, that supreme end, the infinitely wise God, the

T 2

Maker of man, and thereby the total and absolute
Proprietor in and Owner of his all, and that end of
living to God, and glorifying him; vanity, I say, in a
wholly missing his end and chief mark. For who
can take aim at any mark, that eyes it not, or looks
not earnestly and evenly at it; that either looks quite
another way, or looks with a regardless eye at the
best? The blessed apostle tells us he looked with
another eye, Phil. iii. 13, with an eye that looked not
off, or looked easily ; but the best mark had the best
aim, he looked for life.

The Scripture calls a sinner a " vain man," James
ii. 20, for his living beside his main end, ever in
every thing missing that chief end ; which rises from
being wanting in aiming right, and that want of
aiming is for want of minding. Never can aiming,
which is an act of the will, (intending is an act of
the will, aiming is the intending of a mark,) never
can aiming be right, unless considering or meditating
be right, be due and earnest, with evenness and constancy : that heart which comes not to be reduced to
minding its chief end, will miss it utterly at last.

The reason why there is so much vanity in the
best, is partly, yea, greatly upon this little minding,
this slight, uneven, and seldom looking well at the
main mark of God and happiness.

2. Disadvantage, sinful security, a sleepy soul
state, and heart hardening, a sinking and decaying in
godliness, is grounded much upon disuse of meditating ; especially meditation of review and self-re-
flections.

" No man repented, every one turned to his course,"
Jer. viii. 6. Not considering is the foundation of
both sinners' and saints' security, and growings worse.

If fallen asleep, if falling and in a declining state,

awakening and recovery must be by self-bethinking, 1 Kings vii. 47.   No wise man but hath need of frequent reviews, and weighings again over and over, of the best of his doings, much more of the errors of them.

3. Givings way to evil and vain thoughts will follow your neglect of good thoughts.

The mind will be ever busy, if not in good, then in evil: giving way to vain thoughts is very dangerous ; men by giving way to vain thoughts provoke God to leave them, to give them up to a walking in the vanity of their minds, Eph. iv. 17 ; and at last, as to a customary vanity of mind, God may give them up to judicial disrelishing and abhorring holy things, and the thinkings of them, and so perish in them.

Oh let therefore the good hand of my God so stay up and act my weak and warping spirit, with the strongest and most efficacious reasons and inducements, in this so greatly important and necessary, so sweet and blessed an ordinance, this heavenly meditation, that I may ever prove a better artist in it, a better Christian by it !

PART III.

THE IMPROVEMENT.

CHAP. I.—*Of the Improvement of the Doctrine of Meditation, by way first of Instruction.*

THIS being so concerning a work, and having so strong an influence upon the whole course of Christianity, let us now endeavour to beat out this gold, extend it, and make it applicable to the state and condition of all sorts of persons, in all the useful ways we can.

Then if meditation on spiritual things, and earthly in a spiritual manner, in such seriousness, searchings, and dwellings of the thoughts upon them, for such high and holy ends, is so needful for all Christians to exercise, we observe, that it serves to hold forth a light of instruction to all that own the Lord Christ, the golden sceptre of his word, and the obligation laid so indispensably on them, to see how they are called upon to own and observe it, and to walk continually in this sweet and pleasant path, this so righteous and good way.

Divers there are who call themselves Christians, and would be counted good, if not so good as any, which yet lead a life of inadvertency, and quite overlooking of it, mind not this meditation; as if it concerned them not, as if they were not at all obliged, but free from any such engagement of their thoughts, any employing of their serious thoughts this way. Oh how many are there to be found, that never considered what that noble eye of the understanding was given for! They use it as if it were to look only downward, or any other way but upward and heavenward; they lose, contentedly lose, the principal end of that so rare faculty, made most peculiarly to mind and contemplate heavenly beauties and excellences.

What was said by Duke Alva, that he did not use to look up to heaven, may be said of too many, yea, they may say it of themselves, they do not use to look up to heaven, by meditating on the things above. Ah, sad eye, and sad frame of spirit, but saddest state, not to have God nor the things of God in the thoughts; to have an eye made purposely for them above all, but uses to look from them, not towards them, that fixes on the earth, that hath their eyes' all, and heaven the allowance of a nothing.

Others mistakingly think meditation may concern some sorts of persons, but not them; they have no leisure, they have no learning, as others have. We read of a king, when a treatise of happiness was presented unto him, would not look on it, but said he was not at leisure. Oh how many are there too like him in this, they are not at leisure! They can find time for looking every way, on every thing fond fancy carries them to, but it is for others who have time and a mind to it, thus to employ it in meditation.

Others there are who think religious seriousness and musing on things heavenly the greatest folly, the worst bestowing of thoughts and time; they loathe all trouble of consideration this way, license their thinkings to a roving, ranging liberty, let their thoughts fly, as children do their arrows, any way

and every way, but to no certain mark at all. With
such any way is vanity but " walking in the vanity
of their mind," Eph. iv. 17 ; with them no thoughts
are savoury but such as are remotest from heaven.
A seriousness, and fixing their thoughts, is a fetter-
ing to their freeness of fancy; all stay of thoughts is
a mere tediousness ; and the more spiritual the things
are they are persuaded to mind, the more unkind entertainment they meet with.

Oh that ever that eye, which the great Soul-maker
bestows, purposely and principally, to act its seriousness and best mindings on best things, should be so
strangely perverted to an only minding the worst!
Oh what a wonder is it, that the great Giver of this
great talent of the thinking power doth not totally
take it away, doth not let it quite quench in a seizing
stupidity, and loss of reason's use, as it happens to
some by sad diseases; or that the wildness and
wickedness of fancy be not revenged with wildness
of phrensy, and striking all such wilfully mindless sinners mad, as sometimes some are, and it may be
partly on this account!

Oh let every one take heed of provoking their God
in such a sort, and set themselves to ponder what it
is, not only to forget God carelessly, but to refuse to
remember him purposely and designedly ; purposely
to refuse minding those things of heaven, which, like
the lights of heaven, have purposely the greatest
lustre and glory, that they may have the greatest
eyeings and lookings upon.

Every one therefore should learn this great truth,
feel the great necessity and importance of this duty,
see it most clearly Christ's blessed way for the frequent and constant walk of his thoughts, to improve
communion with God, and perfect holiness by.

Lord, clear up my eye to see daily more into the excellences of this heavenly way, and have my spirit lifted up and enlarged in it. Oh let me not faint and grow weary, but have the loins of my spirit girded with strength, my goings held up in this path of pleasantness, unto the end.

CHAP. II.—*A second Improvement of this Truth by way of Conviction, and for deep Humbling.*

LET this serve for conviction and deep humbling of every one for no better discharging this obedience to the Lord of our spirits, and that thinking power of them. The natural faculty for thinking was given by God, chiefly for spiritual objects, and for acting itself in a spiritual way; as the bodily eye is given much more for beholding the light of the sun, than the light of candles.

That so precious talent of the thinking power was not lent us by our Lord to embezzle and ravel out, but to employ and improve for his best advantage; not to be as water spilt upon the ground; not to be as a spring of pure excellent water, which empties itself into some near noisome ditch, or is swallowed up in some bog or quagmire. Oh no, it was given us for excellent ends, to act and be in exercise, to put forth its strength and vigour upon things most excellent and high in themselves, and most sweet and suitable to it.

Therefore let every person look back, and be

greatly humbled for those times of childhood and
youth, and that excessive vanity of thoughts, and
evils, continually evil imaginations, as Scriptures
charge all with, Gen. vi. 5.   Oh let us learn much to
be humbled, for being so long under the total neglect
and daily exclusion of all thought seriousness, not at
all complying with, but disrelishing, but refusing all reducing of the thoughts to any due mindings and ponderings of heavenly things.

In that forecited sixth chapter of Genesis, the Lord
when he was threatening the drowning of all the
earth, he saw the wickedness of man was great, and
then, among others, when he is making a review and
looks back to former times, the times of men's youth,
he casts into all the sum of sins; the youth's sins of
thoughts, the then evils of its imaginations, with the
aggravations; reckons not the ways only, and wildness
of youth discovering itself to others, but the evil
thoughts of youth, and punishes for them with other
sins; I say he drowned the world for youth sins, yea,
youngest time's thoughts.   Though youth be least
considerable, and youth's thoughts least of all considered, yet the holy God puts these mites into the
black bill, makes the weights of thought sins to help
cast the balance, hangs these about the sinners' necks
to help drown them in the flood.

Oh let us then look back to them, be duly humbled
for them; humbled for that all of the evil of imaginations, humbled that there was then no consideration,
nothing of this so incumbent duty, this then, even
in youth, so needful duty.   Oh what a sad time was
that which did not, would not meditate, that could
not, would not spare time; time from pleasures, play,
vanities, and follies; time from very toys, trifles, poor,
petty, despicable things, yet so eagerly minding them,

and being so taken with them, enslaved, led, and be-fooled by them.

Ah, when the holy God at the great day before all the world shall bring forth the eager mindings of youth, the toys, vanities, fancies, and follies of youth, set them all in order, and then show what the things of heaven and happiness discovered and tendered are, all the so rare and most inestimable things proffered in the gospel together;—I say, when all the trifles and vanities of youth, and the bendings of the mind unto them, wholly to them, and all spiritual things in the Scriptures, in their natures, and heights of ex-cellency, and the not minding, but refusing to mind them, shall be laid together; oh what will be the un-speakable shame and confusion, silence and stoppings of the mouths of mindless sinners! Oh what to such as are snatched away in their youth, in the heights of their minding vanities, and so foolish re-fusals of meditating on spiritual things, as not being at leisure yet, as not thinking it proper and seasonable to be serious so soon!

Ah, then, if the case of youth, mindless youth, will be so sad at the great day, when things shall appear as they are, when an infinitely wise and right-eous God will make every sin appear in its exceeding great sinfulness; how now should it humble all for their youthful regardlessness, refusals to allow time for heavenly thoughts, to let precious youth be so embezzled! If we mind not sins of youth, God may soon make us to possess them, Job xiii. 26. If we are truly humbled for them, this may, as it were, spare God a labour, save us that heart smart in troubles and terrors, which, like gravel in the tender eye, or smaller motes there, may occasion great pain.

Those little things of youth, and which by many

are resolved into nothing, or have a pardon of course; ah, these sometimes God blows into the eye of conscience like clouds of dust, that we may feel how great a weight of trouble, how hot a hell the least sin can bring upon us. The least arrow in the quiver of God's wrath, dipped in the least measure of its venom, bred by the least sin, can wound, torment, and drink up our spirits. Oh, therefore, sadly sometimes let every one look over the time of youth, which so long, for intending vanities, disintended and considered not things serious and spiritual, but put them by; put them by as mere niceties and impertinences, yea, as very burdens and yokes; but chiefly having been called so often upon, by the word without, and the Holy Spirit's sweet motions, together with the frequent calls of conscience within.

Oh the time of youth may for ever humble all, cause us to look upon it with great self-loathing and heart-breaking, with fresh runnings of the spring of sorrow and shame for our follies and frowardness in refusal of returning, and to cry out with the psalmist, Lord, "remember not the sins of my youth," Psa. xxv. 7. O give a free and full pardon for that time so foolishly wasted, without consideration acted upon any spiritual concernment, to any purpose, but all lost.

CHAP. III.—*Another particular Cause of Humbling, for so long Neglect of Meditation.*

FOR humbling greatly every Christian, in that at the best and soonest we began so late this seriousness of thoughts, this duty of meditation, which challenges of all the very first consideration and pondering; the very first buddings out, and first blossomings of the considering power, should begin with our spiritual concernments, not letting it act blindly, ignorantly, evilly, and impertinently, but knowingly, wisely, and in a right manner: the rule allows not taking the first step, nor any other after, wrong.   Ah, how long hath it been, how long have the best of saints, the soonest blossoming and ripened young Christians, how long was it before consideration and meditation began in their hearts, before the sceptre of Jesus Christ, held forth in the laws and commands of meditation, was attended, would be yielded to!   How long ere any of our foolish and froward spirits would cease their vanities and wildness, follies and impertinences of thoughts!   When wisdom in any one begins to act, then consideration begins: no hopes of young heads, till they begin to put forth and act consideration; then begin they to be wise, or give hopes of a being hereafter wise, when they prove considerate; then begins that which is wisdom for thyself, when thou comest to consider, when thy spirit begins to beat the golden path of meditation.   Ah then let it humble us, it was so long before the first and fundamental meditation or consideration, before that first engaging the heart to seriousness and a due minding, that initial and introductive considering for true turning to God with the whole heart.   Formerly, in one of the grounds of this point we mentioned the necessity of consideration, and pondering our unspeakable misery by sin and God's displeasure, in order to conversion to God.   As all that are truly converted are truly humbled, so all truly humbled and converted are made first truly serious and self-bethinking, reduced to this meditation of their inexpressibly miserable condition. Conversion to God stands as it were on two feet, comes about by a double inlet, of a twofold consideration or meditation.

1. A serious meditation of now seen and felt unspeakable misery, that load and burden of sin and God's wrath laid on ; and this must be deep, sink down into the soul and press it, and soak through the soul, in sorrowings, in meltings, in weariness of spirit, and in willingness to be eased of the present pressure.

2. Then a most serious meditation and pondering of the rich, free grace of God the Father, reconcilable in a full Saviour, offered in a free, firm covenant and promise of salvation, to every sinner without exception.

These two great considerations are the foundations and inlets of the great heart mutation and conversion. Therefore these are of the greatest concernment of all other considerations ; yea, these are such considerations, that no other are to be reckoned upon, till they have been performed effectually.

Ah, therefore, how exceedingly should this humble all persons whatsoever, for their former so long neglect of this introductive and fundamental consideration ! God cries out, " How long will it be ere they attain to innocency !" Hos. viii. 5. Ah, how long was it with any, with the very earliest self-bethinker, before he used the eye of his mind in consideration ! consideration to view, not what was far off, but what was, of all others, the nearest; to see himself, and himself also in his nearest concern of all others, that eternal condition of his immortal soul.

Ah, what a humbling charge should this bring up to every spirit, to every bosom ! Oh how should it shame thee and me, and every one, to think how long it was before we began to do what might be called thinking, before I once began to think to any purpose,

how long my thinking and considering power was
merely abused by me, was both diverted and debased
by a continual running like water beside the mill,
ravelling out like a golden thread, spoiled as fast as
spun, by a neglect of winding up and right using!
Ah, how sad and self-abasing reflections should this
often occasion to us! Ah, think we sadly, how long
so noble a faculty as the understanding is! how rare
an acting the acting of its consideration is! how high
a concern eternity of happiness is! how necessary, in
order to happiness, conversion is! and how needful
consideration to conversion is! And yet to lose all
the right and best use of this considering power, this
meditating, by engaging it in impertinences and very
nothings, mere shells and shadows, instead of realities
and things of worth, true worth and excellency; to be
so long, like the prodigal, before we come to ourselves,
were seen sitting in our right mind, entering upon
meditation for that great soul affair, conversion.

CHAP. IV.—*For Humbling those that are totally
yet to begin Consideration for Conversion.*

AH then, in the next place, as it was for great shame
universally to all persons whatsoever, for so long neglecting consideration, and meditating of their souls'
condition, and for conversion; so how far more should
it humble all, that never as yet so meditated to that
great and principal end conversion, so as conversion
followed consideration; never had the first corner-
stone laid of that consideration, which bottoms and
ground sconversion; that hitherto have had all their

precious thoughts scattered in rovings and wanderings
of spirit, acted and wasted upon vanities and follies,
things that perish, that cannot profit in the day of
wrath, that will prove sorrow, shame, and anguish of
spirit in the latter end !

Ah, how many are there who for improving that
great talent of the thinking power, employing it for
those so high ends it was peculiarly designed to and
given for, for wisdom to salvation, and glorifying God
the Giver, that have daily all their thoughts either vile
or vain ; that walk in the vanity of their minds, that
is, in a constancy and prevalency of mind vanity,
vanity exclusive of good thoughts and all right seriousness, and productive of nothing but the weeds of
evil and vain thinkings ! The way of their thoughts
is a successive taking step after step in vanity, one
vain thought follows close, treads on the heels of another for haste ; all the walking of that so working,
active, busy mind, is nothing but continued vanity.
Oh how sad a frame of spirit is this, how sad a sign
and symptom, if not healed by a new frame of heart,
symptom of deepest danger of ruin and destruction
hastening on apace !

Some diseases in that so noble part the head, are
most dangerous, the cure is hard, the killing quick :
when vanity seizes the mind, when men, from vain
thoughts arising in them, come to allowing of them,
and from allowing to a walking " in the vanity of
their mind," vanity of thoughts becomes a habit ; and
when it becomes habitual, then the danger is great.
All habits, evil habits, are like old, rooted diseases,
hardly, if ever, cured. Oh, when men walk in the
vanity of their minds, God may be provoked to a
giving them up to walk on, and so be at last ruined
utterly for want of a timely returning from it.

Oh how should this awaken such, that have so this way ravelled out their youth; it may be, lavished and lost their best days of riper years, yea, peradventure, are arrived at an old age, and are old withal in this way of vanity of thoughts! Old and vain is sad to purpose. Ah, when younger, when elder, yet never could allow or would find time to become serious: a young head, and a vain head, all wildness is a sad beginning. A grown man ripened in reason, but not yet beginning, not so far as budding out in consideration, not arrived at the wisdom of minding soul concerns, that is worse, and a sad sign. But for a man to have grey hairs here and there, and to be yet to begin wisdom for himself, in self-bethinkings, never to have laid the foundation of meditating on the highest soul affairs, thereby to seek conversion, oh this is dreadful, sad beyond all! ah, to ravel out the most, the best, the all almost of thy time, and never, never to interpose one time's, one hour's serious meditation, or never to meditate to purpose, so as to turn to God truly, but be still to begin to return to God, contenting thyself with a just nothing done, of that greatest, and which should never be the last, but first despatched, business of all others!

Ah, but what will all prove at last to all younger or elder, if there be a going on without consideration, without conversion? Young, and strong, and old, are all liable to death, yea, to a death that may be on thee suddenly; who can (all things considered) think in any wisdom he can be so secure, that he needs not yet be ready for dying! Ah, if that black serjeant, death, claps thee suddenly on the shoulder, serves an arrest upon thee, presently to come away and give up thy account, in what woeful case wilt thou then find thyself, what terror and confusion will instantly seize thee!

It will most certainly come, that thou knowest; but when it will come, that thou canst not know; oh think therefore of it beforehand. Make it thy case as now come, and as if the symptoms of it had really seized thee, that thou wert now drawing on, hadst but a few hours or minutes to continue in this world, and then be cast upon eternity, be cast upon eternity, and before thou ever hast come to any consideration which issued in a real conversion, and thereby to make some sure provision for thy eternal salvation. Oh put this case, this dying case, put it soon enough, and close home to thy bosom, let it stay upon thy heart, let death as it were lay his cold hand on thee, and conceive that thou feelest it touch thee, and take fast hold of thee to carry thee instantly away, and so cut thee off from ever having one opportunity, the shortest space imaginable, for consideration, any possibility of conversion to God more; that time and means must now be no longer, because thou must be no longer in the land of the living.

Oh but then think, oh seriously think what immediately must follow after, ponder thy particular doom, thy soul's sentencing to an everlasting state. Think not only of thy soul's leaving its old ruined tabernacle, but of its launching forth into that ocean of eternity. Think what an eternity thine eternity must now be, who wasted all thy time lent thee for eternity, and that so precious talent of opportunity trusted with thee, to trade for eternity, for a most happy eternity, and making that sure, 1 Tim. vi. 12; 2 Pet. i.

And to affect thee more abundantly, and work

upon thy spirit to purpose, think, oh think of, besides thy own particular day, of that great day fixed and appointed by the great Governor of all the world, for judging of every person, every work of every person, the secrets of that person's heart, yea, every secret thing, good or evil, Eccl. xii. Imagine then that great and terrible day of the Lord to be come, thou seest the heavens departing as a scroll, the elements melting with fervent heat, the earth with the works therein burnt up ; imagine thou seest the Lord Jesus descending from heaven with his mighty angels, coming with the voice of the archangel and the trump of God, seest the dead arising, the living all changed in a moment, and all persons whatsoever assembled and brought before Jesus Christ the Judge, such a Judge as never any was in any degree to be compared with, so unspeakably excellent and glorious, sitting on his high throne, in highest and most transcendent majesty and glory, as there cannot possibly be greater.

Among all that are to be judged, imagine thyself there appearing at the judgment-seat to make thy personal answer, and take thy eternal doom ; that presently thou art called, Come, thou sinner, come, hold up thy hand at the bar, answer for thyself; that thou hearest the Judge call, read the indictment, read it aloud, and answer, thou sinner, to every part of thy charge.

1. Thou that standest here at this bar to be tried, thou hadst a noble faculty of reason and understanding, and with it a power of thinking and meditating given into thy soul, and that, above all others, to meditate of heavenly things. Thou answerest, It is true, Lord, I cannot deny it.

2. Thou also hadst my word, a perfect rule, to

direct thee, my ministers to persuade thee, my Spirit to draw thee, thine own conscience to call upon thee, which also called loud, often, and earnestly upon thee to consider. Yes, Lord, thou answerest, it is most true.

3. Time also and opportunity thou hadst, space sufficient allowed thee to meditate and consider, if thou wouldst have done it; a time of youth, and time enough then; also a time of, it may be, riper years, and old age; a time of many years, great patience, waitings on, and strivings with. True, Lord, thou answerest, I had many opportunities to consider.

4. But when thou should have remembered thy Creator in the days of thy youth, thou didst forget him, wouldst not think of him, of his word, of his ways, thy own state, and thy soul's concerns. Thy first fresh years were spent in walking in the sight of thy eyes, and minding vanities; thou couldst find time enough to think of thy pleasures, thy play, sports, and pastimes, thy excesses, filthiness, looseness, but not of thy God, or thy soul's great affairs. At such a place, in such a year, such a month, such a day of that month, such an hour, or such hours of that day, (is it not so, sinner?) there and then thou wert thinking, musing, devising for such a pleasure, such a sport, such a vanity, and such a wickedness; and the following day, at such a place, and such an hour, doing the like; and so day after day thy thoughts were lavished, lost, let out on impertinences and mere vanities, but purposely taken and turned from all religious seriousness, all soul matters. Was not this thy usual way to ravel out that thy youth's time in never minding thy God, and the things are holy; never to consider any thing to any purpose indeed? What sayest thou, sinner, to all this charge

acting the seriousness of them upon things that challenge it most, till thou comest to thyself, as Luke xv. 17, comest to humble thyself greatly, to say with deepest sorrow, self-abhorring, and shame, Oh what have I done! what have I been! how many years have I run out, void of all due consideration! how many and many millions of steps have I taken in the great road of vanity of thoughts! Ah, how near am I come to the end of my days, or how near may my end, for aught I know, be; and so for want of thinking and meditating, I may perish for ever! Ah, at how low a rate have I set my precious soul, set my body, my whole person, my hopes, my God, his Christ, his Spirit, his grace, heaven, happiness, and all my high concerns, that never thought them worth a thought, or a few thoughts in this way, this holy way of meditation; never weighed them so in the balance, unless to find them too light, outweighed by every worldly, every bodily and carnal concern! Oh unwise, silly wretch, that I have all this time been, that I should deal thus by myself, be so cruel and so heedless, the most foolish adventurer, the most idle sluggard, to live in a lothness to be at the pains of a sometimes meditating and thinking, though the gains be, or might be, beyond all thoughts.

Ah, now therefore, now, now, if it be not too late, by the Lord's help I will begin to bethink myself, now I will set myself to do my utmost, now to make haste and use all the means I possibly can to repent and reform, that I may be recovered from my vanity of mind and conversation, and at last be wise unto salvation.

CHAP. V.—*Of being humbled for Negligence in this Duty of Meditation, after experiencing the Fruit and Sweetness of it.*

ANOTHER improvement of this doctrine, is for due humbling of all such who after experiencing the success and sweetness of heavenly meditation, both that first soul seriousness, into which they were drawn, drawn by the Holy Spirit in effectual vocation, and grounding their so happy conversion to God and believing in Christ; and then likewise after their usual and daily exercising holy meditation, that whence they have had so sweet communion with God, those rare hours wherein they have been rapt up, with that blessed apostle, into the third heaven, and tasted of those glorious and soul-ravishing pleasures and joys that are unspeakable.

Ah, Christian, to experience so often the surpassing sweetness of this happy way, this path and walk to heaven, and tread it no more.

1. To fail so frequently in that so needful daily meditation, do it so little or so slenderly.

2. To take so seldom into that path of occasional set and solemn meditation, that also of so great advantage, large incomes of light and wisdom, warmth and quickening, strength and encouragings.

3. And to act no oftener that so easy, quick, and expedite ejaculatory meditating, whereby thy soul may give encumbrances and overcharging business the slip, take breath, ease itself, mount up to heaven, make a short visit, and return refreshed, quickened, and enlarged.

A student never does himself such wrong, as when

he reads much and muses little; for then he either receives in, or retains nothing, or cannot manage his notions: we never order and despatch affairs worse, than when we meditate least. And so a Christian never loses more labour, does his soul affairs worse, than when he muses not, and warms not himself by this exercise of meditation. Divers profess a faculty and ability, as in sciences and ways of learning, in mysteries and ways of trading and dealing, yet are but slender proficients, can do little but bungle, because they study and muse no more to know their own way. Many Christians are but bunglers to what they might be, make a large disproportion between their profession and their proficiency, their practice and their profit, because they meditate no more to understand their way.

The great, not only ignorance, but dead-heartedness and spiritual chilness, with the brokenness and unevenness of Christians in their walkings, arises much from a negligence in this meditation; either negligence of not doing it, but ceasing sometimes, or negligence of slackness and slothfulness, in ceasing fervency and industry for the manner. David's manner of meditation, in the fervency and the constancy of it, will keep up David's affections, fervent and flaming affections, and David's constancy and evenness of conversation.

Little meditating also makes lean Christians, of little life, little strength, little growth, and of little usefulness to others. In Heb. xii. 12, there is mention of feeble knees, which also occasions the going with no steadiness, and the not making of straight steps. As it is often in the body thus, from a failing in the head, obstructions of the fountain, and feeder of sense and motion; so this among others, this failing in meditation, is a great occasion, (though there be divers other causes,) a great ground of Christians' weak feet, and going no stronger and steadier. Meditation, that should influence, stir up strength and motion, is obstructed, disused, and neglected. Meditation must still lend a hand of help to every spiritual undertaking; first ponder, then proceed. We can perform nothing well in worldly affairs, without well considering; so in spiritual matters, what duties can be well performed, what graces rightly exercised, what in all religion that can be named, can be rightly ordered, if you mind not seriously, consider not before the doing it, as well as mind and attend it in the doing!

Serious thinking is fundamental to all right doing. Oh what are the innumerable advantages that thy constancy in this course would still bring in! and what have been thy losses by neglect, and will daily increase upon thee by it! Oh therefore consider, be awakened, and strive to be humbled for all thy failings and neglects; especially thy fallings off from and disusings of this so necessary and excellent duty: look to thy first beginning in it, and thy making no better entrance into it.

First undertakings, if not so well and thorough, prove great inconveniences; and if not looked after and amended, may occasion a less seriousness and care ever after; but, however, they require a making up and bettering: that which serves a young, weak, and unexperienced Christian, must not serve a grown Christian, one old in his way.

Be humbled for thy improving no more in this art of meditation, for being no better artist, for having so little of this heavenly habit and heart readiness, from thy frequencies and constancies of not only acting, but

earnest and vigorous strivings, which intend and
strengthen, improve and increase the habit.

Be humbled for no higher attainments in this
happy way, which we should be most perfect in and
ready for; in which we should still have an increasing
and heightening complacency and pleasure to perform,
with a striving to do it better, as to heart readiness,
better as to heart power, and purpose, resolvedness
against oppositions and hinderances.

Ah then look, mournfully look we, and with shame
and self-abasings, on all and for all our failings, and
for all our guilt contracted for this duty neglected.

(1.) That our progress and improvement hath
been so small.

(2.) Our inequalities and unevennesses so many.

(3.) Our fallings off and desistings, and lyings so
long, or any space of time, before returning and recovering, and by our disusing, contracting an unwillingness, a spiritual lothness, a doing with more
difficulty, or by refusals and denying of doing this
duty, to thereby aggravate our sin.

Therefore, I say, for all these admitted and added,
let us be deeply humbled before God, and mourn
over so many and great neglects he hath observed in
us. Ah, therefore, say, I have sinned greatly in that
I have done, 2 Sam. xxiv. 10: say, I will do no
more, Job xxxiv. 32. Ah, so to slight, to forget
the concerns of God and my soul, to let my eyes be
in the corners of the earth, to let my soul lose so its
lookings, by eyeing vanity; to embezzle my precious
thoughts upon the by, and overlook the main.

May not my God come and challenge me for great
unkindness, unworthiness, and folly? What, thou, my
child, to be so vain and unwise, when thou hast to
contemplate thy God, in his infinite all-sufficiency;

x 3

thy Saviour, in all his matchless beauty and fulness; thy Sanctifier, in all his operations and consolations; thy perfect rule, the Scriptures, with all the treasures of heavenly truths in them; and when thou hast all the excellent and admired works and ways of a God, the condition of his church and people, thy own soul's state, and eternal salvation, together with all such things that continually stand full in thy view! Ah, to have so many paths for the feet of thy spirit to walk in by meditation, so many rare objects for thy eyes' entertainment and employment, and to thy sweetest solace, largest satisfaction, and yet in any degree to miscarry the golden seasons of this so heart-enriching meditation.

Ah, may not my grieved God, and his grieved Spirit, grieve and sadden my herein so sinning spirit? May not my neglects of meditation, not seriously and frequently thinking of him, and such things that nearly, highly concern him, justly occasion my God's neglecting of me? Neglecting me, by withdrawing his hand from his blessed impulses, infusings of heavenly thoughts, judging it not meet to give down good and holy thoughts into a spirit distempered, diverted, by too usual admittance of earthly, evil, and carnal thoughts, and disuse of holy meditation. Who will plant the most precious flowers among heaps of poisonous weeds? Who will mix their richest, purest wine, with puddle, dirty water; or their gold and diamonds among dirt and dung?

Ah, this is the way for my God not only to withdraw himself, but to let Satan the foul spirit loose upon me, to trouble me, to haunt me, to follow me, with all manner of disquieting and discouraging thoughts, with temptations of injury and stealing, revenge and cruelty, uncleanness and filthiness, and sinful sensualities, and such like evil thoughts against others.

Ah, may not this neglect of good thoughts and due meditation be justly met with, and expose me to the blackest and most horrid thoughts and temptations, such as those of blasphemy, thoughts as thick as hail, and that daily haunt me, darting horror and hell into my spirit, making my heart to tremble, and my hair to stand upright on my head?

Ah, may I not (if I amend not the sooner) come to that so sad and dreadful temptation, so contrary to nature, the temptation of self-destroying, thinking it may be best to be rid of my trouble, though it be so horrid and unnatural, and will render the case so dangerous and dubious?

Yea, may I not have self let loose upon self, my own heart to worry itself; my bosom opened, the book of my conscience held open before me, and my eye held to a looking continually into it, seeing my sins set all in order before me, making me a Magormissabib, fear round about, a terror to myself?

And to all, may not my God plunge me into the depths of desertion, set himself against me, let all his waves pass over me, let me see and feel nothing but his wrath and hell; that I who would not meditate as I should, shall now nothing but meditate as I would not, meditate nothing but terror?

Oh therefore, to prevent all this, or whatsoever may befall me on carelessness and neglect, oh let me call to mind my former times, my former tastes and sweet solaces, had in my walking up this hill of meditation; those rare hours, sweet enlargements, strong consolations, happy and encouraging experiences I had when I kept up my vigour and constancy, as in others, so in this blessed way and exercise of holy meditation; and being greatly humbled, let me keep closer to and walk with an evener foot in this heavenly path.

CHAP. VI.—*A Persuasion to all such as never accustomed themselves to this work of Meditation.*

IF meditation be so necessary a duty, let this then prevail with every one that hitherto hath done nothing in it as yet, or that which hath been to no purpose. Oh that this sin can be laid to thy soul's charge, that yet thou art to begin to meditate of the great things of thy God, and thy own soul! That thou shouldst have so rare a power in thy soul, of thinking and meditating, a power also that is so active and busy continually, and yet never employed aright; so great a talent intrusted for use, and either hid up in a napkin, or wasted and ravelled out in vanities, impertinencies, and wickedness.

1. Seriously, I beseech thee, consider, thou canst be no good Christian, no truly godly person, (whatsoever thou or others think of thee,) that hast been and art no complier, but a refuser in this particular. Ah, this strikes thee home to the heart, dashes quite thy confidence and hopes, grounded on thy calling thyself a Christian. That clear passage proves it undeniably, The blessed man meditates in the law of God day and night, Psa. i. 2. The least that this place can hold forth, must be a doing this duty in a course and way. He that is a blessed man, is not only one that pretends to religion, but practiseth and uses medita-

tion, hath an inward delight in the law of God; and from delight in it, meditates on it, in a constancy and ordinariness: not acts a now and then bare thinking, when others mention it, ministers preach on it, or in the reading of it; to think of it then when it cannot well be avoided; but a serious and purposely meditating, a keeping up a conscientious and complacent constancy in it. If, therefore, continual meditation of the law of God, his word, and the excellences in it, be the character of a godly person, think well of it and thy own condition; flatter not thyself with that kind of false godliness, which falls short of the true character of true blessedness.

2. Consider, thou canst be no true subject of Jesus Christ, that dost not submit to this law of Christ, this meditation. It is in Scripture made one of the imperial laws of the King of the church, who gives every subject of his this charge, lays this command indispensably, and repeats it frequently, records the examples of the saints, who practised it diligently, as David and others; therefore thou disownest this law, thou disownest the Lawgiver Christ, and so he takes it.

3. Ah, then, what is it that reigns in thy heart, that sits in the throne and sways, but the tyrant sin, sin that hath dominion over thee, sin that is the great obstruction and hinders thee, sin that is the great bias of diversion that draws thee quite another way?

It is merely the vanity of thy mind, in which thou walkest, that keeps thee from walking this way.

It is thy sinful folly; the wise in heart will muse and consider, and most consider things of the most concernment: what is it which hath made all the spiritual fools, but sin? The Scripture fool is the sinner; and wherein is the folly seen more, than in not considering things most considerable?

Thy not meditating, it is from the tides and currents of unmortified lusts; lusts in dominion and reign, lusts that engross thy thinkings, lusts that engage and set thy thoughts on work, and fill them.

In every predominant lust there is a predominant scope and tendency, an end and aim that gives the rules and laws; as therefore the lust's aim lies, so all the thoughts and seriousness are levelled; as the lust's aims and marks are, so are the mindings: if lusts of sensuality, riot, drunkenness, uncleanness, and voluptuousness; if these or any of these be predominant, all the strength of the mind and its musings run out at that leak, that passage. If covetousness and worldly-mindedness be predominant, all the studyings and thinkings run down and are carried away by that outlet. If pride, vain-glory, and affectation of honour bear sway, then the thoughts and contrivances act up all that way, climb up that hill.

Thy serving lusts and pleasures, being enslaved by them, is the ground of thy thought's subserviency to them; they set up an exclusion of good thoughts, shut the door against all godly seriousness, turn the engine of the thinking power into an instrument and forge, for themselves to act a sinful seriousness, to further only the satisfying of them.

I have read in Pliny, that the Romans, attempting a discovery of some more unknown places of Africa, could not proceed and succeed in it by reason of the innumerable sorts of serpents and poisonous creatures which filled the country. Thy heart is like that country, full of dangerous lusts, which overrun it; there is the true reason why thou wilt not, canst not meditate, because the predominant lusts in it engross and enslave the whole thinking power; lusts rule thy lookings, thy heart's sinfulness hath seized thy seriousness, sweeps all thoughts into itself and service. One lust shares now one proportion of thoughts, another lust goes away with another part, and so among them all, who take their turns in thy heart, they gather up, and appropriate all thy seriousness and vigour of thoughts, all that are to any purpose. All other thinkings are so short, slight, seldom acted in comparison, that they amount to nothing; millions of them make no more than motes in the sun would contribute to make a mountain, because there is commonly nothing of seriousness in them; when they are acted toward things spiritual, they are but smoke or chaff that flies away. And consider why lusts have thy thoughts so enslaved to them, it is because lusts and sin have that empress of thy heart, thy love; for as thy love is, so are thy thinkings: thou pretendest thou lovest God, and with all thy heart, but it is no such thing; that which hath the love most, hath the eye most: who ever could truly say they loved any person most, and thought of that person least, but of other things every day and hour more?

O consider this well, how evil it is thou meditatest not by reason of thy reigning corruptions and lusts that will not let thee meditate; and lusts have thy thoughts from having thy love.

4. Why as to thy own frame of spirit is there a neglect of this holy duty? it is from sin reigning in the relishing part, the palate of thy soul; sin that takes away thy taste, and makes godliness unsavoury: Those that are after the flesh, savour the things of the flesh, Rom. viii. 5. Ah, not to meditate from such a sad cause, from a not savouring the things of God! finding no suitableness, no sweetness, no pleasantness in spiritual things! none in the word and ways of God, in the precious promises, heavenly graces,

glorious privileges, given to the children of God! none in an infinitely sweet and blessed God, Father, Son, and Spirit! none in the things above, but all in the things below, not because they have no savour or sweetness in them, but because thy carnal heart hath no principle of savouring of them!

5. Nay, is it not from sin that lodges and breeds in thy bosom a hellish enmity against any thing is holy? "The carnal mind is enmity against God," Rom. viii. 7, and so against every thing that comes from God. Ah but, sinner, this is the blackest thing in thine or any bosom, this is the loathsomest thing in all the world, it is the chief feature and lineament in the face of Satan, the most abominable part of Satan's heart, and the very worst thing in all hell; nothing is or will be more evil in hell, than their enmity, boiling up and running over continually against God.

6. But who is he that hath unhinged thy heart, in respect of this duty of meditation, that acts thee to this awkwardness, and bars the door against it? is it not Satan that dwells and rules within? Satan that is thy soul's implacable enemy, and the great adversary to this meditation? And what is his reason of hindering thee, his grand reason, but that he knows this to be the way of coming to a man's self, and turning to God?

Of all such things that are dispositive and assisting to conversion and faith, Satan is the grand enemy to this consideration and meditating of a man's spiritual condition. If thou wilt do Satan's will, and gratify him the best thou canst, if thou wilt give him the best security of utter undoing thyself, let him see and know thou wilt not consider and muse on thy soul's concerns, but look quite another way.

7. Whither do thy thoughts sink and soak, but

into the base earth, and in the base things of it? He
that looks with his bodily eye, if he looks not upward,
may look many other ways than downward, right forward, on the right or left hand; but thy soul's eye,
if it look not to things above, it looks downward to
the things below, Col. iii. 5; the base, dry earth
drinks up all thy thoughts.

8. When wilt thou begin to think, to think to any
purpose indeed, when will that time be? Shall it be
when thou art most timeless and heartless? when
thou hast least leisure, least fitness, bodily fitness and
disposition, of ease, strength, spirits, and senses?
when thou hast least heart fitness of desires and willingness, which with time will wear away and be less?

The longer thou disusest thyself to good and serious thinkings, the less fit and disposed thou wilt
every way be, and the more will vanity of thoughts
grow upon thee, dye thy mind into the grain colour
of habitual vanity; the more will thy heart grow up
and ripen in an averseness from all good thoughts,
harden and grow more sinfully and desperately set
against seriousness, all such meditating as is necessary
to true repenting.

9. Wilt thou defer thinking and considering till it
be too late, till time and the season of grace shall be
no longer, till life, and soul, and heaven be irrecover-
ably lost? Wilt thou lose this short time here, till
thou comest to an eternity of time, to think of thy
neglects of thinking? to muse when it will do no
good, when musing on thy not musing and meditating, will turn into torturing and tormenting thee for
ever?

Ah, therefore, now while it is called to-day, now
while thinking may do thee good, good to converting
and saving; ah, now bemoan thyself, and sad, so sad,

dreadful, and dangerous state. Never rest or be quiet till thou becomest a serious person, one that useth his thinking power to the right end, and in the right manner, to meditate thyself home, as the prodigal did home to his father's house, to be received with great joy.

Consider therefore, 1. This is one part of wisdom indeed, of wisdom for thyself, when thy soul concerns have their allowance of due consideration. 2. Never expect a cure of that worm, that wolf in thy breast, of those gnawing, grinding pains, and terrors of conscience, until thou by consideration come to convert and turn to God. 3. Never wilt thou taste of peace of conscience, joy that is unspeakable and full of glory, until thy thought vanity be healed, and thou becomest a seriously meditating person.

Therefore begin at that first meditation of thy unspeakable misery under sin, God's wrath for it, death eternal awaiting thee, and which by death's soon coming may seize thee, and seal thee up in it for ever.

Also, labour that consideration may rightly issue in an awakening thee out of thy deep security, in a contrition of spirit, and a right preparative humbling, dashing thy pride and carnal confidence.

(1.) To fear exceedingly for thy so great misery and danger, by being under so great wrath of a God, and the curse of his law, Acts xvi. 29.

(2.) To sorrow and mourn deeply for this thy misery, thy mirth and laughter being turned into heaviness, Jam. iv. 9.

(3.) To despair of help in thyself, see the insufficiency of thy own goodness and righteousness, and of thy own ability of wisdom to devise, will to choose, or any power of thine to save thee.

(4.) To come from former carelessness and negligence, to an earnest care and desire to be eased and delivered, Acts ii. 37.

Then being weary and heavy laden, endeavour the second consideration of the way of relief and help.

[1.] By pondering the infinite love of God, his willingness to receive broken-hearted sinners to mercy, pardon, reconciliation, adoption, and full salvation.

[2.] The fulness of redemption in Christ freely offered to all.

[3.] By pondering the promises of salvation, righteousness, so perfect and glorious pardon, so full of all graces and happiness : Christ must be received in the promises, rested upon as sure, good, and free.

[4.] By earnest, often praying for grace, faith, and other graces, a new heart, and new principles, which will introduce a new power, and make godliness in all the duties of it, and this of meditation, sweet and easy.

CHAP. VII.—*An Application to such as are Godly, and have tasted the Sweetness of Meditation.*

THE next persuasion and instigation is of all such who, from a right principle planted in them by heart-changing grace, and their experience from often and usual practice of meditation, have tasted the benefit and sweetness of it ; to take heed of neglecting it, and to endeavour a constancy and improvement in it.

As there is nothing harder than to hedge in the thoughts and govern them, so how hard is it to make them keep and beat this path of meditation, to have the soul go, as with hinds' feet, most readily, and with enlargements of steps in it ! The holiest heart is too apt to flag and be weary in the best pathway to heaven. Meditation hath a strong and active enemy in every bosom ; when any would do this good, evil is present, in backwardness to it, regret and reluctance rises up, puts in a caveat, hangs a weight and clog to hinder, which watchfulness and resolution must spy out and cast off. " Lay aside every weight," saith the apostle, Heb. xii. 1. Every weight the flesh casts upon a duty, the spirit must cast off, and then run : sin at all times can easily beset us, and now at this time we may easily find it. How easily will sin beset us with excuses ! how easily with whole troops of arguments will it charge us ! how easily with swarms of diversions, diverting thoughts, purposes, affections, will it seek to warp us ! this thing, and the other, and a third, and a thousand, that fly about as thick in the heart, as motes in the sunshine.

1. Meditation is harder than some other duties of godliness ; for in other duties the body comes in as an assistant to the soul, and lends a hand of help. As in praying, there may the voice come in, which is a great furtherance, keeping better up the mind's intention, and keeping better off deadness and distraction. In reading, the eye is exercised, and the mind is the better, as to attention and heeding, if not to heat and intention : the eye affects the heart. So preaching hath the ear to convey and make the better impression. But in meditation the soul acts singly and unassisted, without a stirring up, or exciting by any sense, or any help from the body, and so it is the harder, as the condition of our nature now makes it : in the state of imperfection, we need the body's help to further the soul in its workings in some sort.

2. Meditation hath least opportunities of coming

under observation of others, and thereby less provocation and encouragement for doing well, by either bad
or good, before whom, in other cases, our light should
shine, and God by them be glorified.

3. Meditation is hard, in that it is an acting of
the quickest faculty, and the most slippery part of the
soul : nothing is nimbler than the thinking power, no
act in the world quicker and of more expedite motion
than that of a thought, and nothing sooner slips off
the object, or thing acted upon, and makes a way
faster to a new, than the thinking faculty ; like the
bird put wild into a cage, the door is no sooner open,
but she is gone.

Meditation is harder, being not bare thinking, a
flash, a fit for an instant, a touching ; but a fixing and
stay of thoughts, a detaining them, which otherwise
are as oil in a man's right hand, that will not be
retained. A carnal heart counts all ordinances and
spiritual engagements but coming into bonds, tyings
with cords, longs to break them and be free ; so doth
it by this cord and tie of meditation ; it is harsh work
to the flesh.

Oh it is a most high attainment, to be able to say,
" O God, my heart is fixed," Psa. cviii. 1 ; fixed as to
the purpose of heart, the choice and intent of the will,
so to have the head, the mind, to cease the rolling,
ranging vanity and slipperiness, and to act fixedly in
the way of seriousness ; not be a light-headed, but a
musing man, a person of ponderings, and thought
stayings ; like the bee that lights on the flower, and
stays to have the honey with her ere she removes.

4. Meditation is the harder, in that Satan hath
greater power upon, and more immediate passage to
the faculty of imagination, than other faculties of the
will and affections ; he works not so immediately cn

the will and affections, as upon the imagination, and there he endeavours interruptions by his injections and suggestions; there he endeavours diversions to think quite another way from the work in hand, and disturbances, casting in by-thoughts, and sundry objects of different or contrary nature to the duty we are in. As Satan filled Ananias's heart, but first by filling the imagination with thought of covetousness; so he can cast suddenly into the best heart thoughts and apprehensions, when about the best work, to disturb and hinder. Besides, consider his malice is great against meditation, knowing how great advantage comes to us by it, and how much disadvantage to him.

Satan is much prejudiced by ponderings; he ever watches when this work is taken in hand, and therefore, Christian, thou hast greater reason of taking the greater heed, to watch him that so watches thee, to fight him that fights against thee, and so envies thee the help of this ordinance, that would not have thee enjoy the freedom of one good, one serious thought, but is casting the dust of evil thoughts in the eyes of our minds, when they are looking up to heaven; but principally he envies and opposes seriousness, searchings, and dwelling of thoughts upon spiritual things.

Satan deals with us here, as deceitful courtiers and counsellors have done with their masters, diverting them from minding their affairs, and all right seriousness, by pleasures and new devices, under the pretence of freedom from encumbrances and trouble, and enjoying themselves; but that hereby they may more securely prosecute and compass their own private interests. Satan had rather we should do any thing than keep up a seriousness in meditation, (or any other holy duties,) which may keep us awake and in a watchful posture against his enterprises.

5. Meditation is the harder, by reason of the exemplary mindlessness of so many we daily meet and converse with, who refuse and slight all seriousness, as unnecessary niceness, or neglect it, out of slothfulness, and lothness to trouble themselves. Bad examples are very infectious, apt to convey a secret poison into men's hearts, when they heed them not: by touching this pitch, the best are ready to be defiled.

6. Meditation is like the road or passage where many things meet us, jostle us, and are ready to turn us out of the way. Cares strive to come in, businesses and multiplicity of affairs, sudden emergencies, and sundry things, that may attempt to interpose; and these, if our watch and guard be not the stronger and stricter, will make the duty miscarry.

Yea, sometimes one duty may drive out another: often we let holy duties interfere and cross each other, hearing, praying, and the rest; sometimes there is hastening from one to another, sometimes letting one detain us so long, that others are cut short, and so helps are turned in part into hinderances, opportunities for some duties into obstructions to others, when godly prudence allows every thing its season and due proportion of time.

The external hinderances to meditation are many from common business, and things of this life; and we often create our own hinderances by our sloth and imprudence, not carefully redeeming and wisely ordering our times and opportunities.

Ah then, my soul, if meditation be so high, so hard, as to its spiritual nature, and hath withal such enemies and oppositions, look to it then I must the more cautiously, but not less resolutely perform it.

The moralists say that difficulty is *cos virtutis*, the whetstone of virtue, the incentive and heightener of magnanimity : to a great and heroic spirit nothing must be so great as to outlook it and discourage it. The greater and braver fish swim against the stream ; the noble Christian by difficulty and opposition is cautioned, but not cowed out.

If there were nothing to set against and weigh with the former cautions and arguments from enemies and opposition, if no high inducements and advantageous arguments to put into the scale of persuasion, to weigh against such as fill the scale of dissuasion, it then might the more reverse and turn the edge of thy courage (yet arguments from evil and mischief in many cases are sufficient alone) ; the danger of an armed enemy's approaching, as in Jacob's case ; the danger of deadly poison prepared for thee, or infection coming very nigh thee, is enough. But we have encouragements, and those in full measure, pressed down and running over. As Elisha to his servant discouraged, when encompassed in Dothan, We have more with us than against us. What if there be a principle of flesh that makes opposition ; yet thy principle of spirit and grace, is a real ground of hope and help. If thy grace, Christian, be true, though but a grain of mustard-seed, it will live, and hold, and act, and grow, act into endeavour and striving till it overcomes. A principle will help thee.

(1.) Consider, a principle introduces an inclination, a bent and tendency of heart against the inclination and contrary tendency of corruption, Psa. cxix. 112. And it is a principle must live, and the contrary carnal principle must die ; Rom. vi. 11, Reckon yourselves dead unto sin, but alive unto God. Sin as to the purchase of Christ is dead in the saints totally, and it is dead in the habit and root initially and in part, in respect of the communicated and inherent grace of Christ, which upon union with Christ, begins the death of sin in mortification, Rom. vi.

(2.) A principle, besides inclination and tendency, introduces power and ability; as the flesh hath its power, so the Spirit and grace hath its contrary power.

(3.) A principle introduces facility; though the flesh makes duties hard, yet the Spirit is ready, and makes godliness easy.

(4.) A principle introduces delight and complacency; the flesh acts reluctance, the Spirit delight and pleasure, Psa. cxix. 47.

(5.) A principle works holding on and constancy, Gal. v.; as the flesh lusts against the Spirit, so the Spirit against the flesh; not only begins, but holds on; a principle will help you to hold on, for God will hold that on: " He that hath begun a good work in you, will perform it until the day of Christ," Phil. i. 6.

(6.) A principle is blest, by the using of it, with progress and growth; the flesh, that shall decrease and waste, but the grain of mustard-seed shall grow to a great tree, Matt. xiii. 32.

(7.) A principle shall be crowned, by contending and striving, with glorious conquest and victory; the Spirit wars against the flesh, and it conquers in the issue by its still warring; judgment is brought forth to victory, Rom. viii. 37.

Ah, never be discouraged for any thing within; be very sensible of sin within, and the stirrings of it, but sink not under the sight of it; take thou encouragement, Christian, to fight it, and to subdue it. If thy heart's badness appear, its backwardness and crossness to any duty, know you can get nothing by giving way, but by going on and striving; and use this herein as thy rule, wear out thy own backwardness to and weariness in a duty, by doing it in a resolved constancy, wear out the indisposition to duty by doing that duty, and doing it fervently.

Also, if Satan be such an enemy, yet have we not more and stronger with us than him? we have the Holy Spirit that helps to pray, and he will help us to meditate. If he sees we are labouring to get up the mount in meditation, he will give us his hand to help us up ; if Satan and all hell be against us in this or any other duty, he will be for us, yea, Father, Son, and Spirit are and will be all assistants to us. Do we not use to say, God came in at such a time, in such a duty ? He delights to see how the pulse of thy spirit beats heavenward, how the eye of thy soul looks upward, how it fixes its looks of heavenly love upon him ; he delights to help up thy heart in its holy meditation, to help it tower up to heaven, to taste of those surmounting glorious delicacies prepared for his beloveds' entertainment and highest solace.

What others in their exemplary carelessness hold forth what their mindlessness is, must not have any impression of discouragement, or prove to us any impediment. It is no staying till we can take every one along with us in our journey to heaven. Neither must the example of any, the highest, the greatest, the richest, the wisest, and most learned, the nearest related, the dearest affected, nor any under any consideration whatever, have that ill influence upon us, either to discourage or divert us, weaken our hands, or hinder our making straight steps in this blessed path of meditating diligently upon heavenly things. Neither let the cares and pleasures, business and affairs of this world, hinder this soul great affair of serious meditation in the seasons of it.

The saints of Christ in all ages have found a way to this duty, as well as others, and that through the

throng and multiplicity of crowding and jostling occasions.   As it is said of our Lord Christ, in Luke
iv. 30, when they of Nazareth, angry with him, thrust
him out of the city, and would have cast him down
headlong, "he passing through the midst of them
went his way," the saints of Christ have made their
way, passing through the midst of businesses and
emergencies, troubles and disquiets.   They had a
wisdom given them to find out a way, they had a will,
a purpose, and resolvedness fixed, so as to overlook
and overcome obstructions and lets, from throngings of
business, and multitudes of still successively interposing diversions.   That holy David, who had so
many highly urging and pressing occasions, as no
man now, whatsoever he be, can have more ; yet he
made his way continually through all the throngings
of so high importances, and most urgent affairs : he
had a wisdom given to find a way, and a will to resolve to meditate, and he did it daily.

He says he will meditate in God's statutes, Psa.
cxix. 48 ; when he so determined, certainly he did it
not rashly, and without consideration of his many occasions and weighty affairs, and those great diversions
which he might after meet with at home and abroad,
in peace and war ; yet thus he resolves.   And Psa.
cxix. 97, he saith it, and to the Lord himself, that he
did it, and all the day : first he saith he will, then
saith he doth meditate, and saith it to the all-knowing God.

It therefore hence appears how feasible and prac-
ticable this duty is ; notwithstanding cares, business,
troubles of all sorts whatever, from the world and
living in it, there is an attainable will.

(1.) A godly heart may come to say I will, may
set a universal purpose of heart, a firm purpose, and

a purpose of equal extent, to the whole latitude of gospel duties, and whatsoever the word requires.

(2.) And likewise he may have a latitude of wisdom, to understand his way, every way he is to walk. "The wisdom of the prudent is to understand his way," Prov. xiv. 8. "Thou hast made me wiser than mine enemies: I have more understanding than all my teachers," Psa. cxix. 98, 99. There David discovers he had wisdom for his way, and how he arrived at such a height of wisdom, and directs us how to come by it.

(3.) And as a Christian may come to say he will do such a required duty, and arrive at the wisdom of doing it; so by grace he may come up to an answerable extensiveness of practice and performance, walking in all the ways of the Lord, as Zacharias and Elisabeth, Luke i. 6. David often professes his both universality, as of his heart purpose, so of his practice, as the 119th Psalm, and others, abundantly show.

Yet first fixing our purpose in the strength of Christ, then following after the wisdom of our way, making it a grand scope to attain the wisdom, the right and sure wisdom of our soul affairs, to be artists in religion; and then falling close to practise what we resolve and understand: this with Christ's help will make our work, any work upon our hands, to prove easy. They are all plain to him that understandeth, Prov. viii. 9; "*easy*," the old translation hath it. We have a saying in divinity, "The way to godliness is within godliness;" that is, the way to learn it is to act it, and the way to facilitate and make it easy, is by exercising ourselves still in it, setting upon and keeping up the practice of it. He that doth much in it fervently and frequently, will come to perform with increasing facility: slack and listless doing, slight and negligent performing, may come to loathing and leaving, end with the disadvantage of a far worse temper of heart averseness than there was at the first. Formality in religion ends often in falling first off from it, and then falling out with it; contrarily doing with care and fervency increaseth spiritual strength, and the increase of strength makes the work more easy.

In using to do it earnestly, we arrive at a doing easily. Oh therefore let every one be highly encouraged to hold up our constancy in this excellent duty, to walk with an extensive and increasing evenness and equality in this so pleasant high road to heaven, both in daily meditation; in that for the entrance, and that other for the ending of the day; in also the occasional solemn meditation, that rare way of spiritual improvement in wisdom and heavenly warmth; and in that way of meditation, by short and sudden ejaculations. This threefold cord will draw strongly heavenward, will make thy soul go from strength to strength, from warmth to warmth, from pleasure to pleasure; make thee keep upon the wing, mount up aloft, and not be weary by the successive varieties and the abundant sweetness flowing hereby into thy bosom.

Is my heart dead at any time and listless? how soon will meditation quicken it, and reduce it into activity!

Is it barren and unfruitful alone or in company? what rare rich matter can meditating bring in and spread over the barren soil of my spirit, and make it soon put forth fruitfully!

Is it chill and cold, without wonted warmth and vivacity? what fuel can it fetch to kindle a fire on this hearth, fuel from heaven and earth, from the word and works of God, and all sorts of objects whatever, spiritualizing them for my use, what sparks can it strike, what coals can it kindle and blow up into a flame to thaw my frozen heart!

How high a preparative is meditation to prayer, to enrich it with choicest materials, to enliven it, and make it burning hot in holy fervency!

How rare a dispositive to hearing the word of Christ, to open the everlasting doors of the heart, to widen the heart for a letting in more freely of heavenly truths, and increasing the good heart's treasure, to make us swift to hear, to hear with the largest and liveliest affections, readiest purpose, most raised and fixed resolutions, to receive and obey the word in every thing, most abundant readiness to be moulded into the form of doctrine that shall be delivered!

What an efficacious helper is meditation to spiritual digestion, and reducing divine truths into sound and good nourishment, which miscarry in others for want of due meditating!

And what a mighty assistant is it to holy duties! what is there performed wisely and with vigour, unless directed and assisted by meditation?

For to make the instigations more full, we may look back to the ends of meditation, and the afterward grounds were given and enlarged upon, which being many, will be too long to repeat.

CHAP. VIII.—*Of the Evidences of a due Meditation.*

FOR the evidences of a due and right meditation, it must have the nature, properties, and attendants of it; and therefore it is not to be taken up as a custom, as a thing made to stop the mouth of a calling and urging conscience, or a mere acting for notions, a study and search of curiosity, to know novelty, or to know much, and be able to hold discourse with others. But it must have a higher nature, purer ends, and be performed in another sort, than an only wise or a learned man, yea, than any formal Christian can act or compass of himself. And for the characters of a right holy meditation, there will be no need to fetch any other lights of discovery, but only to take up and hold those to this intendment, which were opened in the discovery of the nature of divine meditation.

1. As making it our real and high obedience to God, the sovereign Lord of our souls, and to the golden sceptre of his word in that express law of his, laid upon the thinking power, and grounded upon the high and infinite obligations he hath on us, to impose this thought tribute and homage, a pure obedience to him, and doing his will herein.

He that meditates aright, hath been taught and learnt to obey God, to yield it to him as his due. I am under my God, saith the right Christian, and infinitely obliged to all which he commands me. This, among others, is one of his righteous and holy laws, one great signification of his royal will; I must not, will not deny it, dispute it, or put it from me, but comply

z 2

freely with it. And this comes from that spring, that root which lies at the bottom of the heart, that super-eminent love to God, (the holy heart's chief good,) and the great ground of all right obedience. "Love is the fulfilling of the law," Rom. xiii. 10, and so is it the fulfilling of this particular law of holy medita-tion ; love to God, so infinitely excellent in himself, and who hath so unspeakably loved the holy soul. Therefore if it be the right and genuine obedience, it hath this high, this warm spring of love running in this channel, this of meditation, an overpowering, con-straining love that produces this thinking, this look-ing of the soul in meditation.

O therefore try if this heavenly love hath first been planted in the soil of thy heart, if from a new heart circumcised to love the Lord above all ; that thence thou comest to love meditation, because thou lovest the Lawgiver first, who writes his law, and writes this particular law in thy heart by love to it, by making thee a lover of meditation.

2. If meditation be genuine and right, then is it from a choice of will, wrought by the power of holy love subduing and mortifying carnal and formerly predominant unwillingness and stubbornness, reluct-ancy and refusals of this work, and framing it to will-ingness, freeness, and fixedness of purpose to do it and hold it. "I will meditate," saith the holy psalm-ist, Psa. cxix. 48. Meditation arose from resolu-tion, from a will fixed, and that arose from love acted, and working the will to resolution. Therefore in the 97th verse of this psalm, he speaks it to God him-self, Oh how love I thy law ! and what fruit doth this noble root of love put forth ! it is my meditation all the day. Meditation of the law proceeds from love to the law.

Love lay at the bottom, and that engaged the will into a firm resolution to meditate. Never is the will freer, and its purpose firmer, than when love inclines and engages it. The highest and strongest resolutions that ever were taken up by any holy heart, were the rare products and sweet fruits of heavenly love, love efficaciously exciting the will, winding it up to the top, and then fixing it fast.

3. Where the work of meditation is right, the aims and ends of it are pure, spiritual, and holy; it is carried beyond and above self; it is an acting with self-denying: self is neither the total nor the predominant ingredient in this undertaking. That which Christ calls for, of denying a man's self, Mark viii. 34, in the extent of all Christianity, must particularly be performed in this duty. Self-seeking must not be uppermost, not the main intent or inducement; for this is the sphere an unsound heart moves ever in. The aim and end in the best natural man is never higher than self, and no other really than self, and that because he chiefly loves himself. But a right work must be aimed and acted above all to the living God. Therefore, Zech. vii. 5, God tells them their fasting was not right, because they did it not to God; so is meditation or any other duty not right, if it be not to him, aimed above all at his glory.

In this respect, therefore, religion is in Scripture called godliness, because it is a frame of spirit acting above all self-ends and inferior respects, unto the living God above all. So Heb. ix. 14, "To serve the living God:" works not done to the living God are dead works; a living work is aimed and levelled to the living God.

The end more particularly must be the glorifying God; "Do all to the glory of God," 1 Cor. x. 31.

If eating, drinking, and such inferior things, then much more holy duties, must be done to God's glory. There must be an inward powerful principle that can aim so highly, really, and an acting of that principle that God is actually glorified.

It is not enough to say we do, as many erringly affirm they aim their duties, when they never had first that right principle of holiness wrought in their hearts. Without the principle of holiness it is impossible to have holy aimings, holy ends. It is impossible without an eye to see to level at a mark. Wheresoever there is a right doing, there is a potent elevating principle, that sets the spirit above the predominancy of self-seeking, and acts it into a reality of God exalting above all, that kindles and inflames the soul into an ardency of desire, love, delight of glorifying God in every undertaking. This is unspeakably sweet and heart-gladding; nothing pleases a holy heart more than when the heart below can run in some degree parallel with the hearts of saints and angels above, in hallowing and advancing the highest God and his name. Try we therefore if our meditating be a real acting up to the grand scope and highest end, the exalting of God, if his honour be indeed the preponderating inducement and greatest soul aim.

Happiness and our own salvation was the next aim formerly mentioned; happiness propounded and declared in the gospel, and no other. To this next subordinate end must all the golden lines of holy duties tend, here they must centre. Every right duty must be a real levelling at gospel happiness, that which God proffers, and Christ hath purchased. If meditation be right, it is a part of true wisdom for ourselves, Prov. ix. 12. Wisdom to salvation, as really aimed at it, as any marksman aims at his mark. God, next to himself and his glory, allows and requires us to look and seek, labour and strive for eternal life and happiness; and all our duties, as they are subservient to his glory, so our own happiness is complicated and wrapt up in it, yet not above it, or equal with it, but next under it. Accordingly, therefore, in this duty, as in all others, our aim at happiness must not be a mere self-seeking, it must not terminate only in ourselves; but our own happiness must be aimed at for glorifying God by it.

We must aim at happiness, and being in heaven, thereby to be in a most perfect state, that we may attain the most perfect principle for the highest exalting of God. Although in heaven seeing more, and tasting more, and having the vessels of body and soul filled up with glory and happiness, makes our state more glorious; yet the end of that seeing, tasting, and all enjoyings there, are to put us into a most perfect capacity, highest heart readiness, and alacrity, upon the most overpowering incentives, to lift up to the utmost the glorious praises of God. This then is a very considerable particular, that besides glorifying God, the supreme end, aiming at our own salvation must be more than for ourselves.

We use to speak of several spiritual ends relating to our own spiritual good, which we are allowed to set up, and seek, and strive after; yet all these must have this reduction, must all have this glory of God for their chief end. The last end, as hath been said, gives the rules to all both subservient ways and ends. Therefore in our examination let us take in all the spiritual ends before spoken of, for heavenly light and larger knowledge, for a spirit of wisdom to be wiser to salvation, to be warmer at the heart, melt off all encumbrances, make up to heaven better, to fix our resolutions firmer, strengthen our grand purpose of still walking with God, to stablish our course, and make straighter steps for our feet, and to press harder to the mark. Are our spirits acted to these aims, and all those other meditation is so excellently and usefully appointed to?

Also, do we meditate in the right way of calling off our thoughts from impertinences and diversions? Do we set a strong guard upon our spirits, and watch them diligently? Do we act meditation in bending our minds to it, strive to act with all seriousness we can? Do we act searching and pondering, and keep up constancy of thoughts, till we both bring our hearts to the heavenly temper, and the duty to the kindly issue it should have, and cannot be content with any thing but that a God who sees our actings will approve of?

CHAP. IX.—*Of the Directions relating to Meditation. First, for such as would begin.*

AFTER some characters given of a right meditation, I shall next speak of directions or rules to be observed about it. The rules must be suited to the several sorts of persons that will set upon this work, or proceed in it with success.

If it be a person who would enter upon this way, being sensible of the sin of hitherto neglecting it, and is now willing to be advised how to perform it; then consider, it is no undertaking it, or hope of doing it

aright, and holding on with constancy, and to the
spiritual advantages of it, unless there be an endeavour after a right principle, a living spring within to
found and still feed a due performance of this spiritual
work.   To undertake it without, thou wilt find it too
high and hard, arrive at the best, at a formal doing, a
slight and careless doing, and in the end grow weary
of it, and cast it off, and so return to it no more.
Therefore thy great intendment, to which thou must
bend thyself and whole soul, (which should not, must
not be given over until it be effected,) is to make sure
of a new heart; this will bring in a new power, a new
principle, introduce a bent and inclination of spirit, a
love unto it, a firm and abiding purpose, a rooted resolution for doing it against all difficulty and opposition.   This will make the duty of meditation easy,
and also sweet; by the pleasure and advantages found
in this heavenly way, thou wilt be encouraged to hold
on, success will encourage thee, that will sweeten the
way to thee, and help to stablish thee in it.

Though thou canst not change thy own heart, and
make it new, lay in a new principle of holiness; but
it must be God who gives the new heart, Ezek. xxxvi.
26, 27, and works the will and the deed of his own
good pleasure, Phil. ii. 13.   Yet as he calls thee to
turn, and in order to thy converting, requires thee to
consider and bethink thyself; so is it thy necessary
and important duty to consider and ponder deeply and
frequently those things, and in that manner and order
which are most effectual to that end, and which God
uses to set home.   For by putting thyself into God's
prescribed way of seriously and frequently considering,
thou mayst meet with a help, with God helping at
last, who helps them that seek him diligently, and
give not over striving.

That relation is remarkable of the bad son whom, his father dying, calls to him, and gets him to make this promise, That every day he should for but one quarter of an hour meditate of some one thing or other, what he would. Accordingly he every day employs a quarter of an hour, or some time, in serious thinking : but this at last most happily issues in serious considering his sinful state, and a real converting to God at last. Thus often it hath come to pass, when persons have set themselves to consider, as God in Scripture exhorts, it hath ended in a true returning ; so the prodigal is described, Luke xv. So Ezek. xviii.

If thou art very desirous more particularly to be here directed what to do to obtain the right principle, and thence the right way of acting this duty and others in the holy and spiritual required manner, I shall mention some particulars more necessary for this so weighty a concern. If really and in good earnest thou wilt engage, strive to purpose for obtaining a sure principle of performing this or any duty aright, a principle of grace and holiness, a new heart, and a new spirit,

1. You must go about it with the greatest seriousness that ever thou canst, and endeavour the firmest and strongest purpose for prosecuting it, till thou hast attained it. But then thou must see thy utter inability without God's lending a hand to help thee in so high an undertaking. It is thou must endeavour, but God he must draw thee. " No man can come to me except the Father draw him," John vi. 44. Thou must strive for, but God must give repentance. " If God peradventure will give repentance," 2 Tim. ii. 25. " Turn thou me, and I shall be turned," Jer. xxxi. 18. " A new heart also will I

give you," Ezek. xxxvi. 26. Yet God must see us, when he calls for returning, to endeavour, and strive, and wait for his giving, who works the will and the deed of his own good pleasure, Phil. ii. 13.

2. Thou must resolve to sequester thyself at times, at fit seasons, from all diversions, not suffering any thing then to interrupt thee : thou must sit alone, as Lam. iii. 28.

3. Do all thou possibly canst to be awakened out of thy deep security, so long and so dangerously rested in. Awake, thou that sleepest, and arise from the dead, and Christ shall give thee light, Eph. v. 14.

For this thou must gather all awakening considerations the Scriptures furnish thee with, concerning the inconceivable misery every sinner is in. But consider, things spoken in general in Scripture, and not brought and set home on thyself in particular, will not work to an awakening. Neither will thy saying and acknowledging thy sinfulness and misery in general serve ; generals humble not, generals hit not home. A single arrow or bullet will not serve against a whole flock of fowls, but scattering shot must be used. Take therefore all the warmest considerations thou canst, and heap them as coals of fire on thy own head, bring them home to thy own heart, to melt down thy frozen frame of sinful security. Do all thou canst by the light of the Scripture, and beg, beg most earnestly the light of the Holy Spirit to convince thee of thy extreme misery. It is he that convinces of sin and misery, John xvi. 9.

Endeavour to thy utmost to rightly found this work, by most industrious striving to see the exceeding sinfulness of sin, Rom. vii. the abounding evil in it, Rom. v. And do this by fullest possible pondering the great transcending evil of the lesser sins, or such

as are comparatively small, and we count not great;
see it in examples : as Uzza's dying by an immediate
stroke for but touching once the ark, 1 Chron. xiii.
10. The Bethshemites, for only looking into the
ark, fifty thousand and seventy persons were slain
by a hand from heaven, 1 Sam. vi. 19. Adam and
all his posterity with him were undone by his eating
of a fruit, because forbidden, which in the nature was
no immoral thing, as idolatry, murder, &c. but sinful,
by a peculiar precept of trial broken. Yea, if Adam,
when he was the representative of all, had sinned the
least imaginable sin in one commission, sinned in one
sinful, one vain thought, it had been his own and
all his succeeding posterity's ruin, nay, in the least
omission. Though there be many sorts of sins, with
sundry measures and aggravations, yet there is none
so small but is high treason against an infinite
majesty.

This is a grand intent of God in the whole Bible,
and also in his punitive providences, to demonstrate
God's heart in his dislike and loathing all sin, that it
might blot out our mistakes, and reduce us, stamp
our judgments and hearts with a suitable impression,
a sense of all sin, or whatsoever is but near to it.
Therefore, among others, that is very remarkable.
The Nazarite, not only by purposely touching a dead
body, or coming to it, was unclean : but if any died
suddenly by him, he was to bring his sin-offering and
burnt-offering to make atonement; which was to
manifest by the type the purity God requires, and his
distaste of any the least likeness or nearness to any
defilement of sin, Numb. vi. 9—11.

Dwell and dive deep as ever thou canst into the
abounding sinfulness of every the least sin. Thence
reason and ponder with thyself, what is thy unspeak-

able misery, who art guilty of a whole lifetime sins, such an innumerable company of sins, in thoughts, affectings, purposings, speakings, doings; in acts, ways, habits, and all thy heart evil that hath ever dwelt in thee.

And if thou wilt overlook them, and not consider them, thou shalt be judged one day for them all. To methodize this grand inquiry and soul search, and to have the kindly issue in a due awakening, strive to avoid all confusion of thoughts, and to do it distinctly, and in the best affecting manner thou canst. Rules of art are not here necessary to be used; but the way of thy best skill, by God's assisting, thou canst take to set an edge and give more efficacy to this undertaking, thou mayst single out first that sin or lust which dares and pinches thy spirit most; touch first where thou art tenderest and sorest; on that which items thee most, flashest fullest, like lightning in thy face, makes thy heart oftenest ache.

It is the counsel of some great divines, to pitch upon some gross sin first; seek ease first where thou art disquieted most, or that is likely to give the first blow. The Scriptures set sinners to consider their doings, especially their ways, which are continued doings. These should more humble than mere particular acts; but both acts and ways should be viewed, as they can be recalled and brought to mind, and then put all into the scale to make down-weight, and contribute to fuller awaking.

But above all sinning any, or divers sins, into ways, and then walking these ways into wonts, those worst defilings and soul enslavings of cursed habits; such as habits of sensualness and intemperance, habitual covetousness and worldliness, habitual pride and presumption, self-exalting, self-seeking, habitual vanity of thinkings, and such like. These great chains thou art bound with and enslaved by, Tit. iii. 3, Serving divers lusts : lusts served are sins formed into habits. These old, rooted soul diseases, these heart gangrenes should well be eyed, and much awaken thee. O it is sad to find thyself going to hell in a custom and by a habit, binding thee and haling thee thither.

To all, as highest aggravations, add the consideration of that sin of thy nature, that emptiness and deprivation of all spiritual life, power, image of God and his glory, conjunction and communion with God and all happiness; with cursed inclinedness to all the sin in kinds and aggravations, that the whole world, hell, and all ever acted, or can act for ever.

And that blackest part of hell dropt into thy heart, the worst, very worst thing in Satan's heart, that enmity and horrid repugnancy, crossness and contrariety to all the extensiveness and dimensions of whatsoever is good, is holy and righteous ; yea, that highest monstrosity and transcendency of impiety; enmity to that God who gave at first, and ever keeps up thy being ; and which is the height of that height, the utmost venom hell could hatch, and heart can breed, that horrid enmity to the very being of God himself. Before grace, no guilty sinner but wishes God were not, and if he could, would dethrone and destroy God utterly. And above all yet intimated, take in the superabounding sins against the gospel, neglectings and refusings of the only remedy and relief of an undone soul, which is the greatest possible soul-wronging: Wisdom affirms it ; Sinning against me, saith Wisdom, he " wrongeth his own soul," Prov. viii. 36. All sin wrongs ; but the meaning is more: he wrongs with the greatest possible wrong, the highest can be done, to refuse Christ's salvation. And, which is yet far exceeding all self-wronging, there sin so touches the very apple of God's eye, strikes so provokingly at his very heart, and dashes down his most darling design, the utmost and highest that he ever went, or will go, the highest exalting of the riches of infinite free love and free grace.

I have heard by a good hand, that one of the dukes of Muscovy, while he stood talking with a poor peasant of the country, pitched a spear he held in his hand upon the poor man's naked foot, there digging with the point of the spear into it, and the slave (for so they are generally) durst not complain. Oh! gospel sins dig not into the foot, or hand, or eye of a God, (if I may so speak,) but into his heart, and the very top and crown of it. Every sin against the gospel kicks so at the very heart of God, so dishonours him in that his tenderest, upper interest, as nothing can higher offend, and therefore not expose to deeper danger.

For further help, take the book of conscience, thy soul's register, and God's remembrancer. Look over all the black items there on the file, that it will certainly one day produce, and set before thy face.

For yet surer assistance, take the perfect rule and glass of the law and word of Christ, therewith duly comparing thy life and frame of heart, that by the law's coming, sin may the more abound.

Oh but the law not only discovers guilt, but denounces a most dreadful curse : " Cursed is every one that continueth not in all things which are written in the book of the law to do them," Gal. iii. 10. And as the law, so the gospel curses with a more dreadful curse for not obeying it in true coming to Christ by faith. Oh what a curse must this then be, to be

accursed first for original corruption in all the hellish
wickedness of it, and then to be cursed for all thy
innumerable actual transgressions! Accursed for the
first act of sinning. Accursed for the next act. And
for every new sin to have a new sentence, be under a
new curse. For every, every evil thought, every evil
affection, purpose, word, work; every commission,
every omission, every day, for all the sins of it, to be
accursed, from the beginning to the end of it. Really
by the curse to be separated to evil, bound over to
death eternal in hell. How should this startle and
awaken thee!

Oh but there is yet what is more dreadful, to be
continually for sin under the hot displeasure and
abiding wrath of a God. "God is angry with the
wicked every day," Psa. vii. 11. "He that believeth
not, the wrath of God abideth on him," John iii. 36.
This God, so angry for sin, how infinitely able is he
to take revenge, and how resolved is he, unless thou
turn to him! Oh what is that death eternal, that
hell provided to punish sinners! How frail is thy
life, by which thou art kept from falling into the lake
of fire and brimstone! How certain is thy death,
and how uncertain is thy dying time! It may come
in a moment, and then thou art cast upon eternal
ruin.

Consider, thy sins, after commission, grow not less,
wear not out, are not less dangerous. Sin is the
same for substance, though thy sense of it be less.
We greatly deceive ourselves herein, as if sin, the
longer after commission, were less; but the guilt of
sin is the same, the defilement the same, the curse
against them is in the same force, the wrath, displeasure, and resolution of God to revenge them full
out the very same, and God's remembrance of them

is ever the same.   " I remember all their wickedness : "
and how is that ?   " They are before my face," Hos.
vii. 2.   If they are not before thy face, as God can
set them, yet they are before his face, Psa. l. 21 ; li.
9 ; that is, seen and remembered as a thing set full in
a man's eye, and his eye full on them.

I have been too bold in thus enlarging.   Oh it is
hard to awake from the deep sleep of sin.   But this
must be endeavoured all thou canst, and God he is to
be entreated to help and do this for thee.   There
must be an awakening by conviction really and undeniably, seeing and acknowledging thy most woeful
condition.

Conviction in the understanding must end in contrition, and a working down to the affections ; in a
fourfold affection, answering a fourfold distemper.
1. Upon fear.   2. Sorrow.   3. Despair.   4. Desire
and care to be eased.

(1.) To tame presumptuous boldness and confidence
in thy coming to fear, that for all thy sin and danger
feared not.   As it is said in that particular case, Jer.
xxxvi. 24.   Though so great sinners, and so severely
threatened, yet were they not afraid, but burnt the
roll.   To say we have sinned is not enough, there
must be real pungent fear, Acts ii. 37, pricked at the
heart on sight of the sin of killing Christ, a real and
deep fear, to a wounding, piercing the heart and thick
skin of security, hindering the feeling of a woeful state,
coming to be as really sensible as thou dost in assured
and great danger : the jailer " came trembling," Acts
xvi. 29.   God by his Spirit, the spirit of bondage,
works this fear, Rom. viii. 15.

(2.) There must be a dashing the usually carnal
jollity and mirth.   " Let your laughter be turned to
mourning, and joy to heaviness," James iv. 9 : this

2 A 3

is all the Scripture calls for. A man condemned to die a cruel death, if persuaded he must die, will not laugh and be merry, but mourn. That mirth used at other times is not to be used now.

(3.) To dash the deceiving, usual, carnal hopes, which are the house built upon the sand. Hopes of salvation on no true foundation, but fond fancy, mere imagination. There must be despair as to all worthiness and ability in a man's self, or any creature, or in God and Christ hoped, as many do in a false way, Deut. xxix.; Psa. l. " What shall we do ? " Acts ii. 37, implies, as I take it, (beside other things,) despair of what formerly they hoped and trusted on.

(4.) To curb and cure carelessness, and a not desiring any other condition than their present; or an only cold, as it is in many, and a fluctuating desire: there must an edge be set upon desire, an earnest great desire to be eased of the trouble and burden of sin, and God's wrath. " What must I do ? " Acts xvi. 30; and, " What shall we do ? " Acts ii. 37, implies an earnest desire to be eased. And accordingly there must be an applying thyself to all the ways thou knowest, and going to others that can advise thee. Praying especially often, and as earnestly as thou canst. Confessing and bewailing greatly thy present condition; upon being truly awakened, and thence made really sensible of thy so woeful state, weary and heavy laden. After the first dispositive meditation, and the impressions made on thy heart through the Lord's help, then a second meditation must next be mightily intended, and diligently followed, meditation on the means and manner of using them, for getting out of thy so sad estate, and coming to a safe and happy. As he, " What must I do to be saved? " Acts xvi. 30.

Here must be laid at the foundation of this work, that so necessary consideration, That none can help himself, and attain the mercy of a God in a meritorious Saviour, unless God the Father by his Holy Spirit, the mighty Applier of Christ's redemption, draw efficaciously the weary sinner to the soul-easing Saviour, works faith to come, and rests on an all-sufficient Christ.

The first step in this great soul concern, must be labouring to divert the eye from a total or too much viewing of sin and God's wrath, and earnestly endeavour to be duly, deeply possessed of the infinite mercy, love, riches of free favour in Christ, in whom he is placable, and infinitely willing to show mercy. 1. Willing, in that he hath, in his abounding wisdom and prudence, contrived the way of reconciliation in Christ, Eph. i.   2. Willing in infinite love and riches of grace; he appointed his own only Son, anointed him with all fulness of grace, sending him, and causing him to work and procure redemption perfectly in all respects, and then in making the most free imaginable and possible proffer and tender of salvation in Christ.

A discovery and tender in the exceeding great and precious promises, promises that are as so many strong yearnings of the heart of a God to sinners; promises most firmly fixed, as being all the engrossed particulars, and the golden clauses of the covenant of grace, signed and sealed with the most precious blood of Christ, and therefore " ordered in all things most sure," 2 Sam. xxiii. 5.   The promises and covenant are by most highly demonstrating (that hardly to be believed and trusted to, by once awakened sinners) that free rich love of God in Christ: by demonstration of it, the intendment is first to found and breed faith in weary, heavy-laden sinners, and after to build it up and perfect it.

Meditation should first fix upon the promises of free justification and pardon of sin : and as humbling arises not from a confused general apprehension of sin, or many sins, but distinct particular viewings of particular evils ; so comfortings and coming to relief must be by singling out and pondering the promises of mercy in particular. As a drowning man that escapes by a taking hold on a particular thing, hand, or cord. But the thing the greatest and highest for producing and founding justifying faith, is first pondering the infinitely all-amazing and adored free love of God the Father, John iii. 16 ; 1 John iii. 1. 1. This is that so rich mine, out of which the most precious Corner-stone, Christ himself, was taken. 2. For principally glorifying this riches of free grace, the earth for a stage was set up to begin the discovery and revelation of it. 3. The great assize of the great day of judgment is chiefly appointed for higher manifestation of it. 4. And the highest heaven, with the state of glory there, is purposely founded and conferred on the saints for the highest demonstration chiefly of free, saving grace ; not angels' glorification, but redeemed saints' glorifying, is for free, saving grace's greatest glorifying, and highest exalting.

Dwell here, till largest apprehensions and highest admirations swallow up and drown all thy fears, doubts, and discouragements, raising thy spirit up to hope, trust, and consolation.

But this so infinitely free love of the Father must be connected with most wishfully viewing, and most earnest pondering the highest proof and evidence of it, in that greatest possible gift, God's own Son, God in our nature. God so loved the world, that he gave his only begotten Son, that whosoever believeth in him should not perish, but have everlasting life, John iii. 16. Here, after all thy black and sad thoughts and disquiets, is the richest, strongest, and surest cordial for a fainting heart. A Christ in whom all fulness of " wisdom, and righteousness, and sanctification, and redemption" dwell, 1 Cor. i. 30. Who out of his own infinite love became man, was in the " form of a servant," performed the whole law, pacified the wrath of God, purchased perfect and eternal life, by laying down his life a ransom. 1. A Christ freely offered by God the Father ; Come and buy without money, Isa. lv. 1. 2. Freely offering himself ; If any man thirst, let him come unto me, and drink, John vii. 37. 3. Freely offered, and to be taken as the bride and the Spirit say, Come and drink of " the water of life freely," Rev. xxii. 17. This free grace must be applied by the promises of grace and pardon more especially and first. Christ is not offered by God the Father, and the Lord Christ offers not himself, nor the Holy Spirit offers not, neither draws to Christ, but on the ground of the promise of forgiveness and salvation. Nor can it be taken by man, as a learned divine expresses it, but *mediante promissione*—that is, by means of a promise.

The promises particularly must be pondered duly, often and often. 1. The goodness of them ; they are good, sweet indeed to a needy, thirsty spirit. 2. The sureness and firmness, by a God that cannot lie, Tit. i. 2, all yea and amen in Christ, 2 Cor. i. 3. The freeness of them. Nothing so free as they that come only from a God, only for his own name's sake. 4. The seal of them, in the rare and abundant examples recorded for encouragement of sinners of all sorts received to mercy. So 1 Tim. i. 16, I, saith the apostle, was received "for a pattern to them which should hereafter believe on him to life everlasting."

The promises must be pondered, prayed often over, as those which are for the wounded, weary, and heavy laden, to produce faith; not only to feed it, but found and feed it also; to begin, and to build it up. Never leave pondering the promises, God's love, and Christ's fulness offered in them, until pondering comes to hope, hope to thirsting, thirsting to highest prizing, prizing to selling all, and buying the pearl, till thou comest to renouncing thy own righteousness, thou cast thyself upon God in Christ, by the promise first rested on, promise leading to Christ first, and to God by Christ; and not only Christ for justification as thy Priest that purges guilt, and makes atonement, but as thy Prophet and King for light and holiness, for a new heart, a new principle, a new wisdom and power, a quickening power, from union and communion with Christ, Rom. vi., by the inhabitation and operation of his Spirit; by faith, that hand which receives all from Christ; when by faith thou art justified and sanctified, and receivest by influence from Christ a living principle. Now thy heart is put upon the right hinge for rightly performing holy duties, praying, reading, hearing the word. And now thou canst meditate aright, in a holy and happy manner, with wisdom and some skill, choice of will, complacency, and constancy. And now meditation will prosper in thy hand. Now, as David's blessed man, thy delight will be in the law of God, and in that law thou wilt meditate day and night.

CHAP. X.—*Of Directions for Meditation respecting such as are young Christians newly
converted.*

OUR next work, after directions to those that desire
to successfully practise holy meditation, having formerly neglected it, is to treat of the directions for
young Christians, who are but entered upon their way,
how best to order their right principle received, to
their best advantage in this way of meditation.

1. Here, as the rule of learned physicians is, in
curing of diseases, that universals are first to be intended ; so first your rule is (to enter and engage
yourselves into that great road, and most ordinary
work incumbent, of daily meditation) herein to contend and strive after an habitual holy frame, to habit
thyself, as thou art able, to the right daily meditation.

1. Habituate and accustom thyself to the morning's meditation, in awaking so still with God, in
serious thinkings of, and admirings, his goodness and
mercy in the night past.

Begin to accustom thyself to first looking up to
God, and that most seriously and earnestly, that so
near as may be God ever may be the first in thy
thoughts. " When I awake, I am ever still with
thee," Psa. cxxxix. 18. And, Give ear unto my meditation. In the morning, O Lord, will I direct, or set
in order, as the word properly signifies, and look up,
Psa. v. 1, 3. He awaked into meditation, and acted
that meditation, in lifting up his heart in praying.
To improve holy thoughts and holy desires of God
being ever the first in our thoughts on awaking, is
certainly more his due and proper right, than any

other things in the world.   It is also the very best
thought bestowing, the best laying out our precious
thoughts for our own profit ; best as to the help and
furtherance of grace ; best for fresh incomes of sweet
peace.   When first we act heavenward, we act freest
and freshest, when the spirit acts upward, before lusts
and corruptions are stirring, before Satan begins to
interpose, and before the world comes in to us, to
hang on its weights upon our hearts.   It is far more
acceptable to the majesty of the high God, to have
the first visit and homage ; likewise more beneficial
to ourselves, to get the start of other things, to give
our hearts first a heavenly seasoning.   The vessel
will be the sweeter, and retain an after better savouriness for the coming day, when this is well and
seriously done.   Visit God early, and he will visit
us early.   This awaking will occasion the Holy
Spirit's awaking and blowing on the garden of thy
heart for the spices to flow.

2. Come then to that meditation relating to the
duties of the succeeding day, this then must be well
attended for making a good entrance into this new
course of meditation.   Here to strive after the true
wisdom of this way, to be an artist in some measure,
a wise meditator.   At the first we cannot be too
wise, nor understand too well a way new begun.   Nor
never can we here be so wise for doing any part of
our spiritual work, but we may learn more.   Also to
have a due temper of warmth, fervour, and vivacity,
this must be minded ; " Fervent in spirit," Rom. xii.
11.   To begin a course dully, act easily, and not
earnestly, this wrongs thee much ; it hinders the otherwise obtainable facility of doing, with that rare sweetness attending a holy seriousness, and the rich improvement of the main stock, that stock of grace

given for increasing.   A habit comes not up by remiss actings, but by earnest actings.   Cold water
cannot be made boiling hot, and kept so, by adding
lukewarm water, but water very hot.   Easy actings
will disintend and abate the habit where attained,
and hinder the attaining where aimed at.   Easy endeavours will settle in a spiritual laziness, set up at a
formality ; but equal and earnest will introduce a
strong habit and high.   Get the habitual fervency by
daily actings of heat, and being fervent in every doing.
So when the apostle urges fervency of spirit, he means
a fervency in all serving the Lord at all times.

3. As you must do this in reference to daily meditation in the general way of it, so habituate and
accustom thyself to meditating of thy chief and supreme end.   To a due and earnest meditating of
God, and glorifying him ; for this gives the laws and
rules to all thy course.   If the question were, What
is the best thought arising any time in any heart ? it
is that which is of God, the glorifying of him.   The
purest, highest thoughts of a God exalting him, must
needs excel all other thoughts more than the sun
excels all candles or least lights whatsoever.   Use
thy thoughts with David and other holy men of God,
to bear strongly and act ardently upon this.   This
lays the foundation daily deeper of thy self-denying,
Mark viii. 34, that so hard and tough work.   Self
would not rise up and float so high in any good
heart, if glorifying the infinitely better God were
more meditated daily upon, and had its more due
and down weight in the scales of the Christian's
thoughts, had more serious musing upon.

4.   Habituate thyself, gain upon thyself as to
serious daily meditation on the next end and scope,
thy own eternal happiness and salvation.   Let not

this so momentous concern want its weight in thy daily
meditating; let it have still some at least serious pondering; and this not only at thy first entrance upon
this way of daily meditating, then when thy fears and
feelings of wrath remain fresh in memory. But here
is the art and frame to be endeavoured, to grow up in
more habitual seriousness of musing on this great salvation. This was the blessed apostle's way; he not
only at first, when Christ humbled him, began it, to
meditate how to be saved, but eyed it daily, accustomed himself into serious, more serious minding it.
Phil. iii. 13, I forget things behind, and press to
the mark. He kept his constant aiming, and aimed
better, still more fully; and therefore the act being
stronger, the habit must be more intended. The
habit of meditating here should not sink and be in a
consumption, decline and grow weaker, or but keep
up alive; but it should root deeper, put forth stronger,
shoot up higher to the mark. Salvation should have
quicker and more lively impressions on us, like the
natural motion, though slack at first, yet quick at last.
That is more natural and genuine which grows still
stronger, like rich wine, more strong and spirit by
keeping close.

5. Contend to habiting thyself to ponder those
particular means making up to the grand ends of
glorifying God, and thy happiness in enjoyment of
him for ever. Namely,

(1.) Accustom thyself to as high and transporting
thoughts of Jesus Christ, his fulness of grace freely
offered, and thy daily putting him on more, and
growing up in him. And this by meditation of the
precious promises and the faith, whereby thou must,
through them, receive from Christ, and live by it.

(2.) So accustom thyself daily to meditation of

the Holy Spirit's dwelling and operating in every good heart, without whose assistance thou canst not perform any good; therefore must not be neglected, grieved, quenched, resisted; but prayed for and cherished, earnestly expected, and highly entertained.

(3.) Accustom thyself to some seriousness of thoughts of the ordinances of Christ, the ways of our communion with God, (we have no other means for it,) and the walks wherein the Spirit comes.

(4.) Use to cast a wishful eye on all such conducing things, formerly mentioned, for which thou canst have opportunity.

(5.) Look to well enter into and fix upon the meditation, daily examination, of review, looking over matters of the day; and if hindered at any time, help it by after industry. I say the meditation of review in the close of the day, to see and judge thyself as to thy heart's frame, and thy carriage in the time of the day.

This at the first is like the working with an awkward hand; this must not be slubbered over, slightly done. But being harsh and unpleasant work at first, thou must so manage it with care and constancy, that thou mayst gain a hand at it, it may become easy and pleasant. Suarez a Jesuit says of himself, that his times of self-reflection, and examining his conscience for matters of the day, were the sweetest part of all the day.

Thy rule must be to perform this work, so as it proves easier and sweeter, and thereby thou improvest in it. The more impartial and sincere you are in it, the sweeter you will find it. The more accurate and exquisite your inquiries and heart-searchings are, and the more impartial towards yourself, the sweeter peace, the higher boldness and confidence will thy heart be filled with. For this brings in the clearer evidence of thy sincerity, thy impartiality.

Nothing perfumes the spirit of a christian with sweeter peace and more heavenly joy, than a clear discovery of the heart's uprightness and integrity, which, by searching our hearts, and impartially judging them, we attain. As David prays, " Judge me, O Lord: for I have walked in mine integrity," Psa. xxvi. 1. And, Search me, and see if any way of wickedness be in me, Psa. cxxxix. 23, 24. This came from his own first impartial searching, and finding his sincerity. Usual and diligent self-searching brings in and keeps up a settled peace and confidence, by a man's being daily more assured of sincerity and heart uprightness. Be careful therefore and diligent in this self-searching.

CHAP. XI.—*Of the Directions for particular Cases of young Christians, how they should do therein.*

BESIDES these more general things, last mentioned, I must next come to the rules of meditation, as to thy particular case and condition.

Here that thy meditation must pitch upon, will be either, 1. The case of thy assurance, either wanting and not yet attained, or else weak and feeble. 2. It must be something relating to sanctification, thy weak grace, and many imperfections here, the purging of thy heart from divers evils, subduing of new rising and stirring corruptions; some particular sin that

haunts and troubles thee ; some temptation which
follows thee ; some cross or affliction lying heavy upon
thee : or any other particulars wherein thou art concerned, here to meditate how to have help the best
and speediest.

1. That is a principal point of wisdom, to study
and ponder the case of thy peace and assurance of
God's love and favour, if not yet obtained ; or but
enjoyed in a small measure, accompanied with divers
doubts and fears ; to meditate how best thou mayst
come to assurance, and be strong and stablished in it.
How to have thy good condition made out to thee,
and thy fears, discouragements, and doubts may scat-
ter and be driven away.

Here thou must be willing to take pains, and resolve to exercise very humble, patient waiting. "Wait
on the Lord : be of good courage, and he shall
strengthen thine heart; wait, I say, on the Lord," Psa.
xxvii. 14. " There is forgiveness with thee, that
thou mayest be feared. I wait for the Lord, my soul
doth wait. My soul waiteth more than they that
watch for the morning," Psa. cxxx. 4—6. I say
humble, patient waiting, until by frequent ponderings
and searchings thou art replenished with such a furniture and treasury of Scripture grounds, gospel reasons, and inducements ; and these so full and clear, as
thy heart now changed by the gracious help of the
Holy Ghost, who assures by the gospel promises,
arrives at the skill and wisdom, as to be able to
answer thy own cavilling, doubting spirit ; and to re-
pel the false reasons that Satan uses to hinder thy
peace and assurance. Assurance is chiefly founded
on our sanctification assured. So divines say, assurance of election, justification, perseverance, and glorification, cannot be without assurance of sanctification,

this being the ground of our assurance in the other four.

In particular, thou must labour to draw forth out of the sure word of Christ, the infallible characters and clear descriptions and evidences of the new creature, and of sincerity of grace; then meditate and ponder so duly upon these sure evidences and right Scripture descriptions given of the new creature and sincerity of grace, as to come to as clear and distinct an understanding of what is held forth to thee as thou canst. I pass divers things might be mentioned, and shall touch on the following.

(1.) As that change and renewing of the mind and judgment, which, in respect of sin, is to have it out of measure sinful, Rom. vii. 13.   The greatest evil in all the world, as that only contrariety and enmity to the greatest good, namely, the infinitely blessed God, his infinite holiness and purity, and all his so infinitely glorious attributes; yea, his very being, with his sovereignty and government; all his most holy, righteous, and good laws, and word, the signification and demonstration of his sovereignty over us, and of his will concerning us.   Hereby likewise manifesting the extreme injuriousness and unrighteousness of sin, in regard of God, whom upon infinite and indispensable obligations we are engaged perfectly to obey.

And as the abounding sinfulness of sin must be seen, so as the judgment disallows all known sin, the very least; so there must be a universal liking, and an allowance of all good, of all known truths, and all known duties; truths as revealed by God, and to be believed by us; and duties commanded by God, and to be performed by us.

(2.) In seeing the fulness, 1 Pet. ii. 7, of beauty and excellency, with the mightiness of Christ to save, in all respects, all that come to God by him by faith, with the vanity of all earthly things to make us happy, and the excellency of grace, holiness, faith, love, and the other required heavenly graces and soul abilities and beauties above all other endowments. This is the first part, the first right change of the mind and judgment. Whereas the natural man knows not the things of God, nor can he, because they are spiritually discerned, 1 Cor. ii.

2. The next part of the new creature, is that change and new heavenly frame of that noble faculty the will. " To will is present," Rom. vii. 18. Often in the Psalms David mentions his will, his choice, his purpose, his firm and rooted resolution. " I will keep thy statutes. I have chosen the way of truth. I have sworn, and I will perform it, that I will keep thy righteous judgments," Psa. cxix. 8, 30, 106. Isa. lvi. 4, That choose the things which please ; God's own description of a gracious frame of spirit, by a gracious choice. On the contrary, a sinful, unconverted heart is described by choosing things that are sinful and provoking. I say the change of the will is a high evidence of sincerity, a choosing of God for our God, choosing of Christ, his offered grace, above all, him to our righteousness and justification, our wisdom, our sanctification ; so coming to, taking of, trusting on him, is an act of the will, in choosing him, a choosing the holy ways of God universally. " Respect unto all thy commandments," Psa. cxix. 6. This not so much in knowing, as purpose of heart for keeping all.

To add but one thing more. The new creature is principally seen in a new will, and a new will in a new aim, altering utterly that old, sinful, carnal aim, of carnal self, and satisfying of it, sinfully aiming at only or chiefly self, and satisfying self in worldly and carnal things. This idol self, the grand aim, is taken down, is no more the soul's master-mark, that gave all the laws, made every thing serve to it, and end in it; eyeing of self chiefly, aiming at, seeking and striving most for self, is changed; and there is a new master-aim, a new mark to which it designs, and principally drives at, God and his glory, serving and pleasing him. This evidently appears in the saints in Scripture. They exalt God, called such as seek God, serve God, live to God, to Christ, Psa. xxii. 26; xxiv. 6, " This the generation of them that seek him," and deny themselves. " Alive unto God," Rom. vi. 11. Live not to themselves, but to him that died for them, 2 Cor. v. 15.

(1.) Universal allowance of all known good in the mind.

(2.) Universal abhorrence· of all known evil; choosing all good, and a universal purpose of will to please God in all things, are the things the sincerity of them stands of those two noble faculties renewed.

(3.) A real change of the corrupt, carnal, and disorderly movings of the affections, to a making them holy and heavenly, to setting them on the things above, and taking them off really from the things below, from their usual sway, rule, violent running to carnal and earthly things, and from their customary and predominant deadness, flatness, and remissness to and in spiritual and heavenly things.

A change really upon the great and leading affection, love, the great weight that carries all. My soul's love is my soul's weight, as the devout ancient said, the strong bias that still leads it. Hence arise the other holy affections, they are acted from love, desire,

delight, sorrow, fear, hatred of all known evil. " Ye
that love the Lord, hate evil," Psa. xcvii. 10. " I
hate every false way," Psa. cxix. 104. A character
it is of a wicked man, he abhorreth not evil, Psa.
xxxvi. 4. But a holy heart, when it comes even new
out of the furnace, is new cast, new made, it is stamped
with predominant love to God and his ways, and with
new self-loathing and sin-abhorring. " A new heart
also will I give you. Then shall ye remember your
own evil ways, and shall loathe yourselves in your own
sight for your iniquities and for your abominations,"
Ezek. xxxvi. 26, 31. I shall add no more particulars. The truth and sincerity of this whole work
wrought first in thee really, and then known, must be
the ground for evidencing of thy assurance, which
must be done by comparing the pattern of the new
creature described in the infallible word of Christ,
and the copy of it drawn in thy heart.

Such serious searching and due meditating, with
praying and other ordinances, must be on thy part ;
thou must " give diligence to make your calling and
election sure," 2 Pet. i. 10. But withal there must
be a due consideration, and praying for the evidencing
and sealing Spirit of Christ the Comforter, and diligent
still attending upon those ways and means of grace
the Holy Spirit uses to come and seal and comfort in.

I know other things might be mentioned, especially
in a purposely handling this doctrine of assurance.
The manner of God's working in such as are effectually drawn to Christ, differs in circumstances, and in
the sensible perceivings of it, accordingly as God
pleases to work : and assurance, as the Spirit pleases,
is given in a different way.

But trying by this change upon the heart in a renewing the mind, subduing, and turning that great

wheel of the soul, the refractory and stubborn will,
changing the main aim from self and the creature to
God in Christ. Really plucking up the affections
rooted in the earth, and finding them set upon things
above ; an evident change, and turning the grand
affection of love out of its old channel, and a placing
it upon God, his word, ways, and people, the saints
above all other things : when these things freely given
thee of God, and by the Spirit of God received, are
made known to be in thee, 1 Cor. ii. 12, this is a
right assurance. O pray, pray for this sealing and
assuring Spirit ; this will help thee against the fears,
doubts, deceits of thy own heart, and Satan's methods,
and clear up thy good condition to thee.

This assurance attained, the next meditation must
be of the best ways of keeping and preserving it,
which must be endeavoured ; yea, of thy growing up
to the riches and fulness of assurance. The preserving of assurance, and growing up in it, 2 Pet. i.
10, must be by care and diligence used about it, and
used for exacter walking in all Christ's ways. Endeavours of mortifying thy corruptions, combating
with Satan and the world, and getting victory. To
him that overcometh, I will give him a white stone
with a new name, Rev. ii. 17. The white stone is
thy justification, the new name is adoption of sons,
both assured upon victory obtained.

There must be a tender care of obedience to and
compliance with the Holy Spirit, and of not grieving
of it. " Grieve not the Holy Spirit of God, whereby
ye are sealed unto the day of redemption," Eph. iv.
30. If thou wouldst have the Holy Spirit a sealing
Spirit, thou must not be a griever of that Spirit, by
any ordinary neglectings and slightings of it, or by
contrary walkings to it : wilful and presumptuous

evils especially provoke and grieve, and will hinder assurance. God will speak peace to his saints, " but let them not turn again to folly," Psa. lxxxv. 8.

This in David, " Make me to hear joy and gladness ; that the bones which thou hast broken may rejoice," Psa. li. 8. Some saints by their falls have felt it long, it may be ever after, as great bruises in the body. Others upon care and fruitfulness have kept their peace and assurance long, it may be to the last.

CHAP. XII.—*Of the next Meditation, namely, how weak and imperfect thy Grace is.*

THIS is a meditation very necessary for making thee very humble, greatly fearful and careful, and highly to provoke thee to contend to a growth and strength of grace, to be rooted and stablished daily more.

When a soul comes to look and search into himself, sees what little grace he hath, what abundance of corruptions, and in what power they show themselves ; when he finds how he is assaulted by Satan, and insnared by the world, and things of it ; he sees how necessary it is to consider what in this case he is to do. This therefore after assurance in some degree obtained, and how to keep and increase it, may well be the matter of meditation.

Meditate then of thy grace received, the weakness and imperfection of it, and how to help and strengthen it, especially thy faith, that great fundamental grace, that serves as the eye to see Christ, the foot to come to him, and hand to take him, lean upon, and to take and receive from him.

1. In the case of weakness of grace, thy meditation must be upon that purposely conferred fulness, Col. i. 19, that fountain-fulness, which is in Christ, to whom by faith thou art united, ingrafted into him, to partake of the sweetness of this Vine, John xv. 3, of the fatness of this Olive. He " is made to us wisdom, and righteousness, and sanctification," 1 Cor. i. 30. 1. Meritoriously, so he hath purchased these. 2. Efficaciously, he imparts and communicates these. " Without me ye can do nothing," John xv. 5; without first a real ingrafting into Christ, ver. 4, without a vital influence from him, and without a new continual acting trust and recumbency on him. But " I can do all things through Christ which strengtheneth me," Phil. iv. 13. Consider thou must that he will help thee. If Christ did first help thee, when thou wert a stranger and enemy to him, now much more will he help thee, being reconciled. If when thou hadst no union, wert no member of his, he made thee a member; much more, being a member, will he supply life, strength, and growth, to make thee a perfect member: he must make his body in all the members perfect at last. They must grow therefore, that he may be a Head perfected, in all his members' perfection. The way Christ will teach thee, seeking to him. The work Christ will work for thee, trusting in him.

2. Then, as thy meditation must be of Christ, the well of living waters, and his fulness, so (because the well, though a living spring, yet it is deep) how to come at it, how to draw. The next meditation therefore must be of our means vouchsafed us to draw, and of particularly that by which all the saints, in

all ages, have drawn out of this well of salvation, and received grace for grace. Therefore this meditation must be of that precious powerful faith, whereby Christ is received ; initially, by our first union and communion with him ; and received also gradually daily, and for our building up to perfection in him, meditation must be, as of faith, to fetch supply from Christ.

3. So of the way faith hath to act, namely, by the precious promises of sanctification, in which Christ assures thee he will not break the bruised reed, nor quench the smoking flax, Matt. xii. 20. That the kingdom of heaven at first is as a grain of mustard-seed, but it becomes as a great tree, Matt. xiii. 31, 32. That the good work in any heart God will perform it until the day of Christ, Phil. i. 6. Thou must repair to the rich treasury of the gospel, gather up the pearls of promises scattered all over it, string them up in meditation, and ponder their infallible truth, abundant goodness, and most transcendent freeness.

4. Next thou must meditate duly of the way to attain the sweetness and helps of the promises. This is by Christ's appointed ordinances, praying, and the rest, wherein thy faith must act upon the promises, and by them upon Jesus Christ ; and so, though that well be deep, faith is thy bucket, the promises the chain, the ordinances the hands to let it down, and draw it up filled with living water for thy thirsty soul to drink.

2 c

CHAP. XIII.—*Of Meditation of Corruptions stirring, and often prevailing.*

THIS meditation must proceed upon the promises of sin-subduing and mortifying. " He will subdue our iniquities," Mic. vii. 19. " Sin shall not have dominion over you ; for ye are not under the law, but under grace," Rom. vi. 14. A man under the law, it gives no strength against sin, Rom. iii. 20. It discovers sin, and irritates sin, Rom. vii. 8, 9, but gives no strength to subdue it. But being under gospel grace, that gives power to mortify sin. " They that are Christ's have crucified the flesh with the affections and lusts," Gal. v. 24. They " are dead to sin," Rom. vi. 2, by Christ, purchasing the total mortification ; and dead by an initial and begun sanctification, that from being implanted into Christ's death, and his sin-killing grace, sin receives its death's wound, and shall bleed to death upon it. But this by applying frequently the promises of mortification, exercising faith by them, exciting faith to rest on them. Let us therefore, as for other cases, so for this, gather up a variety of promises of sin-subduing.

Let thy eye in meditation go from promise to promise. First set one promise before thee, and dwell upon that, look to Christ in that, and thence draw help from him, resting on him, for making it good to thy soul's case, and then go to and dwell upon another, ponder that, and rest again upon Christ in that promise, and so successively upon others.

Thou hast great varieties of promises, that thy eye in meditation might be more delighted in walking in this garden of Christ, among these pleasant sweet flowers ; and that faith might by the variety feed more to the full upon them.

In the case of a particular corruption, sometimes, yea, it may be often too hard for thee. Thy now meditation must pass in a more particular manner. In great pondering of the sinfulness of this sin, as the Scripture in the divers passages of it sets it forth, in the kind and nature, in the degrees, aggravations, and abounding sinfulness of it.

1. In the terrible threatenings denounced against it, which discover God's not dealing tenderly, and handling it as it were gently. What David said of Absalom in his rebellion, and warring against him openly, " Deal gently for my sake with the young man, even with Absalom," 2 Sam. xviii. 5, that we are ready to do with applying the threatenings to our corruptions, loth to apply them too hot, and too home, and let these corrosives continue their time, because of their smart and pain. But we should both get store of threatenings, give them all the edge we can, apply them close, and let them stick fast, and stay their just time, to issue in due fear and awakening, and make thee more willing to forego thy sin. The threatenings of the law and word of Christ are of great necessity and use for godly spirits ; so God and the saints in Scripture used them for humblings, awakenings, and reformings.

2. This sin's sinfulness in examples. In the examples of severity, recorded both of wicked and godly persons, God's severity to them, yea, examples of sometimes high and amazing severities against sins looked on as low and little in their nature, God cannot over-punish any the least sin here. The highest severity is lower, and far beneath the hell due for the least sin. Oh let meditation apply all the engines,

discharge all the great and small shot, give it all the broad-sides, and thunders of threatenings of wrath, death, and hell, cast flames of fire in the face of this sin; get all the strongest arguments, highest incentives, with all possible means and ways to help in this case.

When a ship hath sprung a leak, when the sea hath made a remarkable breach, men presently run, study, and apply all possible ways of stopping it. When thy soul hath sprung a leak, that will certainly sink thee without due help in time used. When the sea of sin hath made a dangerous breach, speedily use all effectual means to heal it. Faithful physicians, when a patient is endangered by that disease which is a case of great difficulty, how do they study and strive, with utmost art and industry, to cure it! When it is a great soul case, of most dangerous distemper; when a tendency to great mischief; when a high disadvantage to peace, comfort, strength, growth, fruitfulness; there should be both hastening and heightening, the utmost intending of thoughts, care, industry in all possible ways. Do it to save heart smart and hazard. Do it to save God a labour of using sharper means, sad, soaking, long, and abiding trouble to make thee consider, make thee willing to part with that member, that right foot, or hand, or eye, whatever it be. Ah! but, above all, take that highest inducement, and strive to be the greatest, most industrious, and exquisite artist, in selecting sweetest, strongest, and most efficacious gospel arguments for aggravating thy sin, and loosening thy heart, unsoldering it from that sin which cleaves so fast.

And let the master-piece of all be the deep and great ponderings of the so astonishing and amazing coming and humblings of the Lord Christ, all his abasings, the deepest that ever were ; all of especially his sufferings, his agony, apprehension, and by betraying, his arraignment, condemnation, derision, buffeting, spittings on, scourging, and crucifying, with the weight of the wrath of God, and his withdrawing for a time, and then giving up the ghost.   All these unparalleled sufferings from most inconceivable love. Lay this great abasing home to greatly humble thee ; this soul exceeding heaviness, to work thee to suitable sorrow ; this blood so precious, to warm thy heart, to melt it, and work it to willingness to leave this sin, that more peculiarly spilt it ; this blood of God, and his life that he laid down for it, to thy free laying down of it, of this peculiar Christ-killing sin.

Chap. XIV.—Of Meditation, in respect of Temptations and Assaults by Satan.

THERE is thy meditation and considering, in reference to thy case, as tempted.   It may be thou art under sad temptations, frequent and fierce, dreadful and horrid things injected, that make thy heart ache and tremble, that amaze and confound thee, that haunt thee that thou hast no freedom or quiet, that storm thee so violently thou knowest not what to do.

After peace and assurance is obtained, and power also in some good degree gained, the Lord sometimes lets Satan loose, in several ways he in infinite wisdom judges fittest, for most holy purposes, as referring to himself and his own glory, for most gracious ends, as respecting his own children, their

2 c 3

spiritual great good. If thy case be thus to be tempted, it may be very sorely assaulted, consider that now thou art not to be scared and disturbed, as at a strange thing, unusual with God's children, though new to thee. Thou art not to be saddened and dejected with sorrow and discouragement, not disturbed and confounded, as neither heart nor head, resolution or reason, grace or experience, counsel or any thing can help and be effectual.

1. But now one excellent and proper way in this case of sudden disturbances from sudden assaults, is a turning from thy imaginations, thy sudden and short thoughts, that are raising hurries, violent passions, and disturbances in thee ; to endeavour serious and deliberate thinkings, to do what in us lies to check imagination, and fancy, and hasty apprehensions, thence flashing and flying like sparks from a blazing matter ; and to let the sunshine of reason, serious and religious reason, put out the fire and candles of fancies and imaginations, to quench and slack their heat and haste. There is nothing our foolish hearts are apter unto, than these short sudden thoughts, flashes, and hastiness, without heedings and stay.

Hastiness of thinking comes on us as lightning sometimes on the dry thatched house, sets it instantly on fire ; and comes as lightning with an after thunder-clap, strikes all into fears and confusion, shivers and scatters all confidence and consideration into such confusedness and discomposure, that nothing at that time will prevail with us. Like the sea, when a strong wind hath raised the billows high, it rages and roars, and cannot suddenly rest.

The way in all cases of troubles by sudden apprehensions and short thoughts, is to help ourselves by thoughts of depth and length. Depth of seriousness, things soaking first into thy mind. Length also of abode and staying with thee a fit space of time, that allowance of time which a serious and weighty thing ought in full to have. Thus the relief of temptations working discomposing impressions, from Satan's sudden and thick dartings, and our sudden receivings in imagination and short thinkings, and thence coming quick upon the minds, passions, and affections, must be ejected by contrary seriousness, and time-taking in thinking.

Until we can in some sort cease to be sudden, short, and hasty in our apprehensions, until fancy and imagination sway less, and judgment in seriousness and pondering prevail more, that we are habituated and accustomed to weigh wisely things that come into our minds, Satan will be too hard for us, by making our hastiness our hurt.

This was one reason of David's miscarriage, when he was under temptation in Psa. cxvi.; he tells us, ver. 11, he said " all men are liars." But he found the reason, it was in his haste. His being foiled by the temptation, was by the haste of his spirit in imagination, thought too short, too sudden, and passion was stirred too soon. He did not ponder what God's promise was, and the experiences he had to stay him. Thus the blessed apostle Peter, whom Satan winnowed ; he came thick with his darts of temptation, Peter was too short in consideration, which made him so sudden in fear, and that occasioned his fall. If he had used such consideration, as led him to repent afterward, had used consideration in the time of temptation, he had not been led into it.

Thus divines give the account of that fall that ruined Adam and all his posterity. He did not duly

consider; he acted imagination and incogitancy, not
wisdom and prudent pondering.

This was one way the apostle used in the case of
temptation by affliction, Heb. xii. 3, 5—9. They
considered not, but were too hasty, too forgetful, and
therefore so discouraged at the cross. Therefore he
endeavours to bring them to consideration, to extinguish short apprehension and sudden thoughts, which
occasioned fears and discouragement.

This is a right way to relieve disquiets from any
sudden imaginations, and from the subtle, quick dartings of Satan. Let that which comes suddenly be
thought on seriously, viewed over and over.

Creatures apt to start and fright, as horses young
and of high mettle, we bring them close to the things
they dread, make them look on them often, and touch
them, that time and looking may teach them not to
start. If temptations were entertained not with sudden short thoughts and imagination, but with abode
and seriousness of thoughts in consideration, this
would much advantage us in times of temptation, and
disappoint Satan's designs.

2. And this leads us to another effectual way, and
in part illustrates the former particular, namely, that
help of diverting the mind, earnestly striving when
suggestions and injections charge thee, to think quite
another way. Take in good thoughts, and be as
earnest and intent as thou canst, that Satan may see
thou art not at leisure, hast no mind to parley with
him, there is no room for such a guest, the door is
barred against him. This is a good rule in reason,
to make a diversion of the thoughts: when any
thing troubles us, and proves a disturbance, a diversion is the cure. When Satan comes, thou hast ways
enough for thy thoughts to divert by things of excel-

lency in abundant variety, to entertain and detain with the highest pleasure and satisfaction thy most serious thoughts.

3. But another help, and that our Lord Christ hath taught, when Satan would tempt him: fly up to heaven by prayer. "Pray, lest ye enter into temptation," Mark xiv. 38. When hell rises up, arms and charges against thee, this is ever a ready help, to fly up to heaven, to charge him, complain of him, and call for help that is stronger than Satan, the mighty Spirit of Christ, against that malicious spirit. Prayer is a both rare diversion of thoughts, and a piece of artillery that will do execution most effectually, and never fail, if used in faith and fervency. Satan fears nothing more than prayer, and feels nothing more. If he can discourage prayer, he triumphs. But as our Lord, when in an agony he prayed more fervently, and had an angel sent from heaven to strengthen him, Luke xxii. 43, 44 ; so if thou art in an agony, a sad buffeting of Satan, pray more fervently, and an angel from heaven, yea, the God that is the strengthener will help against this angel from hell.

Meditation in this case of temptation must be ordered by Scripture rules, by having such apprehensions of Satan and his temptations as the Scriptures teach, which hold forth the sure notions and considerations of things concerning our spiritual state and affairs. Ah! when we are guided by our own notions and conceits, Satan will be too hard for us by his subtleties, methods, depths, and deceits, which he hath and practiseth. He can outwit us, far out-reason us, when we have never such parts and perfections of reason and learning, and all human accomplishments. But when we take the Scriptures for our only rule, then have we the most sure and supereminent wisdom, the infinite wisdom of a God against the narrow wisdom of a creature, the infallible wisdom of a God against the falsehoods and lies of a creature. The apostle bids take the shield of faith to quench all the fiery darts of the wicked one, Eph. vi. 16. No shield is proof, and large enough to cover us, and quench his fiery darts, but that of the doctrine of faith in the Scriptures, held forth by the grace of faith in the holy heart; this will do it.

This was the way the Captain of our salvation used when Satan so boldly tempted him. He might have dealt divers ways with him, and at first sight dashed him. He might have told him it would be utterly in vain to tempt him; it was impossible for him to prevail; chid him for his audaciousness to assault the Son of God, reasoned with him, and disputed him quite down, ruled him, and commanded him out of his presence so pure and glorious, as he so often afterward rebuked him, restrained him, and dispossessed him out of so many. But he only looked to the Scripture, used and held forth the Scripture, and nothing is recorded else. Three darts the devil throws, three different temptations he uses. Those three some of the learned (which in 1 John ii. 16 are called the all in the world). 1. Sensuality, in that, Make these stones bread, to feed thee. 2. Pride, in that, " Cast thyself down," to presume proudly. 3. Covetousness, in that, " All these things will I give thee, if thou wilt fall down and worship me," Matt. iv. 3, 6, 9. He tempts him to covet all the kingdoms of the world, contrary to contentedness with his present poor condition. But the three darts of temptation are quenched with the using a threefold scripture; so Satan is disappointed, and goes away shamefully beaten. Beaten by only using this weapon of the word. The word must be thy help in all cases of temptation.

The word must be as thy only sure directive and guide for all right conceiving of Satan and his temptings. We must not misapprehend, misimagine Satan and his workings. As we must not frame any false imaginations of the most blessed God, so we should not frame in our minds any false imaginations of Satan and his temptings of us. But this we do, and must do, when imagination goes alone, and takes not the rule of Scripture, but takes the foolish and feeble principles of a dark and deceitful, and of a dastardly and slothful spirit, loth and unfit to combat. The notions and discoveries of Scripture are our sure way of help. Observe,

(1.) What the Scripture infallibly manifests Satan to be ; as to his nature, he is a spirit, but not a God. He is exceeding wise by nature, crafty, and very subtle by long improved experience, but infinitely, O Christian, below thy God. Though he hath a depth of policy, yet he hath not the master-reach. Though he hath a very extensive and an abounding experimental knowledge in many things, and knows men, and much of particular persons, can look far into them ; yet hath he not the advantages which the heart-maker, and the heart-searcher, Jer. xvii. 10, and the heart-knower, 2 Chron. vi. 30, the only heart-knower. He cannot see with any direct looking on, and into any heart ; but he sees by an indirect eyeing, guessing and gathering by circumstances, and going by consequences, and not by infallible arguments. Both indirectly and imperfectly also it is he knows any heart, and the workings of it.

(2.) As to his power, though he be mighty in strength to make impressions upon elementary natures,

and things belonging to men, as houses, goods,
cattle, any enjoyments of such a sort; and upon
bodies and lives of men, when God pleases to permit
him, as we have it most evidently in the 1st and 2nd
of Job; yet he hath not such power to work upon
the souls of men, as to destroy them, or to disturb
them, or to discern and discover their hearts, their
thinkings, affectings, aimings, or any actings of the
reasonable soul.   Neither can he hurt the soul, either
to destroy it, or to defile it, or to force it to think, or
affect, or purpose.   He can force no man to sin in
the least commission of evil, or omission of good.
He cannot persuade, terrify, or trouble, without first
our giving leave, and giving way.   He gets ground
by our first giving ground; he leads when we let him
fasten his chain, and draws when we suffer ourselves
to be drawn.   " Every man is tempted when he is
drawn away of his own lust, and enticed," James i.
14.   Satan casts forth the bait, but we first catch it
before he catcheth us: he cannot make us take in the
bait, any more than the fisher can force the fish to
bite and swallow his bait; he tenders only, and the
fish takes it of its own accord.   Satan can throw his
dart, but it cannot enter unless we will; if we will
yield, and not encounter with our arms, but walk un-
armed, and not fight.

(3.) Though Satan hath the greatest gall, deepest
and most highly improved hatred, of an irreversible
edge, boiled up to the highest hell-dyed implacable-
ness; yet this serpent is not so formidable as the infinite love of God to thee is comfortable.   What can
his malice weigh against the goodness of thy God
that endureth continually ?

(4.) Though Satan be unweariedly busy and sedulous, yet he is not, cannot be so industrious, careful,

wakeful, working for thee, and disposing all things for thy greatest good, Rom. viii. 28, as thy God is. He never can outdo thy God : his doings against thee cannot outdo thy God's doings for thee ; no, not in any heat or height of any temptation. When he tempts thee, buffets thee, haunts thee, he must not be looked upon as one at full liberty to do what he lists. He is not the ruler of all things, governs not the world by himself alone. But he is under thy God then when he tempts thee ; yea, thy God governs the very temptation. Satan can cast out no more of his serpentine venom than thy God permits : he casts not out one drop, or the least quantity, without thy God's first giving way.

(5.) As thy God governs by still giving Satan leave, and limiting him when he tempts, as he limited him in Job's case ; so his letting Satan tempt is not for him to have his will, but that thy God may have his own holy will, both to teach thee and better thee much, to support, encourage, and yet humble much thy spirit, that thy God sees is needful for thee.

Though temptations are like fire to melt the metal, yet not to mar, but mend it, to purge it, cast it into a new mould, that it may be polished and brightened, and so fitted more for thy God's praise. Though the best physicians sometimes use severe and sharp remedies ; yet the trouble, pain, sickness caused by corrosives, caustics, cuttings, and such like, are not intended for themselves, but for recovery, soundness, strength, and the good of the patient, though at present he may not so like or believe it. So is it in thy God's suffering thee to be tempted sorely, and long buffeted ; and this must be considered and believed. Thy God's suffering thee to be tried is only for gracious ends, which after the temptation is well

over, will clearly be seen, and thankfully acknow-
ledged.

Ah! thou wilt say, I could not have been without
this temptation, or these trials, in this nature, manner,
measure, so sharp, so long, so many. Never had my
experiences been so rich, my faith and trust, love
and cleaving, hope and waiting, humility, patience,
courage, contentedness, and other graces so appeared,
so improved, acted so high, to the praises of God,
and reflected and brought in such peace and joy to
my own bosom. Ah! how out of this evil God hath
wrought my good! Out of this roaring lion this
eater brought meat, out of the strong sweetness, as
Samson of the honey found in the lion he van-
quished, Judg. xiv. 14.

(6.) Though Satan be such an enemy, and his
molestations so great, yet meditation must gather up
the reliefs and encouragements the Scripture supplies
thee with. All discouragement arises much from a
single or too much pondering and poring on a present evil, without a due looking to the means of relief,
escaping, or enduring. Therefore meditation here
must, 1. Eye God as well as Satan, his love, faithfulness, pity, power, and all things making for comfort.
2. The purchase of Christ, buying victory by his
blood. 3. The presence and help of his Spirit
against the evil spirit, and the defence he will be sure
to make of his own house and temple, and the things
of it, to save it from harm.

(7.) Lastly, thy meditation must look up, and
labour to write after the copies of the saints, that have
courageously combated, and gloriously conquered,
especially upon thy Captain-general, who overcame
not by his mere infinite power, but by means at hand,
and ready always in thy power.

CHAP. XV.—*Some Directions as to occasional and set Meditation.*

SOME directions might be next inserted, concerning that meditation used on special occasions, and which is therefore more solemn, and at larger leisure. As in the law, besides the daily sacrifices, there were particular solemn times, where the work was much more; more sacrifices offered, more rites observed, and time spent in those services was more. This meditation must be performed according to the nature and scope, and such rules as godly wisdom can best suggest for it.

1. As choice of the fittest season and opportunity, doing it when we are freest from avocations, and fittest as to frame, temper, and strength of body; when we are liveliest and freshest, and not sunk, tired, dispirited; that the good and lively present temper of body may the better help and assist the soul, and the soul thereby more orderly and vigorously, more intensely and deliberately act.

2. Choosing the fittest place is a prudence and great advantage for avoiding disturbance and interruptions; and to have the golden thread of meditation run smoothly on without breaking from any diversions. We must, in faithfulness to our own spiritual interest, wisely watch, and strongly resolve, to put by every thing that may divert or disquiet us in our now intended meditation.

A darksome place, or that is purposely made something dark for avoiding distractions from the eye, and to be better composed, more serious and intent, is a good furtherance to meditation, if we are not timorous,

and apt to fear. Isaac went out in the evening to
meditation, Gen. xxiv. 63. It may be the duskish-
ness of the time might be part of his purpose, because
he could less see about, which the lightsomeness of
the day would not so suit.

All things which prevent scatterings of the thoughts,
and abate seriousness, which may conduce to intending the mind, and quicken to the duty in hand, should,
so well as we can, be considered and applied, until by
frequent practice we get a hand at this work, that
thou provest an artist in it, and arrivest at a heavenly
habit, to work readiness, easiness, and constancy in
doing it. The prophet saith, " His heart was ready,"
Psa. cviii. 1, so the old translation hath it; the present translation, My heart is fixed. The word in the
Hebrew signifies, first, ready or prepared. Then,
secondly, it signifies fixed. We first fit, prepare a
thing, sharpen it, before we drive it into the ground,
and then drive it in and fix it. So act seriously and
often, that thy heart may be ready, and may also be
fixed, and this by a habit which brings readiness and
fixedness, as in other holy duties, so in this of meditation.

Chap. XVI.—*Of Directions, in reference to short
and ejaculatory Meditations.*

1. Heed here must be taken, that neither these short
and quick actings of the soul in ejaculations prove
exclusive of the more serious and solemn, or take off
from it, from either the daily meditation, or the

solemn occasional formerly spoken of. Nor that we lay more stress upon these short and frequent dartings up of the heart, than upon our daily meditation, or the other; that this short thing be not made to stand for all, or almost all else meditating.

The heart of the best person is deceitful and slippery, inconstant and fickle, dull and slothful, under a lothness to do good, especially that which is high and hard, that comes not off easily, and that which must have time, a space, and good proportion of time. This we are ready, at least in our hearts, to call tedious, and think too long; although there be but bare allowance of so much time as the very necessity for the well-doing the duty requires. As naturally a slightness and shortness to have a serious duty quickly over pleases much; so some portion of this, yea, too much of this carnal hastiness is in the best. Any spiritual performance we would often have over before it be on, and get into the heart, before it be warm in the heart, kindle it, quicken it, draws it up to heaven, and hath its efficacy and real ends.

Things that are hard, and work trouble, we are ready quickly to call tedious; and because other occasions may call loud, our corruption present hath a desire for any duties being over, ended so soon as begun. Therefore thou must take care that this short work get not ground of the other more serious and solemn meditation, that a help convert not itself into a hinderance; that it jostle not out the solemn, or rob it of its due.

Holy duties are to be all links of the same golden chain, pearls all strung upon the same silken thread; the greater must not keep off the less, nor the less the greater. Both must have their just allowance of place, come all upon the thread, make up the chain entire, and be all our helps in their connexion. Holy duties must not clash, not be their own hinderers by opposition, one set against another, or derogating one from another. But like the noble parts in the body, and the meaner parts, which have all their several places, offices, uses for the good of the whole ; yet with their diversity act not contrariety, but a sweet harmonious subserviency mutually to each other, and to the whole.

2. Neither must this sort of meditation be slight and remiss, grow into and settle in a mere customariness and formality. It must not on the one hand shut out the more solemn meditation ; nor on the other hand fix in an easy and slight performing. But must have its true and spiritual, warm and lively acting with reverence, care, pure aiming, to have heart, for the shortness of time, to ascend up to heaven, making a short visit, for meeting with some soul-refreshing, by a sight and taste of the pleasures and delicacies set ready for all that travel this road of heavenly meditation.

We must see that it is a right work, how short soever ; that it be the use of our spiritual archery, from a right principle, to take a true aim at the mark, fly round up to it, by acting spiritual skill and strength, some wisdom and warmth, as the nature of the work will admit. That it be not a flash, a fit of fancy, a mere custom which calls on us, and carries us, but a spark of the holy heart fire within flying up to heaven.

3. This being a short visit made to heaven, a journey of less charge and labour, and of a quick despatch, it therefore should be done the oftener, and with greater frequencies. From friends that are near, we expect more frequent visits. Common and easy things we look to be done more constantly to us.

What thing in the world is so cheap as a thought? What is so short, and of so quick a despatch? A thought visit is the easiest visit. God expects of us it should be frequent, very often; and reason urges to a greater frequency, for making up that which this sort of meditation must want of the more set and solemn. As they say of gold, that it is found either in the ore mixed, or in the lump and small pieces, (pippins as they call them,) but purer; or else in sand and small dust, very pure and good. But the small golden sands, when they are many gathered, and put together, may make so large quantities for use, as that is found in the ore, or lump and greater pieces. Many golden sands of precious ejaculations will amount to much, and help to make a Christian rich at last. Though great gains in trade fill the purse sooner, when ordinary; yet light gains, when thick, will make a heavy purse also at last.

CHAP. XVII.—*Directions for more grown and elder Christians.*

1. You must daily contend to better establishment and confirmation in this way and work of meditation. " I will meditate in thy precepts," Psa. cxix. 15. David had formerly meditated, accustomed himself to this rare practice, was not now to begin to resolve or do. Therefore his meaning must be a fixing his resolution and purpose stronger. The apostle Paul often, for the establishment of those he wrote unto, prays earnestly, " Stablish you in every good word

and work," 2 Thess. ii. 17, in every duty of godliness.

The best Christians, and most established in their
way, have always need of more establishing, as to
their graces and frame of heart, so to their duties and
whole course of godliness. There must be an earnest
care and striving, as you have begun and practised, so
to be stablished. Not to begin, and then draw back,
nor yield to do with a weakness, weariness, and unevenness ; but here to say as David often, O God, my
heart is fixed, I will meditate. Meditation is heavenly, but hard in itself, comes off sometimes harder.
The best heart is a slippery thing, that sometimes
not only flags and falls low, but sometimes also fails :
the purpose within, and the practice without, may
have their stops and falterings. The watch may want
winding up. There may be failure in the practice,
from a failing in the purpose ; a fit of dying away may
come upon thee, if there be not a constant care of
stability. A good man's heart must be like Solomon's temple with the two pillars set up in it, Jachin
and Booz, establishment and strength.

2. As thou must endeavour establishment, so strive
for improvement. Growth is necessary both in
graces and duties, as the Scripture shows.

There must be care to improve in the art and skill
of holy meditation. To understand thy way better ;
" The wisdom of the prudent is to understand his
way," Prov. xiv. 8 ; not only with an initial understanding it, but a progressive understanding of it.
Not only to know in the same degree, and to be
always alike at the last as at the first, but to understand far better. As the wise artificer, that contents
not himself with the same measure of skill in his way,
but, to be a better artist, proceed to a perfection. If

a Christian be trading for heaven in good earnest, he will strive every way to excel. Not like a bungler, that does in a poor pitiful manner, just to live and no more ; but as an artist and man of ingenuity, to live plentifully. I must study how to study better, to comprehend the whole wisdom of my way, to live more fruitfully to others, serviceably to God, comfortably to my own bosom. Not to only just so much skill as will serve to get creeping, but for flying to heaven.

Also, learn how to kindle a fire in my heart, and do my work warmer. Strive to more affectionate meditation. To have things have a quicker passage from the head to the heart. That the spiritual things meditated on come sooner to my heart, kindle it quickly, and make me all on fire " Fervent in spirit, serving the Lord," Rom. xii. 11.   It is not to be taken only for real fervency, but growth. He would not have them no warmer and fervent at last than at first. So meditation should heap hotter coals upon thee, make thy fire a flame. This by meditation's applying warmer and more heart-quickening reasons and arguments. We call motives (reasons for doing a thing, a duty of religion) incentives. Meditation should strike fire, and blow it up into a flame. Strive to have meditation more heart-warming ; not only to have it more notional, but cordial ; not only a shining, but a burning light, as it was said of John Baptist. That is meditation to purpose, when the head moves the heart, brings in light and heat also. The moonlight is pleasant, but the sun's is best, because chiefly it is with vivifying heat, it is the world's warmer. Therefore see, search in meditation for such things, and manage them in such a manner, as may warm thee at the heart most, make thee daily warmer.

Be warmer in that grand affection, that strong spring of spiritual operation, love. Love to the work of meditation, love to heavenly and spiritual things, the lovely, beauteous, and glorious things which meditation brings and sets before thee, highly to treat and entertain thee. Principally most inflamed love to the highest beauty and glory, for whom most peculiarly that best affection, the best part of thy heart, was made, the most blessed God, Father, Son, and Holy Spirit.

Be warmer in ardency of desire to keep in and improve in this heavenly way of meditation. " My soul breaketh for the longing that it hath unto thy judgments," Psa. cxix. 20 ; which soul-breaking was for looking into them by reading, reading for meditating to present and supply new heavenly matter, that he might exercise himself there by meditation, know God's will, and be better affected, more resolved and enlarged. That desire so earnest was greatly (among others) to be at that his rare mind exercise of meditation, the best way of thinking that possibly can be, none like this ; this had this holy man's chief heart-workings ; nothing had that share of constant seriousness ; here were his longings to breathe his soul up this hill ; he grudged the time that gave stop or interruptions to this best thought work.

Be warmer in meditation as to delight and complacency, to not only burn and be fervent in love and desire, but to flame up in joy and delight. Generally, men like a fire best when it flames. The holy prophet, " I will delight myself in thy commandments," Psa. cxix. 47. Meditation in the word is the holy heart's walk of pleasure, a broad, large walk. " Thy commandment is exceeding broad," Psa. cxix. 96, so our present translation ; exceeding large, so the old. We so far live a duty as we act delight. When David saith he will delight, he meant not the mixture of a mere drop, or smallest spark of delight should be stirred up; but a great, yea, growing delight. Delight in meditation should not only live and have a being, some moving; but should thrive and grow. As every ordinance should prove a still greater pleasure ; so meditation should prove a more refreshing soul-eye walk, an ascent from delight to delight, to higher delight, till we come to the top in raptures and highest attending admirations.

CHAP. XVIII.—*Directions more particular.*

WHATEVER thou meditatest upon, let it not be only an intuition, or eyeing a thing, or a mere recognition or remembrance. Or if divers things come before thee, let not thy work be a bare enumeration, or as it were a telling them over, to be able to say, I have thought of such and such things in particular ; but let it be a review with something that new is, with some new considerations, as thou art able. Something fresh, which may bring the better savouriness and sweeter relish, that may set a better edge, and quicken things more upon thee. Meditation, though it be not for feeding fancy with curiosities, yet should be so ordered, as to season and sweeten, suit and prepare things to more spiritual delight, and to a larger perceiving of that extensive and abounding savouriness and excellency in holy things.

Every meditation should endeavour a more exquisite

preparation, better still reducing things that we ponder, both to spiritual advantages, with spiritual pleasure accompanying. To do this most easily and effectually, our way is to improve and quicken meditation by our gathering up the graciously afforded varieties of Scripture passages relating to those things meditation is to be upon, gather the varieties of Scripture passages about that particular subject you mean to meditate on.

The Scripture, in the diversities of passages about particular subjects, is like a rich banquet, where are set before thee great varieties of rarities : there are all manner of subjects ; all things to be believed and practised in order to salvation. There are great varieties of heavenly truths, for knowledge, and wisdom, and right believing. Great varieties of precepts, rules, and directions for due practice. Many promises and many threatenings to back the precepts ; sundry patterns and precedents to assist them, and make them (and thereby the precepts) more effectual on us.

Often in Scripture the same things are expressed in a various manner, in a different, a new mode and fashion, in new trimmings, as it were, and new dressings, to both edify and also please us. Variety in expression carries often variety of notion, holds forth something more to be learned, and affords something that may gratify our spirits, as to pleasure and delight. So the same thing hath, it may be, varieties of arguments and reasons for conviction and demonstration, inducements to persuade and lead. Arguments and inducements, with the highest art of reasoning, with the best improvement of rhetoric and persuasion.

Thus if thou meanest to meditate upon God, or Jesus Christ, or the Holy Spirit, upon faith, or love, or any grace, upon any duty, any sin, any affliction, thy way is to see what the Scripture hath and holds forth in the several passages of it ; as concerning faith, of the nature of it, of the effects and properties of it, privileges coming by it, reasons to persuade to believe, to live by faith in all conditions : how great variety of expressions have you for all things relating to faith, so of other particular subjects ! By this variety, taking up one expression after another, at such times as you can best, how may thy meditation be carried on with great delight and to great advantage !

1. As one excellent way to order and improve thy meditation, take varieties of Scripture passages about any particular subject thou wilt meditate on.

(1.) For Scripture expression hath a foundation of sure and infallible truth, which comes from God that cannot lie : your meditation goes on sure ground.

(2.) Scripture expressions are suited for us by the so infinite wisdom of a God, who knows how best to declare his own mind, and how best to convey and teach it to our capacity and condition. None can speak so to me as God in the Scripture doth.

(3.) Yea, Scripture expressions are sanctified by God, to enable us to sanctify him in this and all other duties. This therefore is our best way to feed on these rarities, this rich banquet of such great varieties, when we are to meditate. Hereby we may ever have matter abundantly to meditate ; never be to seek ; and for the manner, perform it with great delight and pleasure, which will otherwise be a weariness.

This certainly was the way of the highest artists in meditation, David and other holy persons upon record in Scripture. They could not but see the same things to be repeated, yet often in a various way of expression ; therefore must conclude, that the holy

inditer had his wise intendment in such various expressions.   Therefore their godly wisdom must teach
them when they meditated, to go in that way the
Spirit's condescending intent led them : so let it be
thy rule, for thy help, for to make thy meditation
pleasurable and profitable together.

I will mention some instances.   The grace of faith
is thus variously expressed.   By trusting in God,
" Trust in the Lord with all thine heart," Prov. iii. 5 ;
Trust in the Lord Jehovah, Isa. xxvi. 4 ; and in other
places.   By rolling our way on God, Psa. xxxvii. 5.
By taking hold of God's strength, Isa. xxvii. 5, and
divers others.   In reference to Christ ; by seeing the
Son, John vi. 40.   Coming to Christ, Matt. xi. 28.
And believing on and in Christ, often.

Love of God is variously expressed.   " Love the
Lord thy God with all thine heart, and with all thy
soul," Deut. xxx. 6.   Love thy God with all thy heart
and soul ; and a third is added, " with all thy might,"
Deut. vi. 5.   Christ adds to the three former, " with
all thy mind," Mark xii. 30.   Certainly these vary-
ings had their intent ; they were that when we meditate of these or other graces, we should furnish our
meditation, and improve by them.

Thus things cited in Deuteronomy are variously
expressed from those very passages and particulars in
the former books.   So the Chronicles express differ-
ently things in the Kings, and the four evangelists
vary the expressions of the same things, both the
matters historical and doctrinal ; and all the Scripture
over this is practised.   Variety of expression calls
for observation, and holds forth often some peculiar
notion and instruction.

2. Be sure frequently and earnestly to meditate
both on thy supreme and chief end, and on the proper

and proportionate means thereto conducing. But do daily something more to purpose in that great meditation of the supreme end, as wisdom teaches, and being that in its nature which deserves the highest and first things; that also which gives rules to all thy other actings and endeavours, that glorifying and exalting God above all. Do very much in collecting together, spreading before thee, well considering, acting the most vigorous and intense meditation of all such things which may reduce thee to higher apprehensions, warmer affections, firmer resolutions, and more earnest and even contendings for glorifying him that is God, and there is none beside him; for him that only gave thee thy all, body, soul, life, and only preserves thy all. That gave his only Son to death, to save thy soul's life. His Spirit to draw thee to Christ, or thou hadst never come. To dwell and work in thee, and do all for thee, as to applying Christ, and all fellowship in Christ, and with him, and hath so infinitely obliged thee. Therefore how sinful, how unworthy not to honour and glorify him, how unkindly he takes it, and how it grieves him! Let meditation gather up, and industriously strive to improve all it possibly can.

Ah! how that holy apostle was looking and striving this way, how near was this glorifying God to his heart, how much in his eye and endeavour, how oft is he speaking of it, how earnestly doth he provoke all he had to do with to it! Whatsoever ye do, if " eat or drink, do all to the glory of God," 1 Cor. x. 31; acting all to it must imply an always minding of it.

Lay sound stress likewise in meditation as to that thy next chief end, self-saving; to have more serious thoughts, and industrious pressings on hard to work

it out, and " make your calling and election sure,"
2 Pet. i. 10; to work it out against all difficulties
and oppositions, look more earnestly up to heaven,
and into heaven. And it is good when thou thinkest
of heaven; be then so bold with thyself, and faithful
to thyself, as to lead thy thoughts to think of hell,
and ponder that place and state, taking often the
weight of the crown of glory, the worth of the jewels
of that crown, and think in greater earnestness of the
riches of that kingdom of glory, thy own unspeakable
happiness, with that rare, rich, annexed jewel eternity. The losing of it is from not looking on it;
most losing it from looking aside to the world. The
best go but slowly to heaven, because they mind it so
remissly, and move so easily. A way, the best way,
to be the best marksman at heaven, should be every
Christian's great study. This is wisdom for thyself
to meditate, study thyself into the art of winning the
crown of glory. Weigh hell and heaven, unspeakable, insufferable, and eternal, eternal torment and
woe, with inconceivable and eternal, never-fading happiness and highest glory. Represent more effectually,
see, feel more sensibly the fearful and woeful case of
a damned soul, realize it with the best industry and
art thou canst use, and be not so sinfully soft, nice,
and tender of touching, or of dwellings and searchings by this way of thoughts; force thyself to feel the
pains and scorchings of this hell prepared, and the
fulness of God's wrath poured out; and then represent and realize to thyself happiness and glory, with
thy utmost ability and industry, as if thou sawest it
in all the fulness, tasted it, and wert feeding to the
full at Christ's table in his kingdom.

There are strange artifices to get crowns and kingdoms. Ah! act meditation into an ever-growing

more covetous of the gain, ambitious of the honour,
contentious for to have the victory over all difficulties
in the way of this most transcendant crown of glory.
The wise merchant seeks and buys the pearl, Matt.
xiii. 46.   The wise meditator weighs, strives for, and
wins the crown.

3. Improve meditation all you can, as to the grand
and most principal means, be very high and hard
students for that excellency of knowledge, the knowledge of Christ and him crucified, and better applying
of him.   To see daily more what a way Christ is to
the Father, what fulness dwells in him, Col. i. 19,
how freely he is offered, how mighty and ready he is
to save to the uttermost.   Uttermost of guilt, by
righteousness and forgiveness ; of wrath, by reconciliation ; of shame and vileness, by dignity and
adoption through his blood.   To the uttermost of
darkness, by being our light ; uttermost of our errors,
by being put on as truth ; uttermost of folly, by being
applied as our wisdom ; uttermost of corrupt affections and carnal aims, choices and distempers of will,
and sinfulness of the whole soul, by being our "sanctification," 1 Cor. i. 30.   Yea, to the uttermost of all
misery, and to perfect felicity.   Strive to meditate
better, to have meditation issue in a growing knowledge of Christ, sweeter savour, stronger recumbencies
on him, larger receivings from him, more intimate
fellowship with him, and a more worthy walking
with him.

4. Let thy meditation be more improved in that
particular of the great applier of Christ to thee, and
mighty helper of thee, the Holy Spirit ; how to
better entertain him, and by obeying, please and
delight him, and not grieve him ; that he always
may be ready to assist, enlarge, and comfort thee,

2 E 3

seal thee, and shed abroad the love of God in thy heart.

5. Strive after a better meditating on all the precious promises, so as more to strengthen faith, heighten hope, and have the fuller communion with Christ by them.

6. So meditate on the ordinances, as they be more highly valued and endeared, and be more instrumental for thy meeting with God in them, and commanding his blessing by them, of light, warmth, strength, and encouragement.

7. Mightily contend to exacter musings and ponderings of thy heart's great wickedness and deep deceitfulness. Make meditation a better clue and thread to lead thee into all intricacies and windings of that maze and labyrinth wherein thou art so ready to be lost, and art often lost. To know it more perfectly in all its cheats and deceits, but with an earnest looking up to God the heart-searcher, to manifest thyself unto thyself.

So for the methods and depths of Satan thy unwearied enemy, which will not be understood unless studied and minded much. "We are not ignorant," saith the apostle, " of his devices," 2 Cor. ii. 11. He was not ignorant this way, this must be knowledge, by minding and studying of them. Though God teacheth, yet not without our endeavour, setting our thoughts to search and find out his practices and subtleties. If we are careless herein, God may, instead of helping us against him, let him loose upon us, to act his frauds and fury, that our buffetings may awaken us into mindings of him, and endeavours of being acquainted with his devices. Meditate therefore more to be an experienced skilful artist here, and grow more cunning to see into his practices.

8. Meditate more of that enemy the world, that makes the baits for covering Satan's hooks, without which he could not so catch, as often he doth; neither could we be so caught from our own corruptions, if things of the world did not occasion our deceivings. The fuel and tinder is without, the spark and fire is within; the lust is within, but the bait is without. " Every man is tempted, when he is drawn away of his own lust, and enticed," James i. 14. If the bait were nothing to us, there would be no catching of us; if the world were vanity, all things as crucified to us, having no beauty and loveliness in them, there would be no danger. Meditate to a discovery more of the world's vanity, and that insufficiency in every thing but God to make us happy; and to thereby a weanedness of heart from those things that will neither fill, nor fix, nor satisfy us, nor stay with us.

CHAP. XIX.—*More Directions to old Christians.*

BUT more particularly,

1. Thou must earnestly act and strive to improve thy meditation on those things which concern thee in thy rank and age of Christianity.

There are some babes, little children in godliness, others are young and strong men, others are fathers; so 1 John ii. 12—14. The strong men must act according to their age and rank in Christianity, not as babes or little children; the strong Christian must not, does not look to little children's lessons, return

thither, and strive to no more. To use milk, stick at
barely the principles of the oracles of God and doctrine of Christ. But uses strong meat, Heb. v. 12—
14, takes forth the higher lessons in religion, beyond
children. The apostle saith, The word was in them,
and they had overcome the wicked one, 1 John ii. 14.
They were (besides knowledge of the principles) improved to such knowledge of the word, higher knowledge, that they knew what was proper of the word,
and how to use it, as fitted them, to combat with ·Sa-
tan, and overcome him. The strong Christian must
be busied in higher matters ; therefore must act meditation higher, study and learn those lessons, not of
the lower forms, but above them. To learn the horn-
book or primer, and keep there, learn no further, cannot become a grown man. A Christian beyond a
babe must feed above a babe, a younger one, feed on
strong meat, must meditate higher, of growing in
grace, mortifying corruptions which are rising up ;
overcoming temptations when they assault, come, it
may be, thick and fierce. Afflictions that may charge
smartly, and all such lessons which scholars of a higher
form in Christ's school are usually set to learn and
take forth. These thou must make thy study, thy
peculiar meditation, for finding out the best way of
proceeding in these duties.

The young, weak Christians, Christ sets not them
so high and hard tasks at their first entrance into his
school. " I have yet many things to say unto you, but
ye cannot bear them now," John xvi. 12. Higher
matters of knowledge, harder matters of practice ; but
stronger Christians must have stronger meat, and
stronger exercise also, than children and novices. And
this for Christ's higher glory, the stronger Christians'
greater improvement and encouragement. This must

be thy now way of meditation, how to act higher in thy now higher rank. In a word, that thy knowledge, wisdom, strength, courage, all thy graces may be felt more vigorous and improving, be more evident and shining, and Christ in them for his glorifying.

2. Meditation, let it be managed for the best thou canst, as to all particular cases, and there ply most where thou hast most pressing need. Thus David and other holy ones of God endeavoured the exercise of meditation to that particular case which then concerned them, to beat out their best way of help, as often in the Psalms and other places, Psa. xxiii. ; lii. of Doeg ; Psa. lxiii. ; lxxvii. ; cxlii. Particular cases had their particular meditations, as the titles of these psalms or their matter shows.

In a particular case, thou now (it may be) art put upon something new to thee ; here meditation should be used and continued for, and until a right and sure way be discovered for thy best help, the true and sure Scripture way the saints have gone and found relief in. As what Abraham in his trials did, what Jacob, what Job, what David, what many others in the Old and New Testament did, our blessed Lord, his apostles and followers did.

As in cases of diseases, dangers, troubles, a wise man will study the right means and manner how to be helped. Thus in all cases, especially new tasks, trials, troubles, and dangers, meditation should be exercised according to the Scripture directions and examples left us.

If the very particular case, or kind of difficulty, be not to be found in Scripture, then you must by your meditation gather your direction by the rule of proportion. Look what was like it ; look if there be not the same in kind ; yet what is to be found as high and great, not inferior to thy case, if not higher.

1. Thy particular case, it may be, is some prevailing corruption, or that which stirs and much troubles thee, which Christ suffers thee to be disquieted by, sometimes overcome with, to show thee what is in thy heart, to humble thee, and what need thou hast of his Spirit and grace to help thee. Thus it was with Job, David, Jeremiah, and others.

2. Some buffeting it may be of Satan, 2 Cor. xii. 7. Paul had it. So it may be thy temptation is high, it may be horrid against God, unnatural against others, against thyself. This Christ in his wisdom permits, for teaching thee to be a good champion for him, and to experience his succouring and supporting of thee.

3. Or it may be some sore and sharp affliction, some sudden surprisal, which must add to it, as a quicker fire, to refine thee the better.

4. It may be the case of desertion, God withdrawing, hiding his face, leaving thee in the dark, as was David's case ; " Restore unto me the joy of thy salvation," Psa. li. 12. Of Asaph, " Will the Lord cast off for ever?" Psa. lxxvii. 7. Heman's case, Psa. lxxxviii. Look out and weigh what in these cases the saints did, and beat out thy way so well as thou canst.

Chap. XX.—*Divers further Rules.*

OTHER particulars yet may be added to the former ; as,
1. Thy setting meditation on work for wisdom in

that great concern, of keeping thy heart with all diligence, Prov. iv. 23. The art of heart-keeping, one of the greatest skills ; therefore, for the attaining, it must have great study to be in some degree a master in this art, and be better in it. 1. Meditation to learn thought government. Other lessons formerly took thee up more than keeping thy heart, than governing thy thoughts, which among other means must be by, 1. Considering the excellency of the thinking faculty in itself. 2. The uses it is for. 3. The poison of sin that hath gotten up to thy head, and is occasioning such vain and vile thoughts, such wildness, rovings, inconstancies, and readiness to multiply and fix upon either bad or by-things. 4. The necessity of reducing them, dislodging them, those vain and vile imaginations. " How long shall thy vain thoughts lodge within thee ? " saith God to the Jews, Jer. iv. 14. They should neither lodge, as in wicked men, neither enter nor stay in a good heart. 5. There should be a coming to have, and improve in thee an habitual heavenly-mindedness. Strong Christians must have a power and rule over their thoughts, and not be satisfied without it in some sort, remembering God's pure omniscient eye upon all the thoughts, Rom. ii. 16, and his judging hereafter of them at the great day. 6. Thoughts are the soul's inlet into the affections and will, the rise of willing and affecting, and through them of acting and doing. They are very quick and nimble, yet can be very deep, intense, and serious ; great reason therefore thou hast to study, to meditate, to contend to the due regulation of them.

2. Thy meditation must engage in that hard lesson, the way of ruling thy spirit, as to the affections, pondering and beating out, how to govern them.

Among the heathens, the philosophers and wise men had very rare rules and excellent sayings about the right ordering the affections ; but while they beat the bush, they lost the bird. They had not the word of God, they knew not Christ, nor sanctifying grace, whereby the wisdom and only right principles of governing these so unruly affections can be attained, and they tamed and tuned.

(1.) The task is, how to take them off where they are misplaced, and set them on right objects ; off the things below, and upon the things above, where they are both rectified, and elevated, and truly ennobled.

(2.) As how to take them off wrong objects, so to take them down, when they are too hot, high, violent, eager, to turn their edge.

(3.) To stir them up, and make them move, that either would not move, or but slowly, move lazily, and not with due, earnest, and expedite, quick motion when they ought to do it.

These comprise the whole irregularity of the affections. The true and sound cure must be well studied. Although such as " are Christ's have crucified the flesh with the affections and lusts," Gal. v. 24. As to the inward living principle, and the real heart purpose, initially and gradually, in little degree ; for that which is in no degree begun, is not a grain of mustard, is nothing at all. Though those that are in Christ have crucified, as we said, their carnal affections in some degree. The coming in of Christ and grace into the heart gives the carnal affections a deadly dash, like the taking of some incurable poison given to kill gradually. The first taking gives the advantage for death's seizing ; yet this is not enough, as experience sadly shows : there must be a studying and great pondering how to rule the daily discovered un-

ruliness of the affections, and how to cure them, which
is not the philosopher's way, nor the wise moral man's
way, which is to curb and moderate them; but the
Scriptures' directed and commanded way; and therefore the Christian's way that he must use, and that is
to crucify and mortify them.   Mortify your affections
that are on the earth, Col. iii. 5.   The art and sure
way for carnal affections, as so, and then to study to
order these affections which are noble natural plants,
and dispositions of heart, that they may be acted by
grace's principle, and for things heavenly, with a
real warmth and a growing fervency.

3. Strongly thou must resolve, and most exquisitely
endeavour, to study and meditate for the government
of thy will.   The will in its nature and rank is a most
noble faculty, the empress of the soul, the spring of
action, the weight and bias for motion, the door that
opens and admits in choosing, or shuts out in refusing;
that which sets up the mark and aim, every end and
interest, and likewise makes choice or rejections of the
means to the end.   In its corrupt and carnal state, it
is the wickedest part in every person; it sets up the
greatest idol in the world, self, in the throne above
God.   Nothing in Scripture hath so great, frequent,
and high complaints and charges brought in by God
against it, that which is the most hellish and devilish
piece in its repugnancy, contrariety, stoutness, and
stubbornness against God, and whatever is holy; and
the hellish hold-fast of evil, chiefly when it receives
the grain colour and scarlet tincture of habit by
customary sinning.

In hearts changed by grace, it is in a great measure
still carnal, and accordingly in part hath all the forementioned wickedness, and is ready to act it, if it
be not the better watched and ordered continually.

2 F

Being then in the best men so evil, it needs the best
study, the most serious and constant meditation to
find the best way for it, to rule this unruly will. 1.
Especially as to base self-aims, in which it is the
most slippery, and soonest swayed, hastily hurried,
and entangled. 2. And as to the cursed contrariety
and hellishness against the law, will, ways of God,
and God himself.

The art of ruling this ruler in chief is well worth
thy chief meditation; the wretchedness of it will disquiet; the pliantness and obedience, holiness and
purity of its aims, choices, and refusals, will comfort
most, as carrying highest evidences of thy sincerity.

4. Meditation hath great need to act its part industriously and accurately, as to know how to govern
the tongue, that rare instrument, called by David,
Psa. cviii. 1, his glory. But by sin, called by the
apostle, " An unruly member, full of deadly poison,"
James iii. 8; that sets on fire the course of nature, is
set on fire of hell, ver. 6. David prays for a watch
before his mouth. " I said I will take heed that I sin
not with my tongue;" and keeping his mouth " with
a bridle," Psa. xxxix. 1. To refrain evil words requires care; to refrain vain and idle words requires
great care and exactness.

Study this art, not as the scholars of Pythagoras
the philosopher, that had their *quinquennium silen-
tium*, first spent five years in his school to learn
silence; but all a man's life is too little. But there
is more to be learnt than just silence, and that is,
savouriness of speaking. " The tongue of the just
is as choice silver: the heart of the wicked is little
worth," Prov. x. 20. Then and therefore the tongue
of the wicked is little worth, because the heart, out of
whose abundance the mouth speaketh, is little worth.

Study the art of savoury speaking, by getting three things. 1. A good treasure in thy heart. 2. A wisdom to discern times of speaking. 3. A true, godly, humble boldness to speak, and not be ashamed. " I will speak of thy testimonies before kings, and will not be ashamed," Psa. cxix. 46. Meditate for the true Scripture way for speaking.

5. Meditate how so to fill up with heart beauties of graces within, knowledge, wisdom, holiness, and every particular grace, as to have a fruitful, shining, exemplary conversation, suitable to thy rank and station in Christianity. How to walk " worthy of the Lord unto all well pleasing," Col. i. 10. To all fruitfulness in every good work, in all conditions, and in all relative duties, as husband or wife, parent or child, master or servant, and the rest. It is hard to be good indeed, harder to be growing better; hard to become and suit a change in condition never under before, hard to come up to relative duties, and be Christian in them, and so good as a well-grown Christian should be. Some are very heedless here, they too little mind a proportionate growth herein, as in other parts of godliness; but this must be minded. Meditate universal growing, how to honour thy longer standing in godliness, by shooting up and spreading out more.

6. Make it thy great study how to have, suitably to thy rank in godliness, a richer treasury and stock of experiences, useful and rare experiences for thy own and others' advantage: make meditation a great observer, a diligent gatherer, a careful layer up of experiences, choice and precious, to have a large treasury, to bring out of it new and old.

CHAP. XXI.—*Directions to Christians of the uppermost Rank.*

SUCH as are Christians of the highest form in Christ's school, such the apostle, 1 John ii. 13, calls fathers ; not for their long living here, or being long Christians, visible members of the church, as for great growth and improvement in real godliness, much knowledge, wisdom, experience, faith, love, and eminencies of Christianity—their meditation, like the highest artists, must be acted higher.

1. The meditation of such as are fathers, should be higher in all the ways, and concerning all the several points and particulars formerly expressed, and relating to all persons in general, in all the sorts of meditation.

(1.) In the daily meditation, to be more eminently exercised and constant, in drawing out a thread of far exacter evenness and equality, without such frequent breakings off and inconstancies that younger Christians more unpractised, weaker ones not so enriched with grace, usually fail in.

(2.) In this daily meditation, to be more excellently skilful and wise, like an old eminent artist that takes up his work, and performs it with rare skill and dexterity, and little or no study, acting out of a habit excellently, without being to seek, raw at his work, or awkward-handed, as imperfect artists are. An old bungler is a shameful sight ; but an old rare, ready artist is glorious.

(3.) To be more abundantly warm and affectionate, acting with greater fervour, in a stronger stream of purer love, higher flame of all holy affections, aims more spiritual, and richer proportions of all the ingredient assistant graces required. You must be herein (as a meditation so important) an outdoer of such as are in the ranks below thee; and of thy own former attainments and actings, making sure to do in some degree suitable to thy longer standing, and larger opportunities of being a most high proficient in this daily duty.

2. Thy meditation more peculiar and occasional (which in a more signal manner thou sometimes choosest to exercise for thy soul's refreshing and enlargement) must have a more accurate management in thy hand; it should be a singular acting; thy right hand should have her rare cunning.

Oh what work, what rare spiritual and heavenly work doth the holy psalmist David (old in this so excellent and sweet way of meditation, this his peculiarly set and selected solemn meditation) make of this way of meditating in several of the psalms he hath left us on record! In his younger times, the times when he first gave up his heart to God, he soon learned to excel in this art of meditation. He was the sweet singer of Israel, but withal a rare practitioner of heavenly meditation. Not as the too usual way of the world, whose music is often a rather memorizing the heathen gods and goddesses, or that ravels out in mere wanton fancies, but keeps not any due bounds, nor hath any right tendency. But his way and excellency was in psalms and hymns and spiritual songs, for making melody in his heart to the Lord, Eph. v. 19. Not for the temple only, but for his private recreation. This we have appearing, when Saul sent, and they watch the house to kill him, Psa. lix., mentioned 1 Sam. xix. 11. So Psa. xxxiv., when David changed his behaviour before the

king of Gath, mentioned in 1 Sam. xxi. 13. Thus
Psa. lii. of Doeg's wickedness, recorded 1 Sam. xxii.
9. So Psa. lvii. and cxlii., when David was in the
cave, recorded 1 Sam. xxiv. 3. Psa. lvi. compared
with 1 Sam. xxi. 11. On which occasion also the
forecited Psa. xxxiv. was made, and Psa. lxiii., that
so rare and affectionate one, and many others, which
in his way of occasional meditating he penned when
a very young man. Six years he was banished by
Saul, or thereabout ; forty years he reigned ; was
thirty years old when he began to reign ; therefore
he must be between twenty-four and thirty, a young
man, when he penned the psalms about Saul's per-
secutions. Thus, as he recreated himself with all
sorts of music, so he rarely improved it by exercising
himself in a way of holy meditation, reduced his harp,
lute, and all others to heavenly use ; so afterwards,
when he made musical instruments for public worship
in the temple, by God's prescription, he meditated
psalms for that music, assisted by God's inspiration.
But as all along his time he acted meditation, and by
time excelled more in it ; so he came not short of
his former actings when he was old, yea, when very old.

Oh what rare pieces are those last meditations in
2 Sam. xxii ; Psa. xviii. ! It hath a twice recording
for the more full commending to serious considering
of all that read the Bible.

And the next chapter, 2 Sam. xxiii., when he was
to die ; after all his meditatings and songs, we have
his last meditation, set, intended meditation, his swan-
like song, purposely left in the first part of that chapter. He goes not out as a candle in a stink, but
like a rich perfume cast upon fire, in a most sweet and
heavenly rapture. The best wine should be at the
last. Certainly no old Christians should live, act,

or perform at the same rate a younger Christian, a weak, and but little grown person doth; but do higher, rarer things, be ever upon, not only doing, but self-outdoing; not only on endeavouring something, but excelling, still contending to self-excelling. Last works more than first, Rev. ii. 19; that is, better than the first. The formal Christian in a sort may do more; the right fruitful Christian does better last; not more only in number, but in weight, in intrinsic inward excellency, a better way, a better wisdom, warmth, delight, evenness, exactness in all duties, and this meditation does become the old aged fathers; their crown of glory is their exceeding themselves, and evidencing of it.

3. In your short, sudden ejaculations you should strive to excel.

(1.) How thick should these heavenly sparks fly up from thy heart! not as sparks from a common fire, but like sparks out of a burning, flaming furnace, like David, " When I awake, I am still with thee," Psa. cxxxix. 18. So night and day, all the day thy meditation should be carrying thee upwards; make many mountings up to heaven.

(2.) How quick and expedite should this flight to heaven be! not slow, but nimble, as the flight of longer and stronger winged eagles. Thou shouldst have less weight hanging on thee. Casting off every weight, Heb. xii. 1. The weakest must begin to cast off; the stronger must have cast off more; the old Christian must have cast off most weight, have most strength, therefore may mount up quicker and higher.

How pure and spiritual should thy short thoughts be, like the sparklings of the purest and strongest wine long close kept! Yea, thou shouldst be able to draw with the threefold cord of daily, occasional, and

ejaculatory meditation (these interwoven together meditations) draw more strongly off things below, in
fuller diversions, higher despisings of all empty vanities, and draw more vigorously upward.   The setting
thy affections on things above, thy eminent acting
and fixing them, should be by an eminent first using
and habituating thy spirit to heavenly-mindedness.
The strongest, steadiest, and most improved affections
arise from exacter and more earnest meditations. The
deeper the foundations of thoughts, the higher the
stories of thy affections mount up.

CHAP. XXII.—*The particular managing of this
Meditation.—Application general.*

IN particular thy meditation should so be managed,
as to the matter of knowledge and wisdom, as to
render thee the highest artist in thy trade of godliness.

1. To be full of knowledge above the weaker
Christians. I am persuaded you are full of knowledge,
Rom. xv. 14.   The young Christian must get knowledge ; the strong must have much more ; but the
old Christian must be very full to be a teacher of
others, Heb. v. 12.

2. To have meditated so, as to arrive at much wisdom, to understand thy way, and order it best.   A
wise Christian is a person of great excellency ; it is
very highly extolled in the Scripture.   This David,
though not presently, yet attained in time ; as, " I
have more understanding than all my teachers."

" I understand more than the ancients," Psa. cxix. 99, 100.

3. To have the richest treasure of heavenly truths, the fullest stores of precious experiences. Meditation is the greater gatherer of them, and the improver of them on all occasions. It becometh not a Christian of long standing to be poor and unfurnished of holy experiences. The psalmist we may see drawing forth his experiences, and telling them to others. I cried, and he heard, Psa. iii. 4, 5. Almost all the Psalm xviii. ; he puts all the pearls of deliverances (experiences that way) on one silken thread of this one Psalm together. So Asaph, " I call to remembrance my song in the night," Psa. lxxvii. 6 ; what joy he formerly felt, though now he wanted it. Thus often the saints in Scripture. The apostle, Who hath delivered and doth, 2 Cor. i. 10 ; he had his experiences ready.

4. More peculiarly your great exercise (which others cannot so well reach) is to be much employed in the deepest mysteries, the highest points of faith, and the hardest matters of practice. I mean not so much such sorts of difficulties in divinity, those which great skill in the tongues and arts will require, and that must have long time, much study, which the necessary occasions of very many cannot admit, and are not necessary for every man to understand. But such higher matters of godliness, as may more edify you in your holy faith, Jude 20, increase your obedience to a more fruitful and exact walking. " See then that ye walk circumspectly," Eph. v. 15, accurately, or exactly, the word is. Thus the higher contemplations of the nature of God, his attributes, and titles, the works of God, creation and providence, his wise, righteous, and holy administrations and government.

1. Government in the whole world, and all things in

particular in it, to the least circumstance, the falling
of a hair from the head. 2. Government, and that
so rare and admirable, towards the rational creatures ;
but most observable, astonishing towards his church
and his dear saints. This, as some of our divines say
of God's government of the world and matters in it, is
to be one of the great meditations of Christians, that
are by the apostle called fathers, who having obtained
formerly much acquaintance with other truths, of
more necessary use for their then rank and standing,
now are to busy themselves in these high mysteries
for furthering faith and godliness.

The mysteries in the two books of Scripture and
nature, are the two tropics or lines between which
thy meditation should move and bound, run its
course, and keep within this compass, which is useful and safe.

In sum, let thy meditation be improved all thou
canst for the setting up of the main mark, for the
fullest aiming at it, the hardest pressing toward it,
with all contendings for an excellency of wisdom,
eminency of holiness, exemplariness of conversation
and exact walking, together with all industriousness
after that peace which passes all understanding, joy
unspeakable and full of glory, the establishings and
heightening of them, with longings and hastenings
after that appearing of the Lord, and crying, Come,
Lord Jesus, come quickly.

Application general. Then all who know these
greatly necessary things are utterly inexcusable, that
will not comply with the careful practice of them.
Ah ! therefore let every one most earnestly beg it of
God, to write this his law of holy meditation in his
heart ; to give the right wisdom to understand the
way of it, the firm purpose and resolution constantly

to perform it, yea, the practice of it with sweetest solace and highest delight.   Let me say to my soul, Necessity is laid upon me.   It is an imperial law of the great King of heaven ; if I do it not, great guilt will be contracted, great wrath of a God will be kindled, my soul will deeply be wronged.   If I have not, act not good thoughts, my heart will act evil thoughts, will fill with evil thoughts, will fix and habituate itself in them, be quite over-run with them. I shall have a spirit stained, deeply dyed into habitual vanity of mind ; yea, I may be given up to judicial penal vanity of thoughts.   It may be to terrifying and most affrighting thoughts.   That I, who would not be brought to think of the threatenings of a just God and his terrible curses, that would not meditate of that greatest of evils sin, of my heart and life sins, shall have all my sins set in order before me, held and kept staring me continually in the face.   That I, who would not meditate of the most blessed God, his Christ's fulness, his Spirit's sweetness, his heaven and everlasting happiness, shall now have represented to my thoughts, and be made to see Satan, hell, and eternal death continually before me ; yea, to be under such amazements and terrors, to be so haunted and followed, that at last it may be insupportable, and quite overwhelm me.

Oh therefore let me not so sin against my own soul, and for ever undo myself by wilful or heedless neglecting this duty, which lies so indispensably upon me, and may be so advantageous to me !

Oh how many are continually guilty of self-destroy-ing, for want of a timely self-bethinking !   By a slighter thinking, for want of serious thinking.   By a too short thinking, for want of the necessary allow-ance of time and space for thinking.   By a too seldom

thinking, and not using due frequency of thinking. By acting mere fancy and imagination, and not
wise consideration. Adam's first state was good, yet
mutable ; but it was not a sin or imperfection to be
mutable. And though this mutability of his will was
a ground of his fall, yet it was his incogitancy that
was the first blamable cause ; he fell by acting sudden,
too hasty imagination, and not due consideration ; he
considered not all things to be considered. Thus,
ever since, the falls of sinners are generally more by
incogitancy, haste, and hurries of fancy and imagination, want of consideration (though there be sins also
of deliberation, not precipitations, but presumptions).

When God reduces a sinner, he brings him from
swaying fancy and carelessness to considerateness.
Because he considers and turns, Ezek. xviii. 28 ; he
breaks the reeden sceptre of fancy and inconsidera-
tion, and brings in and sets up the golden sceptre of
wise consideration. So Acts ii. 37, " Men and bre-
thren, what shall we do ? " " Sirs, what must I do to
be saved ? " Acts xvi. 30. But oh what a pity is it
that any soul should perish, for want of a little thinking ! Shall I suffer myself to be of that simple sort,
and to be carried away in that crowd to utter ruin ?
If I never yet walked in this heavenly thought-way,
the greater reason I have to hasten into it. But if I
have tasted, tried, and found the surpassing sweetness
and advantages of it, have I not high encouragement
to make a further progress still in it ?

And if by long beating this path, I have largely
experienced the most abundant pleasantness and
sweetness, have I not then the greatest inducement to
go on the more both evenly and earnestly ? Ah !
then, my soul, consider with thyself the liberties, the
latitudes, the pleasures, and satieties which thy eye

may still expatiate and recreate itself in, by this rare art of divine meditation.

Look to thy ways, thy eye ways, their varieties and excellences, which are so many, and of that transcendency, that there never were, nor can be, any so various and spacious, of that delicacy, beauty, and glory. The wise and holy heart hath far the advantage of all the great scholars and artists, all the highest nobles and princes; he hath better walks and rarer eye-entertainments in his happy way of meditation. Ah! then, my soul, how canst thou in the least sort be slothful and backward to this so pleasant performance, and soul-enriching way, this so easy ascent to heaven, by the paths and steps purposely made thee to mount up thither?

See what plenties of rare provisions are made to entertain and take up thy thoughts; what multitudes of fittest objects; what sweet and precious things lie full before thee, to give thee a full employment, at all times, and with a very great variety, to be a preventive of weariness and cloying, and introduce a more fulness of satiety and delight.

Thou hast that great book of the whole creation, all the several most stupendous and glorious works of God, to take and look over all the gilded leaves, and there to meditate on wonder after wonder.

Thou mayst carry thy eye over all the earth full of God's riches; descend into the bowels of it, meet with all the hid treasures and rarities locked up in the Maker's rich cabinet there below. Thou mayst go upon the so large extended waters, through the paths of the seas, see the things of excellency in the one and other. Thence thou mayst ascend up the steps and stories of the air and firmament, the glorious heaven beyond it, with the so glorious lights of such astonishing magnitudes and motions, orders and influences. Thence then mount up thou mayst to the highest heaven, that most holy place, the world's most glorious fabric, that palace of the King of glory, with all his so glorious retinue and attendants of millions of millions of most happy saints and angels.

Oh what an ample provision is this for my spirit's particular help and solace, my eye accommodation and recreation! Yea, how unspeakably gracious must I have declared my God to be towards me, had I only been favoured with the ten thousandth part of the things my meditation can recreate itself upon!

Ah! but, my soul, thou hast more graciously afforded thee by thy God another book, that richest treasure of most infallible, necessary, and saving truths; there may I most highly meditate, and satiate myself with that highest mystery of godliness, all the wonders concurring and meeting to make it up; and among them, that most especially of the so astonishing, so all-amazing mystery of God manifested in the flesh. The very highest thought walk given for a created nature to take its most rapturous solace in. Not only for sinners redeemed by the Lord of glory, but those of that uppermost rank of nature, that never needed a Saviour from sin; yet being mutable creatures, might all have fallen. But in Christ their Head, being given in their election to him, and thence preserved by him. These blessed angels have this mystery of godliness, this Lord of glory, Jesus Christ, their Head of continuation of happiness, the most transcendent object of their highest contemplation and admiration.

Oh what an account then shall I render to my God, if I do not design and endeavour meditation in some good degree proportionate, and answering the so inconceivable eye obligation and engagement herein lying on me.

But, O my soul, this is not all, thou hast yet another book, besides that of the creature, and the other of Scripture; the book of thy own self, state, and heart, wherein with singular advantage thou mayst constantly busy thy thoughts most seriously. And if thou art Christ's temple, knowest his dwelling in thee, thou mayst find it like the so glorious temple of Solomon, built of costly stones of spiritual excellences, overlaid with that pure gold of inward holiness and sanctification throughout. Having in it that fire of heavenly love descended on it, burning in it; the altar for offering thyself by Christ in thee a whole burnt-offering ; the golden Altar Christ for the perfuming of all thy services to ascend as incense up to God, and be pleasing, most sweet, and acceptable with him. There you may find the golden lamps with the seven glorious lights, the Lord of light, thy wisdom, making thee light and shining in heavenly knowledge and wisdom. Nay, there may be found the golden ark with the testimony, the law by the finger of Christ written on the fleshy tables of thy heart, and the mercy-seat or propitiatory, whereby thou art made to God a friend by Christ who is the propitiation, residing in the temple, the hidden man of thy heart ; the cherubims of glory cover thee, and thy whole man made the temple of the Holy Ghost dwelling and working in thee.

Oh what precious matter of meditation may thy own glorious state, and the beauties of graces and holiness, the new creature formed in thee, after the image of Christ, and the Spirit of life and power, to the highest praise of the infinite love of the most blessed God, afford thee ; even that God who in riches of free grace hath thought upon, and from all eternity chosen thee to be a vessel of glory and honour!

Oh how many and many rare objects, as have been formerly expressed, are given and set before thee to improve meditation upon! And to and above all, if there be not enough, large enough, high enough, sweet enough, and satisfying, thou hast to search and dive further into the infinite power of the all-sufficient God, especially his infinite loveliness and sweetness, to take thy highest solace and fullest satisfaction.

O then, my soul, lift up to the utmost thyself in most glorious praises unto thy God, who hath appointed such a way as this of heavenly meditation, to hedge in thy thoughts, wildness, and wanderings; to help up thy thought, otherwise earthliness. Bless him with all that is within thee for vouchsafing and sanctifying so happy a way for thy both thought employment and improvement. Bless him with all heart enlargements thou canst for making thee so spacious and large walks.

Most highly rejoice in him who hath afforded thee so transcending, pleasant, and delightful walks for thy thoughts to take their happy turns in.

Say unto thy God, O " what is man, that thou art mindful of him? " Psa. viii. 4; so mindful of that silly mind of man, as to prepare and fit for him such blessed mind walks, and these in so great variety of excellency, spiritual excellency for such pure pleasure, and rapturous delight.

O then, my soul, never deny the doing of this work, never defer the doing to a better time, when time is now.

O be not heartless and listless, dead and dull, uneven and inconstant in the fervent performance of it.

O daily strive for higher excellency in this heavenly art, to have the wings of thy spirit longer and stronger, to soar a higher pitch, to take a more nimble flight, and make larger returns of blessed advantages, in peace, joy, satisfactions of delights, and highest raptures of spirit; and by this ascent of holy meditation mount up still higher and higher, till thou touchest heaven itself, till contemplation ends in vision and fruition of the most infinitely glorious God himself. Vision is accompanied with plenary and most perfect satisfaction, perfect happiness for ever. To which most unspeakably glorious God, the most infinitely highest beauty and excellency for the eye by contemplation to act and dwell upon; the Father, chiefly in his infinite riches and free grace; the Son, in his infinite fulness of redemption; the Holy Spirit, in his most glorious inhabitation and application of that redemption, be honour, glory, and everlasting praises of saints and angels for ever.   Amen.

Soli Deo gloria.

THE END.